From Motorcycle to Superbike

The History of the Motorbike

From Motorcycle to Superbike

The History of the Motorbike

by

Eric Thompson & Laurie Caddell

New Orchard Editions
Poole · Dorset

Originally published as two volumes by Blandford Press
Motorcycles in Colour Copyright © Blandford Press 1974
Modern Motorbikes Copyright © Blandford Press 1979

ISBN: 1 85079 040 X

This edition published in 1986 by
New Orchard Editions Ltd
Robert Rogers House
New Orchard
Poole
Dorset
BH15 1LU

Printed in Yugoslavia by
Interpoly Ltd.

Contents

Acknowledgments

I wish to acknowledge the generous help from so many friends who have assisted in the production of this book. My thanks to all who allowed me to photograph their magnificent machines and also to those who provided information so readily, namely: Eric Bellamy, Tommy Bullus, Jim Cairns, John Cottrell, Ivor Davies, Jack Harper, Ted Hodgdon, Eric Osborne, Harold Scott, Bob Spreadbrow, Chris Tait, Bob Thomas, and Jock West.

Thanks also to Les Shelley for his excellent line drawings and John Griffith for criticism and helpful comments. The exacting task of typing my manuscript was undertaken by Mary Day.

My grateful thanks to them all.

ERIC E. THOMPSON

6

Author's note

The primary purpose of this book is to convey to the reader the development of motor cycles over the years and illustrate in colour, machines that exist today, which are in most instances beautifully restored and maintained by their owners. I am deeply indebted to the owners of these machines for restoring them for others to enjoy and for making it possible for me to photograph them. Whilst every care has been taken to ensure that dates quoted are correct it must be appreciated that a date may indicate the approximate year or period of some two or three years.

It will be obvious to the reader that to attempt a complete pictorial coverage of the principal motor cycles of the world in the twentieth century in the limited space of one small volume is largely impossible. I have, therefore, attempted within the available 80 pages of colour to show a selection of the foremost models and manufacturers representative of this important industry. As I have taken all the photographs myself and have been unable to travel as widely as I would have wished, the overseas representation has, in some way, been governed by the availability of machines for photography. In some cases too an essential model within this pictorial history may have been photographed under less attractive conditions than I would wish and I must ask the forbearance of my readers if in some cases there is an unevenness of quality. My principle has been to go for the important model rather than for the glamorous photograph. Inevitably many makes that I should like to have included, have, by reason of lack of space been omitted, but the reader will, I trust appreciate that this volume purports to be an illustrated record of several decades and does not attempt to reflect the moods of a particular time.

ERIC E. THOMPSON

Without the research and co-operation given to me by my son
PETER D. THOMPSON
this book would not have come to fruition.

Introduction

The motor cycle is basically a child of the twentieth century although it was conceived in the nineteenth. Historians dispute who designed and built the first petrol-drive bicycle or tricycle. It is quite probable that Gottlieb Daimler carried out some experiments with petrol engines on a motor bicycle before he turned his attention to four wheels, but the only positive and definite claim to the honour and distinction is that of Edward Butler, an Englishman. It must be remembered that in 1884, when this machine was designed, the bicycle as it is known today had not been evolved. The standard bicycle was the 'penny-farthing' and there were a number of tricycles of various shapes and sizes.

Butler's first motor cycle, therefore, had the unusual appearance of a single driving wheel at the rear while the driver sat between the two front wheels, which he used for steering. This machine had two horizontal cylinders which were placed on each side of the steering wheel; a curved connecting rod extended over the cylinder from the forward projecting piston-rod to the crank, which had a chain-drive connection with the back wheel. The piston-rods ran in guides to take the side thrust, while below each cylinder was a reservoir through which passed the mixture in order to heat it. Electric ignition was used, and a float feed carburettor. The valves were of the rotary type driven by chains from the driving wheel. The cylinders were water-cooled with a now most unusual sight: a water tank forming the mudguard over the rear wheel. In order to start this motor cycle, one had to raise the rear wheel by depressing a pedal on the left side which forced two small wheels down on to the ground and thereby jacked up the rear wheel. When the engine was started the rear wheel was lowered again. There were two levers on each side and slightly forward of the seat with which the driver could steer the vehicle.

The advance of the motor cycle in this country was undoubtedly greatly hindered by the 'Red Flag' law, which until 1896 prohibited motor vehicles speeds in excess of four miles per hour and obliged the motorist to be preceded by a man carrying a red flag. The imagination boggles at the thought of similar restrictions enforced on the motorways today!

The turn of the century produced the first practical machines, having progressed through a period of experiments resulting in numerous attempts to provide transport. Quite naturally the pedal cycle (which had now developed into the 'safety cycle' with both wheels of similar size) was the obvious ready-made article on which to attach an engine to relieve the

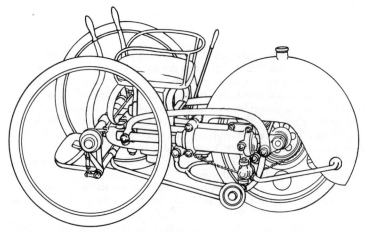

The Butler

rider of effort. It will be realised the engines had to be small and thus were considered to be of assistance rather than a completely independent form of motive power. As cycle frames and components were readily available, many enterprising firms, some quite small, purchased engines mostly from abroad, attached them to frames, adapted as they considered necessary, and offered the complete machines to a doubtful public.

Fuel and oil were vastly different from the specialised products available today. Great difficulty was experienced in starting from cold, due to oils setting in the engine necessitating frequent injections of paraffin to free the piston; poor fuel meant that vaporisation was difficult in the 'surface' type carburettors fitted at the period.

These difficulties deterred the many who looked for cheap personal transport and rather attracted young men who accepted the challenge, buying machines on which to set forth on what proved to be an adventure every time they embarked on even short journeys.

Roads at this time were rutted and abounded in sharp stones, and with horse traffic abundant, nails and flints contributed to frequent punctures in the thin cycle tyres.

The foregoing will convey to the reader that purchasers of motor cycles needed to possess a spirit of adventure as well as the price of a machine, which was about £40 to £50, a considerable sum at the beginning of this century.

Singer

With so many makers with divergent ideas, one of the basic issues was where to fix the engine. The engine inside the back wheel was successfully achieved by Perks and Birch, who took their prototype to one of the biggest cycle manufacturers of the time – Singer. Many were sold in the first few years of the century, and for those who preferred three wheels the 'Singer wheel' was fitted in the front of the tricycle. Whilst other positions were favoured by the leading makes, Werner fitted the engine over the front wheel and drove it by a twisted belt, but the obvious drawbacks were the high centre of gravity: on slippery roads, this made the machine unstable and was feared by many. Positioning the engine in the middle of the frame seems obvious today, but as pedals were considered essential for starting and assisting the engine on hills, space had to be found for both these items. Engines increased in size and performance, due in no small degree to the reliability trials organised throughout the country by the A.C.C. (Auto Cycle Club) which has subsequently to become the Auto Cycle Union.

This club later organised the acknowledged greatest road races in the world: the Tourist Trophy Races, held in the Isle of Man from 1907 to this day. As the title implies, tourism was the prime purpose promoting the event, reliability their aim and with economy very much in mind the regulations decreed that the fuel be rationed.

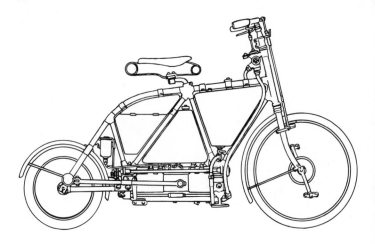

The Holden

Racing and trials have been constantly supported by manufacturers through the years, as the tests have been invaluable in advancing design, and by private competitors, who enter these events for the sheer enjoyment of riding in competitions on their chosen mounts. It is hoped to convey some idea of this development in the following pages and the story behind the production of these marvellous machines. No history of machines can be written without reference to the many men who built, rode, used or even exploited them. To deal with the last first, the name which springs to the forefront of any motor cycle enthusiast's mind is that of the larger than life character Edward Joel Pennington. There was a man who was prepared to buy and naturally sell anything, a man with the eye to the novelty both in the nature of the product involved and the method of sale. An American

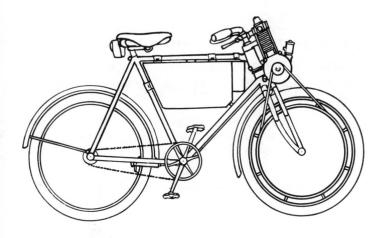

Royal Enfield

Minerva

with a certainly mixed reputation at the end of the nineteenth century, he saw the future of the salesman lay in fields mechanical. He bought and sold patents connected with motorised transport for thousands of dollars but the men he dealt with neither knew his worth nor the value of the merchandise bought. Some was mechanically sound, some worthless. The reason for his success was the selling technique of the man who might have been born in Madison Avenue. His advertising claims for motor cycles sold under his auspices included the boast that they could 'run on kerosene' and 'jump over rivers', neither of which (not surprisingly) was

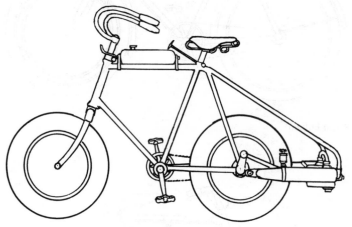

Pennington

substantiated by fact. Pennington was larger than life and trod the tightrope between wealth and bankruptcy frequently but with outward calm at all times. Despite his many financial coups, he died penniless.

The men who have ridden the motor cycles may be a little less extravagant in appearance and outlook, but are perhaps more interesting to the enthusiast. Riders such as Geoff Duke, John Surtees, Mike Hailwood and Giacomo Agostini are racing men known to almost every man and boy, and not a few women. For the older reader the names of Jimmy Simpson, Alec Bennett, Charlie Collier, Stanley Woods and Graham Walker should be included where any roll of racing honour is read. Men who were riders but famous in other fields include Lawrence of Arabia (T. E. Lawrence), who had a great passion for riding his Brough Superior 'Boanerges' and describes this love for motor cycling in brilliant prose in his book *The Mint*; Sir Ralph Richardson, the great actor, and W. O. Bentley, better known for the cars he made.

There are many not so famous men whose feats of riding have endured when their names are long forgotten. Remarkable performances include the many mountain climbs made in the first few years of this century, which developed into races against the clock up Snowdon or Ben Nevis in the 1920s by men riding B.S.A. and Francis-Barnett motor cycles respectively. Extraordinary performances include the feats of the man who rode an Ariel motor cycle across the sea and another who rode a Henderson round a roller-coaster at a Californian funfair. Naturally there have been many speed and distance records achieved over the last seventy-odd years and details of these are given where appropriate throughout this book. It must be said that not all motor cycle achievements are recorded by men, and 'women's lib' would have been proud of Mrs Meeten's 1,000 miles in five days on a Francis-Barnett, Marjorie Cottle's trials exploits and Fay Taylor's impressive displays on the dirt track, all of which helped to put a 'roar' into the twenties. At about the same time two men were attracting attention in the racing circles claiming records in the Isle of Man T.T. races unlikely to ever be surpassed. The names Cowley and Applebee may not be familiar to the present-day reader, but he need not be ashamed for they were not that familiar to the motor cyclists of the time either. These two men raced fairly successfully in the T.T. races when at the age of most men's retirement from normal work. Cowley was sixty-one when he last competed and Applebee fifty-nine.

In Germany it must have been a splendid sight to witness Ernst Henne 'averaging a ton' in 1929 down a Munich highway on his B.M.W. For endurance records it would be hard to better the performances of Cannonball Baker on his Indian, crossing the USA west to east, north to south. These and many other achievements, the men who accomplished them and most importantly of all, the machines that did the work and the men who built them are dealt with in this book. It cannot be complete, but it attempts to show how some of the famous and also some of the lesser-known marques grew up in the twentieth century.

1A   ABC. This rare 1913 model 500cc horizontally opposed twin with hub type gear fitted in the frame.

1B   ABC. A Sopwith-made 398cc HO twin-engine gearbox unit in a spring frame.

1 C ABC. 'Skootamota' designed by Granville Bradshaw, powered by single-cylinder engine with direct chain drive.

1 D ABC. This racing version has a shorter frame than 1 B, but engine unit is similar.

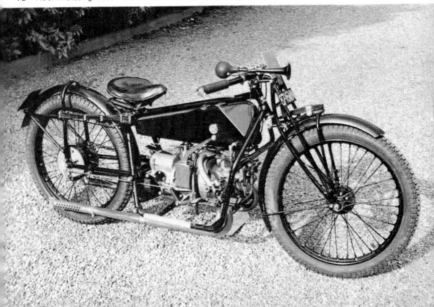

2A A.J.S. This racing machine finished 4th in the Junior T.T. of 1914.

2B A.J.S. Model K7, a production racing machine, with chain-driven overhead camshaft engine of 350cc capacity.

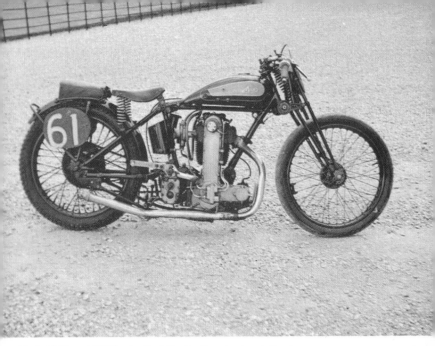

2C   A.J.S. This model M10 is a Brooklands Special with overhead camshaft engine.

2D   A.J.S. A 1950 edition of the 'Boy Racer' 7R. The overhead camshaft engine is of 350cc. Produced from 1948 to 1962.

3A ARIEL. A 1914 racing model. The engine is a side valve White and Poppe, and direct belt is employed.

3B ARIEL. A 1925 500cc side-valve machine with all chain drive.
The lighting is acetylene.

3C ARIEL. An example of the famous 'Square four' of 1000cc. Some early models were of 600cc.

4A ASCOT PULLIN A luxury mount bristling with innovations, made in 1928 The pressed steel frame carries a 500cc OHV engine.

5A BAT This 1910 model is fitted with 770cc J.A.P. engine. A touring sidecar is fitted.

5B BAT A 1913 machine with Armstrong hub gear in rear wheel, driven by belt.

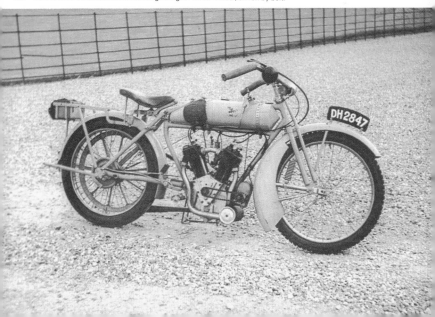

6A B.M.W. This factory has made H.O. twins from the 1920s until today. 500cc to 900cc engines are used.

7A BROUGH SUPERIOR. George Brough's famous racing machine 'Old Bill'. With this 1000cc engine he achieved many wins in hill climbs and sprints.

7B BROUGH SUPERIOR. The Alpine Grand Sports of 1925 with the 984cc OHV J.A.P. engine.

7C BROUGH SUPERIOR. A Sprint special built in 1927 with the 8-55 J.A.P. engine. This machine exceeded 122 m.p.h. on sand.

7D BROUGH SUPERIOR. A 1928 model SS80 de Luxe with Watsonian launch sidecar. The engine is a 980cc J.A.P.

7E BROUGH SUPERIOR. The 1932 four cylinder fitted with 'Austin 7' engine and gearbox, with reverse gear! Twin rear wheels are fitted.

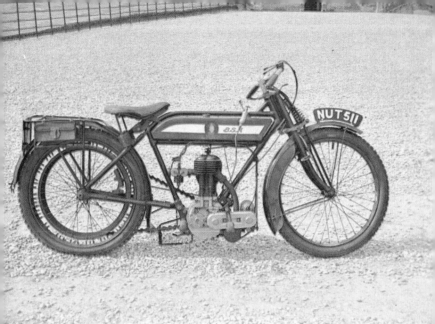

8A B.S.A. A 1913 'TT' model devoid of pedals which featured on standard models. Direct belt drive is employed.

8B B.S.A. The 'Big Twin' sidecar outfit, a popular choice of the family man in 1921.

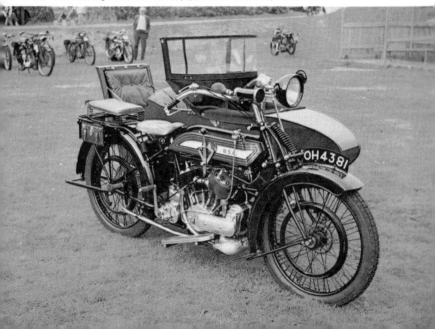

8C   B.S.A. A 250cc 'Round Tank' 1926 version. Adopted by the G.P.O. for telegram delivery.

8D   B.S.A. A touring 350cc side-valve model of 1924. A 3-speed gearbox is fitted.

8E B.S.A. A sporting model with 350cc engine. The B.S.A. gearbox has three-speeds.

8F B.S.A. An example of the 'Star' range. A 1936 edition with a good performance.

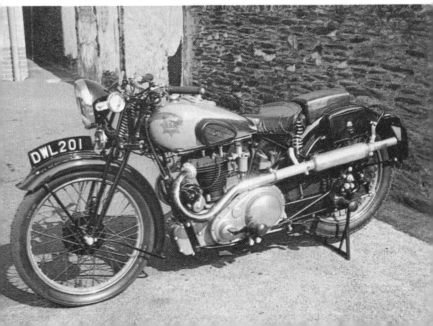

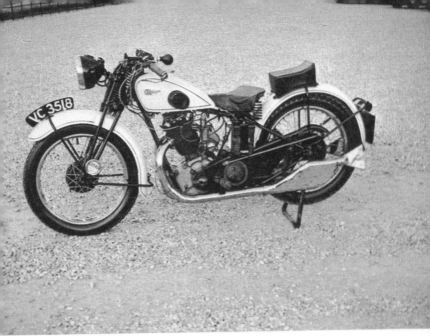

9A CALTHORPE. The 'Ivory Calthorpe' of 1930 was a striking machine – fitted with 500cc o.h.v. engine of their own manufacture.

10A CHATER LEA. The 350cc o.h.v. Blackburne engine was fitted in 1923. A lively sporting mount.

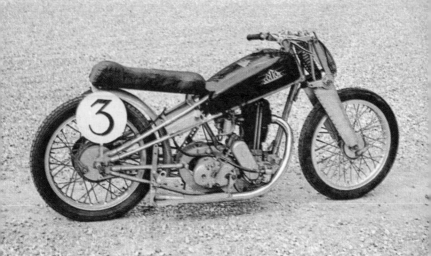

11A COTTON. This Sprint special, built in 1930, is fitted with a 500cc o.h.v. Blackburne engine.

12A D.K.W. This unusual 1938 racing model has a 350cc supercharged engine with 5 pistons.

13A   DOUGLAS. A 1913—2¾ h.p. model horizontally-opposed twin 'two speeder' as used by D.R.s in the First World War.

13B   DOUGLAS. A 1914 racing version 2¾ h.p. model with two-speed gears and belt final drive.

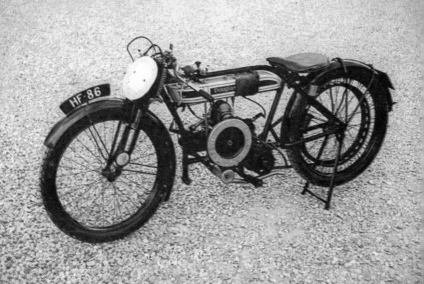

13C DOUGLAS. The racing 1923 machine had an overhead valve 'flat twin' engine of 500cc. Note 'research' brakes (see no. 56).

13D DOUGLAS. A 1928, 500cc o.h.v. horizontally opposed twin racing model. A modified version was successfully used on the cinder tracks.

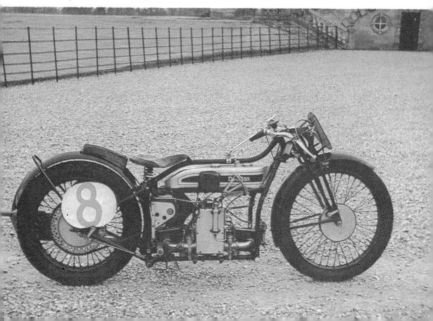

13E DOUGLAS. The 'Endeavour' of 1934 had a 494cc s.v. engine and its many unusual features included shaft drive.

13F DOUGLAS. The Mark III de Luxe, a 348cc – 180° twin with a claimed speed of over 80 m.p.h.

14A DREADNOUGHT. Built in 1902/3 with a 3½h.p. M.M.C. engine and direct belt drive. One of the earliest examples of a 'special'.

15A EXCELSIOR. This is a fine example of the 'Manxman' with the 350 overhead camshaft engine of their own manufacture.

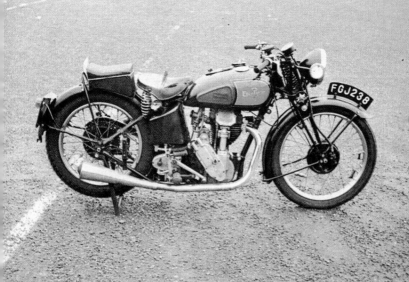

16A FRANCIS BARNETT. The 1928 'straight tube' frame model has a Villiers 147cc and two-speed Albion gearbox.

17A GILERA. The Saturno model of 1951 was a racing special with single cylinder o.h.v. engine.

18A HARLEY DAVIDSON. The 1919 example has overhead inlet valves and side exhaust. The clutch interlocks with the gearbox.

18B HARLEY DAVIDSON. No front brake was fitted until the twenties.

18C HARLEY DAVIDSON. Overhead inlet valves needed tank cutaways.

18D HARLEY DAVIDSON. A 1929 model 'J' with 998cc Vee-twin engine, the last year the inlet over exhaust system was used. Used by many police forces in USA.

19A HENDERSON A powerful machine with four cylinder engine of 1200cc which tended to dwarf most machines of the vintage period.

20A HONDA. A racing 125cc model CR93 using an eight-valve twin-cylinder engine with double overhead camshafts.

20B HONDA. Another specialist machine—this one for trail riders.

20C   HONDA. Similar power unit to the trail — this is in 'everyday' guise.

20D   HONDA. A sports roadster with twin-cylinder engine.

20E HONDA. The 750 'four' with modified forks for sidecar use.

21A H.R.D. A 1927 model with o.h.v. J.A.P. engine similar to the machine used by F. W. Dixon to win the Junior T.T. of that year.

21B VINCENT H.R.D. The 1000cc British o.h.v. Vee-twin with unorthodox spring frame.

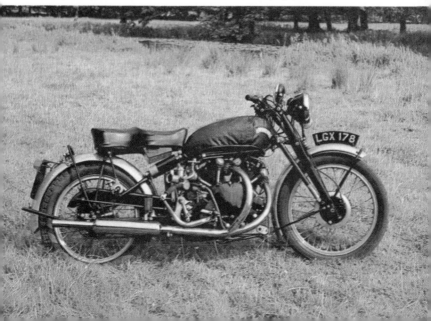

22A HUMBER The 'Beeston' was a popular machine in 1902 fitted with a 372cc engine.

22B HUMBER. A lightweight machine made in 1911 with a 192cc engine.

22C HUMBER. In 1928 this 350cc overhead camshaft engine was of their own manufacture.

23A HUSQVARNA. A 1933 popular Swedish single cylinder model with 3-speed gearbox.

24A INDIAN. This 4-cylinder 'in line' was a development from the acquired Henderson concern.

24B INDIAN. This example of the Four has a 1265cc engine produced in 1934.

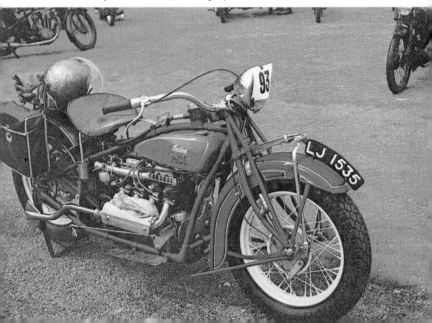

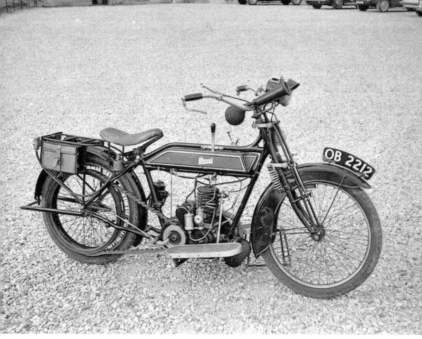

25A   JAMES. A popular lightweight in 1914 with 2-speed gear and engine of 225cc.

25B   JAMES. A 1913 touring mount with 500cc side valve engine. Note complete enclosure of chains.

25C   JAMES. A 1925 Vee-twin side valve engine, 3-speed gearbox and all-chain drive. An overhead valve edition was also marketed.

26A   KAWASAKI. A 500cc three cylinder two-stroke—fast and thirsty.

27A LEA FRANCIS. A 430cc J.A.P. engine is fitted to this 1914 model. The chains are completely enclosed.

27B LEA FRANCIS. This 1921 model is fitted with the Swiss M.A.G. engine.

28A LEVIS. One of the most popular lightweights. A 1926 model with 247cc two-stroke engine.

29A MARTINSYDE. Only a small quantity of these machines were made by the Martinsyde Aircraft Co. in

30A   MATCHLESS. The model 8B of 1914 was a luxury touring outfit. A large M.A.G. engine is used.

30B   MATCHLESS. The G3C was a popular 'Trials' machine. A 350cc engine is used in a spring frame.

31A MORGAN. An early example of the most successful three wheeler. This one, made in 1913, has an air-cooled J.A.P. engine.

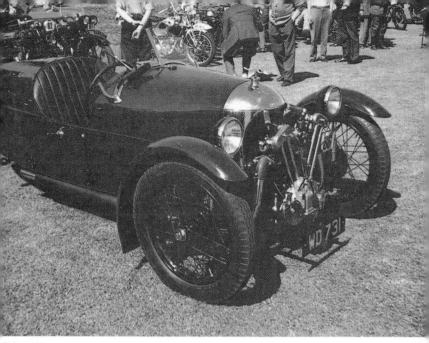

31 B MORGAN. This 'Aero' is fitted with an o.h.v. J.A.P. engine.

31 C MORGAN. A 1933 'Aero' model, fitted with a 'Matchless' engine.

32A MOTO GUZZI. A racing 'four valve' single with o.h.c. engine. Only a few of these were made in 1929.

32B MOTO GUZZI. This machine was successfully raced by Maurice Cann. It is a 250cc o.h.c. single.

33A MOTOSACOCHE. A true lightweight of the day. This 1913 model had a 290cc side valve engine.

34A NORTON. A Peugeot 5 h.p. engine is fitted to this machine which is reputed to have won the twin

34 B NORTON. These sporting 490cc side valve models were capable of 80 m.p.h. Direct belt drive is used.

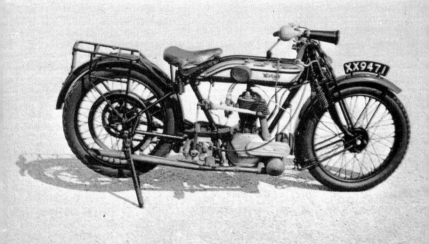

34C NORTON. The 16H model was listed for over forty years, this being a 1925 edition.

34D NORTON. The 'International' had a 490cc o.h.c. engine. This is a 1932 machine.

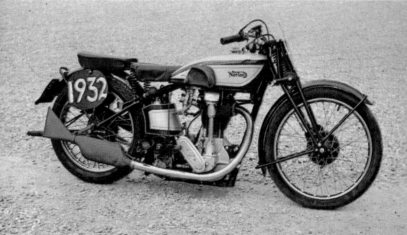

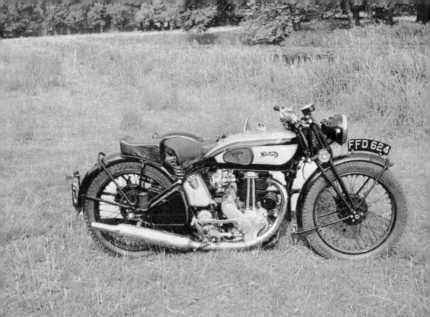

34E NORTON. The ES2 had an o.h.v. 490cc engine. This one is fitted with an 'International' tank, an optional extra.

34F NORTON. The 'Featherbed', so named for its road holding which was a marked improvement on the 'Garden Gate' frame. An outside flywheel was only used on experimental factory models.

35A N.S.U. A 250cc racer from this famous German factory. This model is a 1957 example with double o.h.c.

36A and 36B N.U.T. Two fine examples of these Vee-twins, made in 1925.

37A P. & M. This 1909 model has 469cc engine with automatic inlet valve, two speed gears with expanding clutches. All chain drive is used.

37B P. & M. A 'Panther' model of 1927 with the overhead valve engine of 499cc. A 4-speed gearbox was employed.

38A ROYAL ENFIELD. A glass oil container and dry sump oiling for its 350cc vee-twin M.A.G. engine was very advanced in 1914.

39A RUDGE 'MULTI': 1912 the first year this model was introduced, continuing until 1923. The multi-gear giving constantly variable gear between about 3 to 1 and 6 to 1.

39B RUDGE 'MULTI'. 1915 edition the 499cc engine being similar to the earlier model, but modified frame gave lower riding position — a direct result of a 1914 T.T. victory.

39C RUDGE WHITWORTH. These 'Dirt Track' models enjoyed considerable success on the speedway 1928-1930. The o.h.v. engine had a four-valve head.

39D RUDGE WHITWORTH. This 250cc example was similar to the machine with which Graham Walker won the Lightweight T.T. in 1931.

39E RUDGE WHITWORTH. A 350cc four-valve four-speed racing machine of 1930.

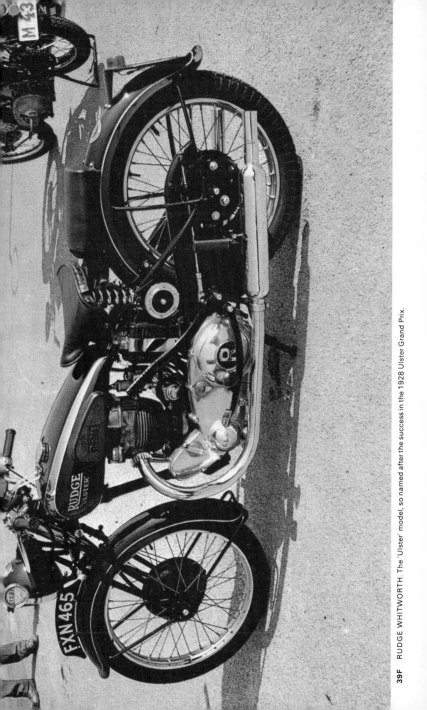

39F RUDGE WHITWORTH. The 'Ulster' model, so named after the success in the 1928 Ulster Grand Prix.

40A   SCOTT. This 1929 Flying Squirrel carried its owner 200,000 miles, many on the Continent of Europe.

40B   SCOTT. A 'Sprint Special' 596cc twin-cylinder water-cooled two-stroke.

484. SUNBEAM. This 1914 model has a 3½ h.p. 770cc engine. A luxury passenger outfit of its day

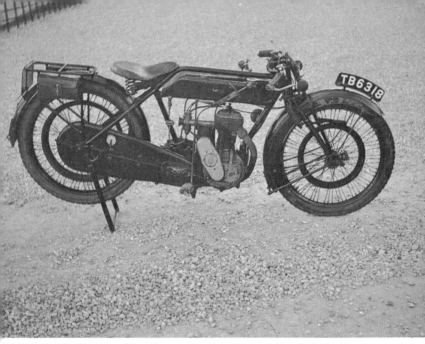

42B   SUNBEAM. A T.T. replica of 3½h.p. similar to the machine which won the Senior T.T. at over 50 m.p.h. in 1922.

42C   SUNBEAM. The 'Light Tourist' model has a 499cc side-valve engine, both chains run in oil baths.

42D SUNBEAM. The model '90' has a 500cc o.h.v. engine with twin port head. A super sports model.

42E SUNBEAM. This 1928 'model 8' represents the last year of the 'flat' tank models. This 350 has a single port head.

42F SUNBEAM. The S7, produced as a luxury mount from 1946 to 1954. A vertical twin engine, shaft drive and balloon tyres.

43A   SUZUKI. Model TS100 a single-cylinder two-stroke engine with rotary disc valve. A 5-speed gearbox

43B SUZUKI. The large three-cylinder water-cooled two-stroke model. A 'Super' bike.

44A   TRIUMPH. This is the oldest known model of this marque, made in 1903. A J.A.P. engine is used.

44B   TRIUMPH. This Roadster of 1910 has the 3½ h.p. side-valve engine, single-speed with hub clutch.

44C TRIUMPH. The 1914 T.T. model with 3½h.p. engine and direct belt drive.

44D TRIUMPH. The model 'H' as used by despatch riders during the First World War.

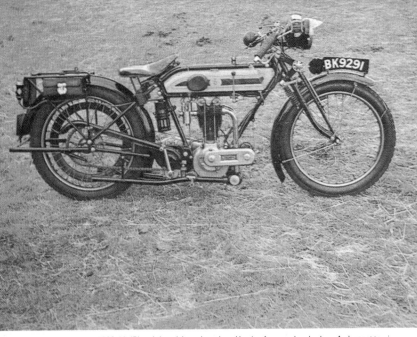

44E TRIUMPH. In 1922 this 'Ricardo' model was introduced having four overhead valves. A pleasant touring machine.

44F TRIUMPH. The 'Speed Twin' with the parallel vertical twin o.h.v. engine. As used extensively by police forces throughout the world.

44G TRIUMPH. A 'Grand Prix' racing machine 500cc prepared for the Manx Grand Prix in 1948, and being rebuilt as we go to press.

44H TRIUMPH. The 'Trident' a 750cc engine with three parallel cylinders, five-speed gearbox and disc brake on front wheel. Capable of over 110 m.p.h.

45A TRUMP. This racing monster, with 1000cc 90 bore J.A.P. engine, was built by F. A. McNab in 1910, to

drive.

47A VELOCETTE. A 1919 211cc two-stroke engined machine, it has a 2-speed gearbox.

47B VELOCETTE. A 1922 Racing model two-stroke as raced in the T.T. Races of 1921 and 1922, gaining 3rd place in each.

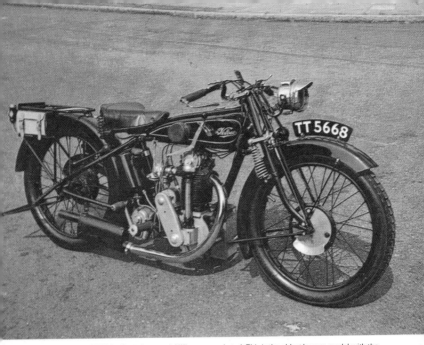

47C VELOCETTE. In 1925 the first o.h.c. model 'K's were marketed. This is the oldest known model with the o.h.c. — 350cc engine.

47D VELOCETTE. A 1931 KTT model, the production o.h.c. racing machine, with 3-speed gearbox.

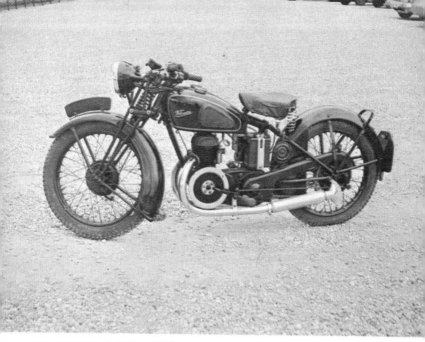

47E VELOCETTE. The 'GTP' model 250cc two-stroke was manufactured from 1930 to 1939.

47F VELOCETTE. 1947 MSS, a 500cc push-rod o.h.v. engine, with 'prewar' specification.

47G VELOCETTE. 200cc Vogue with water-cooled flat twin engine and shaft drive. The bodywork is fibre glass.

47H VELOCETTE. This Thruxton model was ridden to victory in the 1967 Production T.T.

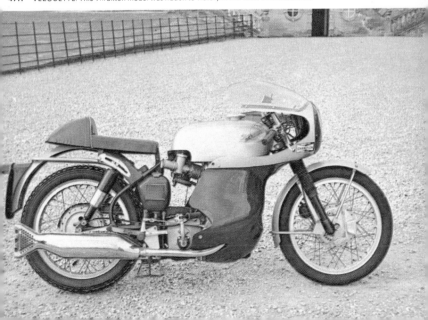

48A WOOLER This is the earliest example of this make, a 344cc two-stroke made in 1911.

49A YAMAHA. One of the many models offered by this Japanese factory.

50A ZENITH. The famous 'Gradua', this 1914 model has 6 h.p. J.A.P. engine.

50B ZENITH. A 1926 combination with 680cc Vee-twin J.A.P. engine and Sturmey-Archer gearbox.

51 FRANCIS BARNETT. Triangulated frame.using straight tubes bolted together.

52 P &M. Method of engine replacing front down tube. Used from 1900 to 1966.

53 VELOCETTE. Overhead camshaft engine produced from 1925 to 1948 with modification.

54 J.A.P. 'Four cam' side-valve 85·5 × 85 mm engine as fitted to many makes of machines including three and four wheelers.

55 SIDECAR. This wicker body was light and strong; very popular before the First World War.

56 SIDECAR. The banking sidecar was designed by F. W. Dixon for the first sidecar T.T. race in 1923, which he won.

1 A.B.C.

Granville Bradshaw first designed and completed the construction of motor cycles for the 'All British (Engine) Company' in 1913.

The frame consisted of brazed tubes and flat steel strip with leaf spring rear suspension. The engine was a horizontally-opposed twin-cylinder placed fore and aft in the frame with side inlet and overhead exhaust valves and a total capacity of 500cc. The gear 'box' was in fact a hub gear by Armstrong with three speeds mounted behind the engine as in later conventional countershaft boxes with all chain-drive. Front brakes were of the stirrup type on the Druid forks but an external contracting band brake was used on the rear wheel. Similar machines were made in 1914, and at the outbreak of war production of motor cycles ceased but the engines were used for a variety of purposes, one being to pump water out of the trenches in France.

It was not until after the First World War that Bradshaw revolutionised the motor cycle industry with the 398cc machine with its over-square flat twin engine in unit with a four-speed gearbox, mounted transversely in a wide cradle frame with leaf springing front and rear. In 1918 T. O. M. Sopwith, with 3,500 employees to occupy (and the large demand for aeroplanes at an end with the conclusion of the war), turned his attention to motor cycle manufacture and Granville Bradshaw. The latter promised a prototype within three weeks to the disbelief of Sopwith, who agreed to manufacture the same when ready, but to back up this disbelief he made a wager that for each day earlier than three weeks he would give Granville Bradshaw £100 and conversely for each day after three weeks Granville Bradshaw would give him £100. Granville Bradshaw came out with £1,000 from that little matter!

The motor cycle was designed with the accent on comfort and convenience, with legshields and under-tray to allow the city man to ride without a change of clothing. It was compact and relatively light in weight. Rear springing was an innovation and a unique design of a full loop frame having a horizontally-opposed twin engine with turned steel cylinders (as in aircraft practice) was mounted across the frame with overhead valves and this made the machine a highly desirable vehicle, which could be ordered finished in grey or black paint.

Unfortunately the motor cycle, which attracted all the attention in its field for its approach to design, struck financial hazards which it found impossible to overcome. Originally intended for sale at a price of £70 in 1919, it soon became apparent that a retail price of £160 was more realistic and from the manufacturers' viewpoint a price under £300 was not going to bring them any profit. The large waiting list was never satisfied, so the enthusiasts not unnaturally turned their attention to less expensive machines and in 1921 the Sopwith factory closed down, after having made about 3,300 machines.

This machine could have been the most famous motor cycle of all time had its various faults been cured, but unhappily this was not to be. The valve gear, a weak feature of design, was rectified by firms offering alternative components, yet for A.B.C. the end came in 1923.

The French firm of Gnome Rhone manufactured a modified version of the machine under licence up to 1925 and a few of these are still running in various parts of the world. Fortunately a number of Sopwith machines are also still running and give great pleasure to their enthusiastic owners.

2 A.J.S.

This is another British manufacturer with a history of achievement over seventy years but unlike many of its former contemporaries it has adapted to the present day needs. Not, it should be added without amalgamation with another well-known make, but the name still lingers on and the influence remains behind the name.

The brothers Stevens – Harry, George, Jack and Joe were so to speak in motor cycle manufacturing from the beginning. As early as 1897 all four had combined to make a motorbicycle from a bicycle frame to which they attached a petrol tank and Mitchell engine and of course a belt-drive for the rear wheel. It was perhaps not unnatural that there should be a high percentage of the family interested in engineering matters as their father was a precision engineer. Perhaps with his encouragement and more than probably with his inherited ability and aptitude the birth of one of Britain's great motor cycle names took place in Wednesfield near Wolverhampton in the midlands of England. They continued to make motor cycles and supply various other manufacturers with their products thereafter, but it was not until 1909–1910 that a completely original A.J.S. was constructed and put on the market.

It was about this time that the T.T. race in the Isle of Man was split into two categories: 500cc Senior and 350cc Junior events. The original A.J.S. was a 298cc two-speed belt-driven motor cycle and entered in the Junior event of 1911. The name A.J.S. was taken from the initials of the eldest brother Albert John (Jack) Stevens, probably because he was the senior partner – in age! By 1912 chain-drive had been introduced to A.J.S. machines and it was not long after that the brothers had their first success in the T.T. – and therefore felt they had made their mark in the motor cycle world – with a wonderful first and second place in the Junior race of 1914. That same year the brothers moved their premises to Graiseley House, Wolverhampton. During the war the factory turned out munitions, but with the ceasefire, returned with a vengeance to the manufacture of successful motor cycles. 1920 saw the introduction of overhead valves which proved a great success on lightweight bikes. A 350cc A.J.S. won the 1920 Junior and the following year went one better by taking both Junior and Senior T.T.s. Howard Davies, who later went into business with his own H.R.D., was the rider in the latter event, having taken second place in the Junior. This achievement can never be repeated as the Senior is now prohibited to motor cycles under 350cc.

The progress of A.J.S. has been interjected with four outstanding models. The first of these was the 'Big Port' introduced in the early 1920s which was modified over the next decade in many ways. Initially a development of the successful Junior T.T. winner of 1920, it was later developed as a 500cc when it became the first machine to lap the T.T. course at 70 m.p.h., with Jimmy Simpson in the saddle. A few years earlier the same rider had been the first to lap in the Junior at 60 m.p.h., again on an A.J.S. By 1929 the A.J.S. held over a hundred world records which itself must be a record! The Stevens brothers aimed at yet another – the world land speed record – and with infinite care prepared a 1000cc V-twin designed by Ike Hatch. Unhappily it returned a disappointing 121 m.p.h. and was abandoned for the next few years until new found enthusiasm caused it to be taken out again and metaphorically dusted down before returning, after the fitting of a supercharger, yet another 'failure' at 132 m.p.h. average when the record stood at just over 150 m.p.h.

But things had changed in that intervening period for A.J.S., namely a small matter of temporary liquidation before being taken over by the makers of Matchless, H. Collier and Sons. With the take-over came a move to London into the Plumstead area. But motor cycles of truly A.J.S. design and manufacture continued to be produced. The trading title was changed in 1938 to Associated Motorcycles Ltd, and in the fifties they absorbed three other famous makes: Norton, James and Francis-Barnett. Before the Second World War such eminent riders as Eric Williams, Jimmy Simpson and Jimmy Guthrie had achieved success on Ajays in major racing events. After the war other notable racers who chose them were Les Graham, Bob Foster, Bill Doran, Rod Coleman, Fergus Anderson, Bob McIntyre and Reg Armstrong. But it was not in the racing circle that A.J.S. really hit the jackpot; their forte was more in the world of reliability trials demonstrated by expert riders like Hugh Viney and Gordon Jackson. Between 1947 and 1961 these two riders each won the Scottish Six Days' Trial four times with several 'placings' on other occasions and in that period on two occasions the manufacturers' award was won by A.J.S. It may well have been this background of success that led eventually to the Y4 250cc moto-cross successes. For it is in that quarter that A.J.S. next found reward and over the latter part of the 1960s in hands of the likes of Malcolm Davis the little Ajay has won new fame which resulted in a factory opening in the United States of America to manufacture this popular product.

Between times, so to speak, the other two outstanding models have been the 'Porcupine' and '7R' otherwise known as the 'Boy Racer' introduced soon after the Second World War. The 499cc Porcupine was so called because its cylinder head finning was of a spikey appearance. The engine lay almost horizontally in the duplex frame with twin overhead camshafts and a feature of this model was that the engine ran 'backwards'! The 'Porcs' had a somewhat chequered career in racing even if not always the first to receive the chequered flag! On one famous occasion, temperamental as ever, two racing machines were in pieces as the third was taken for scrutineering. The time had almost expired for this essential preliminary to taking part in the Ulster Grand Prix. With great presence of mind one machine was presented to the Scrutineers three times with the different numbers of the team stuck on front and side and thereby enabled all to compete! In the 1949 Senior T.T. victory seemed assured for Les Graham, with a good lead over his rivals and only a couple of miles to ride, when the magneto armature sheared, the engine consequently gave up the struggle and the unfortunate Graham had to push the bike in to tenth place. However not all was disappointment for the Porcupine since it gave Les Graham a win in the Swiss G.P. and the European 500cc championship in 1949, the latter being the forerunner to the World Championship.

More successful than the Porcupine was the 7R which was made during the late 1940s through the 1950s and into the 1960s. This 350cc overhead camshaft machine met with early success and was popular with amateur as well as professional racing enthusiasts, on the continent of Europe as well as in Great Britain. Notable amongst the trophies won by the '7R' were several Manx Grands Prix victories, these races being open to amateur or private sponsored riders. The motor cycles are not factory specials and are perhaps therefore better examples of the factories' products since a cynic can argue that the wealth and time devoted to one machine in a particular race may not fairly reflect the time, money and thought contributed to the machines that the factory sell to the public.

Now A.J.S. has been swallowed with Associated Motorcycles Ltd into Norton Villiers Limited. Within this confinement they continue to make a name for themselves in the moto-cross field with the Y4 two-stroke model.

3 ARIEL

Ariel, symbolised by the flying horse, started its life quietly enough as a motor tricycle in 1898 and subsequently leaped into the public eye over the next fifty years until, as with so many other companies, financial needs drove it into amalgamation with other motor cycle manufacturers. The public attention was grabbed by the publicity-conscious men of Ariel with the specific aim of selling their product in a world which had become saturated with too many choices for the potential buyers.

The first Ariel tricycle was powered by a de Dion Bouton single-cylinder engine and the first Ariel motor cycle did not make its public appearance before 1902. The man metaphorically at the helm at this period of time was Charles Sangster, a man with vision and drive. Components Ltd, as it was then called, produced the Ariel motor cycle with a Kerry engine, and Sangster had them on endurance runs such as John O'Groats to Lands End (the north tip of Scotland to the south-west tip of England) with a view to proving their reliability and stamina and achieving his main purpose of attracting public attention.

One of the earliest Ariel motor cars was the first motor vehicle to ascend Mount Snowdon (1904) and gained the organisation further public acclaim. The earliest Ariel motor cycles were between 2 and $3\frac{1}{2}$ horsepower machines ranging in cost between about £35 and £50. This sum of money being the best part of the average man's income for a year meant that sales talk had to be really attractive to encourage purchasers. One such promotion in 1905 was the offer of £25 on 'any last year's models' in a part exchange deal for a new Ariel – indeed a very generous offer. Despite this magnanimous gesture Ariel sales were not greatly improved and the number of models available for purchase decreased during the next few years. By the time of the First World War the range had been made up to include a 500cc side valve single-cylinder engine model and a 6 horsepower (about 670cc) side valve V-twin, the engines being provided by courtesy of White and Poppe. A prototype 350cc two-stroke was announced but never built. After the war, efforts were concentrated on turning out the 6 and 8 horsepower twin-cylinder machines. The post-war period also saw production of a light motor car, the pride and joy of Jack Sangster, son of Charles. But the Ariel motor cycle aspect of the business was not to get its much-needed shot in the arm until 1925 when Victor Moles arrived as sales manager and decided that a complete shake up of policy and action was necessary. He and the newly installed Valentine Page, a former J.A.P. technician, pushed to one side all the models and ideas that were then in production or on the drawing board and brought out their own entirely new 550cc side valve and 500cc overhead valve models under the slogan 'Ariel – the Modern Motor Cycle'. With a guaranteed speed of about 80 m.p.h. on the sports model, the new broom swept the board clean. It is interesting to note that, despite the usual increase in the cost of living, the purchase price of the 1925 Ariel was £55, only two or three pounds more than their 1904 models. The introduction of saddle tanks and cradle frames in 1927 and semi-enclosure of overhead valves and two port engines and the triangulated side-car chassis in 1928 kept Ariel motor cycles to the forefront of British motor cycle popularity, and by 1929 they were making over a thousand motor cycles each week.

Ever keeping an eye out for publicity, Ariel became the first motor cycle to cross the English Channel – entirely under its own power. In August 1929 Harry Perrey mounted his Ariel on floats and with the back wheel driving a paddle rode across the sea to arrive in Calais 3 hours 50 minutes after he had left the English shore line. He naturally had a crew, F. Thacker, who rode on the pillion seat. Not satisfied with this Perrey improved his time on the return journey taking something like three hours, the reason for this probably being that he recognised the route on the way back! This was not the only publicity stunt pulled by the manufacturers and the newspapers were full of pictures of Ariel motor cycles being used by well-known political or theatrical personalities and it is therefore not surprising that the motor cycles used a few years later by George Formby in the famous motor cycling film *No Limit* included a not-heavily disguised Ariel.

The 1930s saw production of the Ariel models with sloping engines and the introduction of the still famous Ariel Square Four, then an overhead camshaft 500cc model. The Square Four with four-cylinder engines of 500, 600 and 1000cc were in production until 1958. The thirties were however an unhappy time for most industrial organisations and Jack Sangster only just succeeded in keeping the company afloat in the financial sense, and in so doing changed the name to Ariel Motors (J.S.) Ltd. The only other models to be produced of noteworthy attention during the pre-war period were the Red Hunter range. These single-cylinder models were gradually developed over the next few years along with the Ariel Square Four. It was a hard time for all those involved in the motor cycle industry, but harder times lay ahead.

Soon after the war, in 1947, Ariel lost the services of Jack Sangster and in the same year merged with B.S.A., but as with the motor industry, machines continued to emerge from the factory with the name of the defunct company, in this case Ariel. 500cc and 650cc vertical twins were made in the late forties and early fifties and in the late fifties a 250cc parallel two-stroke twin-cylinder machine called the Leader was put into production.

In 1962 the Pixie 50cc single-cylinder machine was made to compete with the European and Oriental products, but never found success. However among motor cycle lovers everywhere the name of Ariel has succeeded over the years in earning respect and affection. The end came with a 50cc three-wheel moped which was discontinued shortly before the collapse of the B.S.A. empire.

4 ASCOT PULLIN

Cyril Pullin was renowned in the 1920s for his unorthodox but interesting motor cycle design. Between 1920 and 1925 he designed and helped produce the 'Pullin Groom' motor cycle with a scooter-like appearance and this was followed in about 1928 by the 'Ascot Pullin', which in its time was considered one of the most advanced machines made in England.

It should be clearly established that there was no connection between the Ascot Pullin and the Ascot motor cycle produced by the Ascot Motor Co. in about 1905 and 1906, which used Minerva or Antoine engines.

The Ascot Pullin was thought by most enthusiasts to be ahead of its time and a glance at its many attributes will be sufficient to convince most present day motor cyclists. On the mechanical side the Ascot Pullin had a magnificent 500cc o.h.v. engine gearbox unit horizontally mounted in a frame of pressed steel, which also found room for a large four-gallon petrol tank. The wheels were so designed that not only could they be removed easily in the event of damage or even a puncture, which was the everyday curse of the motor cyclist even in the twenties, but these could also be interchanged one with the other. To assist the rider, an instrument panel was fitted to the handlebars and for his greater comfort, apart from leg shields, a retractable windscreen was attached complete with a wiper. The passenger's comfort was provided for by a seat and foot-rests and all was included as standard equipment although the purchaser was certainly expected to pay one way or another for what he received. Unhappily the machine did not steer as well as a good motor cycle should. While they could be said to be getting good value for money the normal retail price of close on £80 was considered too high by the majority of motor cyclists, with the result that less luxurious machines that had better steering sold in preference to the Ascot Pullin. The present-day reader may well consider that the motor cycle described provided no more than present day standard equipment, which is a classic example of what are considered luxuries by one generation becoming necessities for the next. Unfortunately for Cyril Pullin, the time was not right for the provision of a luxury motor cycle at a luxury price and like so many other makes the Ascot Pullin had left the motor cycle scene by 1930.

5 BAT

The popular belief is that Bat motor cycles were so called because the manufacturer claimed his machine to be 'best after tests': B.A.T. Whether this was to be construed as a not too modest claim that his machines were better than his rivals or that his own machines improved their performance after testing has never been made clear. Actually it is an abbreviation of Batson, founder of the company in 1902. For the short duration of the Bat life, the motor cycles bearing this name (and claim) certainly made an impact on the motor cycling scene. The Bat was made at a factory at Penge in South East London, and the first machine saw the light of day in 1902. From the earliest days they were fitted with spring frames making for a more comfortable ride and better road holding. These early spring frames consisted of a small sub-frame carrying saddle and foot-rests suspended by springs from the main frame. Bat forks were of bottom link design with a pivoted and coil spring-supported U-shaped arm to carry the front wheel spindle anticipating Greeves by half a century.

T. H. Tessier took over the company in about 1904 and he proudly rode a Bat in the first ever Isle of Man T.T. race in 1907. From the very first, Bat dispensed with pedalling gear, claiming that the J.A.P. engine would see its rider safely up the steepest hills, a rare boast indeed in the first few years of the twentieth century.

Later Bats were generally 650cc, 770cc, 964cc and 980cc V-twin-cylinder machines (single-cylinder machines were dropped after 1912). Having entered the first T.T. race in the Isle of Man, Bats were entered in all but one of the pre-First World War T.T. races and, in the 1908 twin-cylinder class, took second place with W. H. Bashall in the saddle, who also recorded the fastest average lap speed of 42·25 miles per hour. Bats were fast and in 1910 the speed set up by H. Bowen in recording the fastest lap of 53·15 m.p.h. contributed to the change of course in the Isle of Man T.T. races. In 1911 the Mountain Circuit was first used for the Senior and Junior classes of the T.T. races. Bowen's lap speed had been regarded as far too dangerous for the short course and safety-conscious officials decided that a change of course would prevent serious accidents. However, fast though they were, another feature of the Bat racing performance was unreliability and more often than not Bat entries retired from the races they entered.

In their short post-war period of production, Bat took over the firm of Martinsyde in 1923 and for the last three years the motor cycle manufactured was sold under the name of Bat-Martinsyde. The company like so many others fell foul of financial troubles caused by increased costs of production and the competition from the newly available cheap, light motor cars and in 1926 the Bat motor cycle company ceased production. Batson's original firm had switched to the manufacture of office equipment in 1902 and duly celebrated its diamond jubilee in 1962.

6 B.M.W.

The Bayerische Motoren Werke, the Bavarian Motor Works, standing in Munich, Germany, represents all that is best in engineering. Founded in 1916, the company has successfully built quality engines for aircraft, motor cycles and motor cars and rightly has an international reputation for such work. The motor cycle was not a serious proposition at B.M.W. until the early 1920s when the first experiments with motor cycles were made. B.M.W. engines were prepared initially for motor cycles made by rival companies and the company did not manufacture their own motor cycle before 1923. The man responsible for this machine was chief engineer Max Friz. From the beginning Friz implemented his own ideas for a better motor cycle. His ideas, like Bradshawe's for A.B.C., allowed the horizontally opposed 500cc twin-cylinder air-cooled engine to be mounted well to the front of the frame and across it, and the engine power was conveyed through clutch and gearbox to a propeller shaft final drive. Shaft drive remained a feature of all future B.M.W. models. Since the first 500cc model came through the factory doors, B.M.W. have generally been associated with big twin-cylinder motor cycles, but apart from these B.M.W. did in the course of time make some single-cylinder motor cycles of between 200cc and 400cc engines with overhead valves. But it has to be admitted that the B.M.W. reputation was certainly earned by the 750cc twin-cylinder with world record breaking speeds, later continued with the 500cc supercharged models. As early as 1929 when the dust covers were hardly off the prototype B.M.W. motor car (an immaculate little limousine), Ernst Henne rode his 740cc twin-cylinder B.M.W. to a world record speed of 100·58 m.p.h. for a standing start mile on an autobahn adjacent to Munich in an incredible 35·79 seconds. Over the following decade, B.M.W. with Henne in the saddle won and lost the world speed records time and time again. Each new record seemed to stretch the machine to its maximum, only for it to be modified to attain even better performances. By 1932 Henne on B.M.W. also held the world record for the 'flying kilo' which means that the machine is already travelling at speed when the timing of the kilometre distance is commenced. The speed attained was 151·86 miles per hour. For his next attempt on the world speed record Henne was given a 500cc supercharged model. It must have been quite a sight for those few spectators scattered in vantage points near the Frankfurt Autobahn (Frankfurt motorway or freeway) when Henne's machine – totally encased with aluminium sheeting to aid streamlining – sped past like a bullet, in both senses, at a record breaking 169·4 miles per hour. The following year Henne improved his performance as he had to, in order to regain the world record lost during those twelve months, with a staggering 174 miles per hour. Speed records were not enough for B.M.W. and in 1937 machines were first entered for the prestige road race, the Isle of Man T.T. in the Senior event. For two years performances were good but not good enough for B.M.W. or indeed the Führer who decreed that the 1939 Senior T.T. should be won by B.M.W. to show the world the superiority of all things German, not least their engineering prowess. There were not many in the motor cycling world of Europe who doubted the superiority of B.M.W. super-charged 500cc motor cycles even if they did not accept Hitler's other boasts. The sixth position in the 1937 T.T. race and the gallant fifth place in the 1938 event had been a little deceptive to all the uninitiated but it was no great surprise to the motor cycling fraternity around the world when Georg Meier on his B.M.W. led the field from start to finish of the 1939 race. His nearest rival, over a minute behind at the end of the race, did not greatly trouble him as it was works team-mate Jock West. The only event to mar the occasion for B.M.W. was the sad death of the third member of the team, Gall, who crashed in practice. The works machines showed many of the standard features of the machine which could be readily purchased by the man with the necessary money, such as the highly developed telescopic coil-sprung and oil-damped front forks which had been standard equipment on B.M.W.s for the previous three years. The finishing victory flag in the 1939 T.T. acted to all appearances as the starting flag to the next major event in Europe, the Second World War. Naturally enough B.M.W. provided motor cycles for the German troops and other machines for the military including aircraft engines and motor cars during the next six years. As far as the motor cycle side of the business was concerned, peacetime limits were imposed by the Allies after the war and in common with all German motor cycle manufacturers B.M.W. made motor cycles of the obligatory 250cc or less. The B.M.W. 250cc single-cylinder looked re-markably as though the company had merely divided an old 500cc twin to make two machines. All parts were suitably reduced versions of the former big model. In time the limit was raised, and B.M.W. resumed manufacture of the 500cc, 600cc and later 750cc models. In the racing world from the mid-fifties B.M.W. specialised in motor cycle sidecar events monopolising the Isle of Man T.T. races for many years and European Grands Prix events as well. With so many victories to their crdit in sidecar events it would not be right to pick out any particular race for comment, but mention must be made of a few of the most successful riders like W. Schneider, F. Camathias, F. Hillebrand, M. Deubel and F. Scheidegger not excluding the British rider Pip Harris.

The B.M.W. factory continues in production and the record book for this company at least cannot yet be closed. With their history and engineering experience many more wonderful B.M.W. achievements can be confidently awaited.

7 BROUGH SUPERIOR

George, the son of William Brough, was born in 1890 and from early childhood took an active interest in his father's activities in the development design and manufacture of motor cars and motor cycles. The first motor cycle that could be truly credited solely to William Brough was in 1902, and at the age of 16 George rode one of his father's machines in the A.C.C. End to End (John O'Groats to Lands End) trial along with his elder brother William junior. Whilst William junior took home a gold medal, George merely had the spiritual satisfaction of having taken part and the physical dissatisfaction of having pedalled his way round most of the course arriving at the finish three days after the last competitor. William Brough's success in motor cycle design and manufacture is illustrated in the achievement of entering seven machines in the London to Edinburgh trial in 1920 and taking home seven medals: six gold and one silver.

George went into partnership with his father, but their aims were different. George Brough, who wanted and intended to make a luxurious machine 'superior' to the average motor cycle, parted company with his father and started manufacture of the first Brough Superiors in Nottingham in 1919. The Mark I was driven by the huge 8 horsepower J. A. Prestwich engine. This V-twin overhead valve engine was known as the '90 Bore' (90 × 76mm bore and stroke). The luxury included heavy plating to prevent rust and special exhaust and silencer design that became a hallmark of a Brough Superior, a muted monster indeed! Another distinctive feature of the Brough Superior throughout its years of manufacture was the bulbous nose tank which contrasted sharply with the angular box shapes appearing on nearly all other makes and it gave the Brough Superiors a smooth streamlined appearance. For these machines with sidecars, an alternative side valve engine was available. The Torpedo sidecar, looking like a miniature R100, was designed to accompany the Brough. The Brough Superior was also superior in price to the average motor cycle and good value though it was thought to be, the motor cycle was not in the price range of the average enthusiast, who had to be content with the advertisements, the records of its achievements, the shop window display and of course in due time the annual view at the motor cycle shows. The Mark II was given the long stroke Motosacoche 748cc engine. The reason for the quiet running of the Brough Superior apart from the exhaust and silencer system was the partial elimination of the usual noise caused by poppet valves and tappets. By 1920 the Brough Superior was already held in high esteem by the lucky owners.

One such owner wrote in eulogistic terms describing the Brough Superior as 'the Rolls Royce of motor cycles' and the letter being published, the phrase thereafter stuck. George Brough was not only responsible for design but also gave his machines the best and only true advertisements by riding them to success. In those days reliability was not a feature of every motor cycle and therefore a purchaser placed greater value on the achievements of machines in endurance trials than in short-term races, where on a given day, for a short time, a machine might just hold together. George Brough took gold medals in the 1920–2 Lands End trials and during his career he won over 200 awards, both in trials and races for he was no mean performer in either field. On his first appearance at Brooklands riding his original SS80 nicknamed 'Spit and Polish' by those who sneered at its well-kept appearance, he won the 1922 Experts scratch race lapping at 100 m.p.h. being the first to achieve this lap speed. Subsequently he won 51 out of 52 consecutive races in the years 1922 to 1923 on 'Old Bill' and in the fifty-second the machine won without him! Leading with only forty yards to go to the finish, a tyre burst on the front wheel causing the rider to fall but the machine continued to finish. The suggestion that 'Old Bill' should be given the trophy was hotly and successfully disputed by the rider who came second but finished still on his bike!

By 1924 the SS100 with overhead valve J.A.P. engine had been developed and was advertised with a guarantee that every machine had been timed over a quarter of a mile at a speed in excess of 100 m.p.h. George Brough had concentrated on the big 1000cc machines and was turning out for public purchase at this period only two models costing between £150 and £170 according to accessories and modifications. A short while later came the Alpine Grand Sports and as the name implies, intended for the sportsman. George himself won the Mount Cenis Hill Climb on the A.G.S. and to his horror upon returning triumphantly to Britain with the trophy found that the Customs men expected him to pay duty on it! The Alpine was followed by the similar Pendine. By 1927 a 750cc side valve machine was being manufactured, which apart from the quiet running expected of Broughs was economical on petrol doing about 80 miles to the gallon. 1927 and 1928 saw two different four-cylinder models at the annual motor cycle show in London with the innovation of the Draper spring frame for greater comfort. In 1929 the Black Alpine 680 (with hand change gear) was brought out and enthusiastically described as being able to 'glide along in almost perfect silence'. One could not always anticipate smooth roads and the 'castle' front forks were a godsend for shock absorbing. These were the result of experiments by George Brough and Harold Karslake whose combined design of a parallel tube with bottom link action was patented and put into production under the name of 'Castle' – naturally derived from Nottingham Castle. Two versions of Castle forks were used, long and short, on most models from 1925 until they were replaced by Monarch for the heavier machines in the mid-thirties. 1931 saw the development of the 'baby' Brough, a 500cc o.h.v. twin which was open to modification for racing purposes and on the market at 100 guineas. In 1933 came the development of the larger Broughs. The 11/50 of 1096cc could cruise with a sidecar at 75 m.p.h. but was still economical on petrol at 60 miles to the gallon.

After the death of his father, George returned to the original works of his father in Basford and from 1935 to the beginning of the war he continued manufacture there. A variation in 1935 was the adoption of 1000cc engines made by A.M.C. of Kent. By 1936 George turned his attention to developing the sidecar. He adapted the Austrian Felbers innovation of a loop frame sidecar, which required no cross-bracing and the body was therefore slung low and sprung on horizontal long semi-elliptical laminated springs, which gave the passenger extra comfort.

All men have dreams, but not all realise them. George devised his 'dream' motor cycle with considerable aid from F. Dixon and H. S. Hatch (well respected figures in the motor cycle world) and turned out the 997cc machine the 'Golden Dream', which incorporated all his ideals and was in fact the last design of Brough Superior. The proposed purchase price was £250, but unfortunately the model never went into general production. The war came and George Brough turned his attention to assisting his country in the best way he knew how. He designed a sidecar which could be adapted for machine-gun mountings or a fire-fighting unit, but the powers-that-be refused it. So his immediate attention went to the manufacture of precision components for aircraft, which were gratefully accepted.

Among the notable achievements of the Brough Superior were the Brooklands lap record speeds of 106·6 m.p.h. with sidecar recorded in 1937 and 124·51 solo in 1939. Both of these records were obtained by Noel Pope. Pope later attempted the world record on two wheels at Bonneville Salt Lake in Utah, USA in 1949, but whilst doing 150 m.p.h. he suffered a fall which left him comparatively unhurt but deterred his efforts. The Brough Superior had held the world record in 1937 when Eric Fernihough clocked 169·781 miles per hour. More recently in the late 1950s and early 1960s

'Bob' Berry made attempts on the world record lying prone on his stream-lined Brough Superior but once again a fall led to failure.

One of the more celebrated Brough Superior enthusiasts was T. E. Lawrence who between 1922 and 1935 owned one SS80 and six S.S. 100s, averaging about 27,000 miles *per annum* on them. He described his Brough Superior as 'reliable and fast as Express trains and the greatest fun in the world to drive' and in his last book *The Mint* the description of a ride on 'Boanerges' his Brough Superior at the time conjures up a word picture of the excitement and pleasure of riding. He unhappily met his death riding his Brough when swerving to avoid a cyclist who suddenly pulled out in front of him.

From 1940 the factory continued as precision engineers, but no more Brough Superiors were made and the machines that remain are jealously cared for by their owners who recognise the worth of the gentle giants.

8   B.S.A.

Many people wonder why it is that one of Britain's foremost motor cycle manufacturers appear to pass themselves off as gunsmiths. At first sight it would seem that the Birmingham Small Arms Company should be a case for prosecution under the Trade Descriptions Act! In fact the motor cycle company was derived from a group of gun makers originally called Birmingham Small Arms Trade Association from the late seventeenth century until the B.S.A. Company was formed in 1861.

Until about 1880 the company continued solely to make weapons, but then branched out into the world of manufacturing cycles. The story is told that a man named Otto presented the directors of the company with his own invention, a bicycle whose merits he proceeded to prove by riding it up and down the boardroom table! Needless to say the directors could not resist such a proposition and immediately ordered two hundred to be made. Cycles continued to be made and some tentative steps were taken in the direction of attaching the new-fangled internal combustion engine to effect their propulsion, but the Boer War once more took the attention of the company whose original interests after all lay in the making of war weapons.

With the turn of the century the B.S.A. Co., once more turned its attention to the production of parts for motor cycles manufactured else-where. It was not until 1910 that the first complete B.S.A. motor cycle took to the road. This was a $3\frac{1}{2}$ horsepower single speed model with cantilever front fork which was sold at a price of £50. An optional extra was a patent cone clutch in the rear hub called the 'free engine hub'. Early B.S.A.

designers paid particular attention to transmission, for example in 1913 the B.S.A. clutch was a three plate job operated by a toe and heel pedal. To start the engine the bottom gear was engaged and clutch freed, the latter being subsequently engaged to take up the drive. Gear changing was done on the valve lifter. It was fitted to machines during the First World War and continued until about 1920.

In the 1920s B.S.A. produced the side valve and overhead valve 350cc models and then the two speed 250cc side valve round tank model. This latter was not only cheap to buy, costing less than £40 it was also economic to run and an enjoyable ride. It was this model which was ordered by the G.P.O. when they inaugurated the telegram delivery service in Great Britain in 1924.

Nortons were not the only manufacturers intent on capturing the public eye with spectacular achievements of endurance and reliability during this decade. In 1924 a young trials rider, H. S. Perrey, led a team of four B.S.A.s on a mountain climb up Snowdon and got there in under twenty-five minutes! The achievement was subsequently emulated by many others but B.S.A. had been first. In about 1926 two men rode B.S.A.s on a round the world trip passing through some 24 countries in a matter of 18 months. Like Nortons the company had a machine built of spare parts gathered from a large number of dealers throughout Great Britain, which started first kick and went on to tackle a trial successfully. Perhaps the trouble with modern cycles is that they are built from parts coming only from one part of the country; certainly it is hard to find a machine nowadays that starts first kick!

B.S.A. were proud, and justly proud, of their Sloper (so called because of its sloping cylinder) which was built from about 1927 which quite by chance introduced the now world famous B.S.A. 'Star' series. Some Slopers had special cams fitted and a high compression piston and to distinguish them from the standard model a red star was stuck conspicuously on them. Subsequently the Blue Star, Empire Star and Gold Star followed them off the factory floor.

From the earliest days B.S.A.s have been used by the Post Office for telegraph boys and deliveries and the small all red lightweight machines have up until recently been in constant use in the communication business.

Apart from the Post Office and many large companies, which have utilised fleets of B.S.A. machines on the basis of their consistent high performance and reliability, the army too has used them in large numbers. But the army naturally expected more from the company than motor cycles when the Second World War started in earnest.

By the 1950s B.S.A. were probably Britain's largest motor cycle manufacturers. In 1953 the company accepted the fact that motor cycles were not just a fanciful sideline and for the first time created a separate division called B.S.A. Motor Cycles Ltd. The B.S.A. Bantam, the 125cc model, was perhaps the most popular small motor cycle of the 1950s, a role now taken over by the Japanese machines such as Honda and Suzuki. With the 1960s the factory turned its attention more to the manufacture of the big engine machines like the Victor, a 441cc brought out in 1965, and the Rocket 3, a 750cc, three-cylinder machine introduced in 1968. The latter had the proud achievement of breaking nine American speed and endurance records in double quick time, and achieving a victory for Dick Mann in the Daytona race of 1971 at a record average speed of 104·7 m.p.h. In fact it was not until the 1950s that the company had either any real interest or success in International racing events. Prior to this there had been notable successes in trials, but nothing spectacular when speed rather than endurance or reliability had been the criterion for success. But in the 50's there were victories in the T.T. Clubman's races and many victories in International moto-cross events and a quite remarkable success at Daytona, Florida, in the USA when they once took the first five places.

As with all motor cycle manufacturers financial problems have forced changes at B.S.A. In 1971 the B.S.A. plant at Small Heath, Birmingham, transferred production to the Triumph factory at Meridan. B.S.A. continued under its own name with the Rocket 3, the Lightning and the Thunderbolt (single and twin carburettor versions of the 650cc twin-cylinder models).

Production of B.S.A. motor cycles in quantity ceased at the end of 1971 and apart from a small number of moto-cross machines no further motor cycles have been built at the B.S.A. factory since that time. This does not mean that the B.S.A. factory became derelict. In fact following the re-organisation and concentration of activity into the three big blocks of buildings at the front of the factory area, they became busier than ever. They continued as principal suppliers in the manufacture of parts and the complete manufacture of the three-cylinder engine, and in addition, have done much sub-contracted engineering work for big companies like British Leyland and Massey Ferguson.

In 1973 the B.S.A. group was taken over by Norton Villiers who formed Norton Villiers Triumph Ltd.

9 CALTHORPE

Like many other manufacturers Calthorpe initially utilised the engines of others in the motor cycles they offered to the public, and again like so many others the J.A.P. (or J.A. Prestwich) engine was one of the main engines so used. Calthorpes first came on the market in about 1910 or 1911 made by the Minstrel and Rea Cycle Company in the Midlands of England and the company name did not change to Calthorpe until just after the First World War. J.A.P. and Precision engines were used in their lightweight side valve single-cylinder machines and by the end of the decade the 147cc Aza was produced. By the mid-twenties they had introduced a new overhead valve 348cc model in which both pushrods were enclosed in a single tube, but by then the machines were being powered by their own Calthorpe engines. Towards the end of the twenties the Calthorpe image was changed with a re-design of its physical appearance. The main change was to put a white saddle tank and white mudguards on the machine to catch the public eye when so many other manufacturers were endeavouring to do the same with chromium plating. The new range of models was called the 'Ivory Calthorpe' and despite subsequent modifications this range continued until the end of Calthorpe production with the accent being placed on the manufacture of the 250cc, 350cc and 500cc o.h.v.s.

However, like so many other British manufacturers, the Second World War effectively brought Calthorpe's life to an end. Just prior to the war the Birmingham-based factory was bought out by Bruce Douglas of Bristol when the firm went into liquidation in 1938, but his plans for Calthorpe motor cycles never had time to see the light of day.

10 CHATER-LEA

At the turn of the century the Chater-Lea company was founded for the manufacture and sale of pedal cycle components. With the increasing interest in the newly developed motor cycle the company started to make frames and other parts for motor cycles, and during those early years experimented with clip-on engines attached to ordinary pedal cycles. But it was not until about 1908 or 1909 that the first Chater-Lea motor cycle, a V-twin cylinder machine, was available for purchase. Like all those to follow up until the First World War, this machine was fairly heavy and of rather robust construction. Chater-Lea did not make their own engines and a multitude of foreign-made products were tried in the early years including the famous Antoine, de Dion Bouton, Minerva and Peugeot, but the company favoured in time the British-made J.A.P. and Blackburne engines. The early Chater-Lea motor cycles were particularly popular for sidecar work, usually powered by J.A.P. V-twin engines of 770cc or 1000cc. The company was at the forefront (not unnaturally in view of their basic interest and knowledge in cycle components) in the development of spring forks, and were fitting them on their motor cycles as early as 1910. Another advanced feature of the Chater-Lea was the dropped top tube of the frame, sloping at the rear until it merged neatly with the saddle tube, making for a lower centre of gravity and greater stability of the machine. This concept was maintained by Chater-Lea designers and was further developed and improved upon during the twenties. One other notable development of the Chater-Lea Company in the first decade of the century was the introduction and subsequent production of a cycle-car. Three-wheel cycle-cars were very popular in those early days of motoring, before Henry Ford made cheap motor cars available to the public.

For 1913 the company only marketed the big twin cylinder 8 horsepower machine, but this featured their own remarkably advanced three-speed gearbox. In the following year, the same model was again available together with a 2¼ horsepower single-cylinder model. War, however, brought production to an end.

Before the war, Chater-Lea's racing success had been rather limited. Sixth place in the 1908 Single Cylinder event in the Isle of Man T.T. races had been achieved but that was to be the beginning and the end of their success in the T.T., retiring on every other occasion an entry was made. However, after the war the Chater-Lea company found considerable success on the race track, particularly in the hands of Dougal Marchant and Ben Bickell. A change in emphasis took place on the factory floor, where, after a brief resumption with the 1914 models, the company concentrated on the production of medium-weight machines fitted chiefly with Blackburne engines while at the same time making and developing their own engine. On the race track Dougal Marchant gained a considerable reputation, being both tuner and racer for Chater-Lea, and nowhere was he more feared by rivals than at the famous Brooklands track, the home of British track racing. In 1923 he won the 200-mile 350cc sidecar race at an average of 57·63 m.p.h., and repeated this success the following year when he also broke the world record for the 'flying' kilometre at 100·81 m.p.h. on a solo machine, which was the first time a 350cc motor cycle had exceeded 100 m.p.h. Unfortunately this did not rank as a world record since it was achieved by riding only in one direction. However, Marchant made up for this in 1926 when he took the world record for the 'flying' kilo for both 350cc and 500cc at 102·99 m.p.h. on his 350cc Chater-Lea with its extensively modified pushrod operated overhead valve Blackburne engine. During the mid-twenties Marchant also developed the 348cc overhead camshaft engine with face cam with considerable success.

On the 'sales' front, Chater-Lea were trend-setters for saddle tanks, featuring them on the 1924 models. During the twenties and early thirties larger Blackburne side valve engines of 550cc were extensively used by Chater-Lea for their sidecar model which incidentally was one of the machines favoured by the Automobile Association for their patrols in Britain during that time. The company, which was basically a family concern, ceased production by 1933.

11 COTTON

In about 1913 a young law student called F. Willoughby Cotton took his hobby of motor cycling not only seriously, but also critically. He was not content with the accepted framework of the current motor cycle which had evolved from the pedal cycle. He realised the shortcomings of the normal unmechanical frame design, which was distorted to accommodate the engine, the tank, the gearbox and other components. He formulated his 'triangulating principle' which was the introduction of a frame on the principle of a triangle with the steering ahead braced scientifically to the rear spindle. His stated 'Principle of Design' was that every necessary tube should be straight and subjected only to compression or tension with full triangulation so that all stress was concentrated at the apex of each set of tubes.

The advantages of this new design were that the motor cycle was light in weight yet free from the previous constant risk of fracture in the frame. With its low centre of gravity the machine was more stable on the road and the rider himself was in a better riding position, the saddle being made lower than on most other machines.

Needing assistance in putting his idea into practice, Cotton turned to Levis who produced the desired construction and were enthusiastic to keep the rights for manufacturing their own machine based on Cotton principles. Taking this as a sign that he had a valuable asset and being in two minds about his career as a lawyer, Cotton decided to make a name in the motor cycling industry. To raise capital for his own factory he sold the rights of a new type of carburettor he had designed to an American firm. With this money he commenced operations in Gloucester after the end of the First World War, the home of Cotton ever since.

Never afraid to take chances, he entered three machines in the 1922 Junior T.T. in the Isle of Man only just over a year after production had started. One of the riders on that occasion was an unknown Irish boy of 18 years of age called Stanley Woods. Woods was given the chance of a ride after a letter arrived on Cotton's desk from Ireland in which it was stated with true Irish 'blarney' that young Stanley was a great admirer of the Cotton machine and had said he could win the T.T. if only he could ride that machine. His claim was justified the year after, when he averaged a speed of 55·73 beating the more famous A.J.S. and Douglas. In that first

T.T. opportunity Woods certainly started with a bang. Having lost a plug at the start and run back to collect it he managed to get into fourth position at the end of a couple of laps. When refilling with petrol the practice was to leave the engine running in case of difficulties in restarting. On this occasion petrol spilled on the engine and both machine and rider were immediately set alight. Nothing daunted, after extinguishing both himself and his machine Woods rode on to come in fifth. The career of the Cottons in the T.T. races was highly successful and in the 1926 Lightweight section, the 'Bobbins' (as they were nicknamed) took the first three places.

Up to the Second World War the engines utilised by Cotton included Blackburne, Villiers, J.A.P. Barr and Stroud sleeve valve, Bradshaw oil cooled and Sturmey Archer. At their peak in the late 1920s, the production of the Cotton decreased in the thirties and suffered greatly with the beginning of the Second World War. Cotton was forbidden to deal with his foreign customers and told to produce for the home market yet was given no specific order to fulfil. Factories do not exist on promises alone and after going into liquidation in 1940 a Government order for machines arrived on Cotton's desk! So production continued. With the end of the Second World War the need of the Government ceased, money became short and the factory ceased to function after producing a limited number of models, one of which was powered by the 500cc side valve J.A.P. twin.

In 1953 two men with an urge to go into the motor cycle production business, Monty Denley and Pat Onions, turned to the Cotton factory and with the encouragement of its founder, opened the Cotton doors for business once more. The obstacles facing them might have deterred two less enthusiastic or able men. From this time on the famous Cotton frame disappeared and the factory endeavoured to put a new face on the machine and compete with the big names again. The new men put the machines in for moto-cross and then road racing with success which was little publicised with the arrival of the Japanese machines on the scene.

Monty Denley died in about 1969, but after a change of premises in 1970 Cotton continued production from a base at Stratton Road, Gloucester, with Pat Onions remaining as one of the directors.

12 D.K.W.

D.K.W. is another European company who specialise successfully in the manufacture of the small lightweight motor cycle. In the German company's case, the very earliest motor cycles they produced were lightweights. Originally D.K.W. motor cycles were designed and manufactured in

Zschopau in Sachsen and then moved to Düsseldorf after the Second World War.

The first D.K.W. machine designed by Hugo Ruppe was in fact a bicycle with a 119cc engine attached over the rear wheel. This was in 1919. Small beginnings for the company which in the next two decades was to acquire the reputation of being the manufacturers of the greatest number of motor cycles in the world. D.K.W. mainly concentrated their attentions on two-stroke single-cylinder machines, with a few twin-cylinder jobs in the 100cc to 500cc range. The company revolutionised the two-stroke motor cycle industry in the thirties by their introduction of a separate cylinder to act as a charging pump. It was in about 1912 that D.K.W. utilised the so called 'loop scavenge system' devised by Dr. Schnuerle, a new system of induction. Briefly the top of the piston was flat (in contrast to other systems), the inlet ports were so angled into the cylinder walls as to direct the flow of mixture during the transfer stroke across the combustion chamber and away from the exhaust port so that it swept the exhaust gas out through the normal piston controlled port. This proved more efficient and generally more realiable than the usual deflector top piston and certainly gave greater power.

Successful factories like D.K.W. were actively encouraged by the new Germany of the 1930s and road racing success was helpful to create a good image. In the late thirties D.K.W. lightweight machines were not only one of the most popular in the world, but also one of the most successful. Significant proof of this is that the record average speed of 78·48 m.p.h. recorded by E. Kluge when winning the 1938 Lightweight T.T. event was not surpassed for twelve years by machines of that cubic capacity. Even the improved standard of engineering design hastened by war did not provide a better motor cycle engine or system than used on this D.K.W. The engine was a 250cc water cooled two-stroke engine of split single design with its third supercharging cylinder. This praise should be qualified as supercharging was pr hibited in international racing after the war, and the poorer low octane petrol then available did not assist the ordinary racing machine to achieve the speeds it might otherwise have attained.

After the Second World War, with a change of premises to Düsseldorf, the factory maintained its policy of manufacturing lightweight two-stroke motor cycles up to 350cc. This of course was a sound policy as the demand for relatively cheap and economical transport was greater than ever before. The recovery of Europe from its post-war poverty and need of economical transport in the late fifties, hit D.K.W. as it did all European motor cycle factories and resulted in the merger of D.K.W. with Zeirad-Union A.G. in Nuernberg. It is interesting to note that the Zschopau factory, now in East Germany, became the home of M.Z. motor cycles.

The latter day fame of D.K.W. is therefore chiefly in the more modest market of mopeds and motor scooters although even there D.K.W. technology evolved the automatic gear change for its Manuhurin model ahead of its competitors. But the D.K.W. factory continues as it started in the manufacture of the lightweight two-stroke motor cycle for which it has always been justly famous.

13 DOUGLAS

In 1905 the Fairy motor cycle was created by Joseph Barter – the 'flat' twin which was to become the world famous Douglas of dispatch-rider fame in the First World War. This Bristol-based firm developed the horizontal opposed fore-aft unit in about 1907 and continued utilising this system until well into the 1930s. William Douglas met Barter when the Douglas foundry made castings for the Fairy engines. The early Douglas models had direct belt drive, but in 1910 a two-speed gearbox with a design based on the back gear of a lathe was added, with the control on top of the tank. This was referred to as the 'tram driver' due to the fact that the lever was actuated fore and aft with a knob not unlike the control used on London trams. The true charm of the early Douglas motor cycles was in their lightness and ease of starting which in the days before the clutch system was developed and accepted, was accomplished simply by sitting astride the machine and giving a slight 'paddle' to set the engine in motion. Traffic stoppages – less frequent in those days – were endured with the engine in neutral, before another slight paddle enabled bottom gear to be engaged and the rider was once more on his way. Another attribute of the pre-war Douglas was its speed, reflected in racing successes such as their overwhelming victory in the 1912 Junior T.T. taking first, second and fourth places. W. H. Bashall, the former Bat-man, took the chequered flag almost five minutes ahead of his team mate E. Kickham who at least had the satisfaction of recording the fastest lap speed in the race. The following year, the best Douglas could do was a second place in the Junior T.T. with W. F. Newsome in the saddle, following the surprise winner Hugh Mason on his N.U.T. with two other Douglas machines in the first nine places.

The next important event for Douglas was in the First World War where many thousand were commissioned for official use by dispatch riders and were said to have performed admirably. After hostilities ceased in 1919 many war-time Douglas motor cycles were re-conditioned and sold to a public hungry for transport, bridging the gap until civilian motor cycle production could once more get into its stride.

Between 1920 and 1930 Douglas motor cycles were once more a power in motor cycle competitions although in a wider range of events, such as road racing, speed trials, hill climbs and the new discovery, speedway. In reliability trials the Douglas team of C. H. King, V. C. King and Spencer were regular winners of manufacturers' team awards during the immediate post-war period. In the late twenties Vic Anstice won many honours for Douglas at sprint events and at the world-renowned Brooklands track.

Earlier Tom Sheard on the new 500cc overhead valve Douglas won the Senior T.T. (the only Manxman to do so) and this combined with Freddie Dixon's victory in the sidecar race made 1923 a memorable year in the Douglas history. Dixon's machine was fitted with a banking side-car of his own design which, prior to the race, had been considered an unsafe device by many officials. However Dixon convinced them of its road-worthiness and proved it with a wonderful win. Freddie Dixon continued his racing career with a third place in the Senior T.T., again on a Douglas, although he was dogged with retirements in further attempts at success on Douglas machines. He was obliged to wait until 1927 for a solo win in the T.T. races. Meanwhile in 1925, on a H.R.D. Douglas, he had another sidecar victory in the Isle of Man T.T. races with L. Parker driving the first combination home.

On the standard production scene 1925 was also the year of the new E.W. model, which retained a modified fore and aft flat twin engine of 350 cubic capacity but up-dated in concept with the gear change for the three-speed box operated through the petrol tank which had an attractive sloping line in contrast with the flat parallel one used for so many years. The famous Douglas silver with blue panels colour scheme was retained and the new model attracted much attention at the British motor cycle show, another attractive feature being its price of £45. Douglas endeavoured at all times to keep the purchase price of their machines reasonable and this added greatly to their popularity in the years between the two world wars. The E.W. was immediately popular and continued with modifications for several years. In the years prior to 1932 Douglas designers always helped (intentionally or otherwise) the purchasers of their machines to save on motor taxes. Before that year there were different rates for motor cycle taxation dependent on the weight of the machine regardless of the engine's cubic capacity, so the lightweight Douglas motor cycles were much appreciated by their owners for this reason if for no other! The tax disc for motor cycles up to 224 pounds in weight cost half the amount charged for the heavier machines, while a sidecar added an extra £1 to the bill. All the Douglas 350cc machines came into the cheaper taxation class and even the C.32 500cc Douglas equipped with dynamo lighting came within the lower limit.

In 1928 speedway racing made its debut in Great Britain and for the first couple of years Douglas motor cycles dominated the tracks. In particular the 500cc o.h.v. Douglas was immediately popular and adapted to speedway purposes because of the model's aptitude for broadsiding due to its low centre of gravity. In time Douglas was superseded for dirt-track racing by Rudge.

The early thirties were significant years for the firm after a change of management and name to Douglas Motors (1931) Ltd., and the introduction of a new Douglas concept in motor cycling design in 1934. The new model was called the Endeavour and had a 500cc horizontally opposed twin-unit construction installed across the frame, as opposed to the in-line unit previously so popular with the factory. The new design fortunately did not commit the fore-aft unit to the scrap yard, as the Endeavour was not the success anticipated. But the Endeavour was an important landmark in the life of Douglas. Apart from the different positioning of the power unit, the significant changes to note were the four-speed gearbox with a hand-change at a time when most manufacturers favoured foot-change; shaft drive to the rear wheel via a spiral bevel final drive; the back wheel itself was quickly detachable for emergency tyre repairs. The engine was made with light alloy cylinders with cast iron liners and valve seatings between the head and barrel. The whole engine was only twenty inches wide when most of its contemporaries were far wider. The single plate fly wheel clutch was so light it could be operated by the little finger. The engine was set in a duplex loop frame and the model was listed originally at £72.10.0. when it made its surprise debut at the British Motor Cycle show of 1934. Despite its many fascinating and original features, the Endeavour failed to hold its own and after a few years the company were obliged to offer brand new models at £25.10.0. in order to recoup some of their losses on this venture. A sad time in the Douglas history but fortunately the set-back did not cripple the company.

Throughout the experimental period the factory had continued production of the popular 350cc in-line model, and with the Second World War the factory again began to assist the forces. In the early fifties the demand for motor-scooters enabled Douglas to manufacture the Italian Vespa under licence which they continued to do until 1960. For the man who preferred a little more power the Mark 3 de Luxe was brought out in 1949. This 348cc push-rod overhead valve transverse twin-cylinder machine was listed by the makers as the fastest standard 350 in the world, capable of 82 m.p.h. Its unusual features included a separate camshaft for each cylinder, a four-speed unit construction gearbox and a reversion to former ideas with foot-change of gears and final drive by chain. The engine was set in a tubular duplex frame with torsion bars supporting the rear swinging forks. The new Douglas forks were worthy of special comment as they were of radiadraulic loading link design.

Douglas motor cycles ceased to be made in the middle fifties and with the continuing success of the Vespas, the company decided to handle the British sales of another Italian motor cycling concern, Gilera. Sadly for the many enthusiasts no more of the delightful flat twin Douglas are coming off the production line.

14 THE DREADNOUGHT

Of recent years many engineers interested in motor cycles have constructed specials or 'one-offs' to obtain a machine incorporating in the specification all items which they consider necessary for a bicycle to perform the task for which it is required.

The Dreadnought is one of the earliest and possibly one of the most famous examples, built in 1902/3 by the late Harold Karslake in the works founded by W. E. Brough (father of George Brough). The construction of the frame was a unique design housing an M.M.C. engine of 3 horse-power purchased second-hand, in good condition, for 25/- (£1.25). It was a larger engine than the average type fitted at that time and considered desirable to avoid the use of pedals. A low saddle position was arranged (to avoid the dreaded side-slip) and many novel devices were incorporated which enabled the builder to accomplish fame as a rider for several years.

The requirements were general purpose use, such as a holiday tour of North Devon and Cornwall during 1906, accomplished on a single-gear machine with $4\frac{1}{2}$ to 1 ratio; two years later he climbed Porlock Hill, but by this time an N.S.U. two-speed gear had been fitted. In 1909 Karslake took part in the M.C.C.'s London–Edinburgh–London trial, but lost his award by being early at the time check at York. Competing in the Lands End Trial the following year, he was unfortunate enough to break an engine shaft, and he retired the machine temporarily. By October 1911, it had covered some 70,000 miles, and so earned the distinction of being exhibited on the Bat stand at the Olympia Show in London later that year.

In 1923 and again in 1927, 'Oily' Karslake, as he was affectionately known (due possibly to his connection with Speedwell Oils) rode the machine again in the M.C.C. London–Edinburgh Trial, now some 400 miles in length and including some formidable hills for that time. In the 1927 event he climbed all except one, due to belt slip caused by passing through the water splash at the foot of the hill, but gained a second class award.

The Dreadnought had the distinction of carrying number 1 in the first Sunbeam Pioneer Run from London to Brighton in 1930, when it was ridden by George Brough, and again on the 25th occasion of this event in 1961, when the author was honoured to pilot it once again to Brighton.

Harold Karslake donated the machine to the Vintage Motor Cycle Club and it can be seen on display at the Coventry Museum.

15 EXCELSIOR

Messrs. Bayliss, Thomas and Slaughter, three gentlemen with a common interest in developing and manufacturing bicycles, combined talents to form Bayliss Thomas and Co., in 1874. From the outset the name Excelsior was chosen for their machines and the emblem was that 'banner with a Strange Device'. The factory was set up in Coventry in the Midlands of England, where in 1896 the company first experimented with motorising their bicycles. Excelsior were the first British motor bicycles on sale to the general public and for that reason alone can claim pride of place in the British history of motor cycling. The first Excelsior motor bicycles had surface carburettors, hot tube ignition and were naturally belt drive. As a publicity stunt the company offered free rides to spectators at the Crystal Palace Exhibition of 1896 and not unnaturally succeeded in attracting all the attention. The early Excelsiors were fitted with de Dion and M.M.C. engines. Looking at an advertisement for a 1902 Excelsior one can see the main improvements claimed and selling features for the machine were the automatic oil lubricator, the 'Bayliss' patent anti-vibratory socket, the 'Bayliss' patent rim pulley attachment and the 'Bayliss' exhaust valve lift. The standard machine was sold with a 24-inch frame and 28-inch wheels with '12-inch Clincher A-Won' tyres. A 'special' was also generally advertised 'suitable for riders of short stature' with small wheels and cranks. What modern-day manufacturer would be so considerate as to cater for such needs? The standard $2\frac{3}{4}$ horsepower model could be purchased in those days for about £45. It would have been on such a model as this that Harry Martin rode in the first M.C.C. (Motor Cycling Club) run to Brighton in 1902 in the company of other early motor cycling pioneers. A year later in less sedate fashion Harry Martin recorded the first mile in less than a minute on a motor cycle (59 4/5 seconds to be precise) at the Dublin Phoenix speed trials.

The company was renamed the Excelsior Motor Co. Ltd., in 1910. Another record for the history books was created in 1913 when the company was responsible for the biggest single-cylinder motor cycle ever in general production, the 800cc side valve motor. Prior to the First World War Excelsior had purchased frames, mudguards and other parts from another Midlands company R. Walker and Son. Reginald Walker was originally in business manufacturing clock and ships' instrument cases but decided to strike off at a tangent and make parts for motor cycles. In 1910 this aspect of the business was doing so well, that Reginald Walker and his motor cycling-enthusiast son Eric decided to market their own complete motor cycle, which was called the Monarch.

After the Great War the Walkers took over the Excelsior company but continued to manufacture motor cycles bearing that proud name and emblem. The plant moved to Birmingham to join the Walkers and the production of motor cycles continued alongside the production of instrument cases. The company tentatively entered the field of manufacturing light cars but ceased production by the mid-nineteen-twenties. Eric Walker was a racing enthusiast and actively encouraged the use of Excelsiors in the major road races. In the hands of people like Walter Handley, Ernie Nott, H. G. Tyrell-Smith, Syd Gleave and Charlie Dodson, Excelsiors had their share of road racing success, highlighted by the victories of Crabtree and Syd Gleave in the lightweight events of the T.T. races in 1929 and 1933. Eric Walker realised that in the racing world he could not expect to win much if he used exactly the same engines as his rivals. So the company developed a four-valve engine built for them by Blackburne for the 1933 race, and Syd Gleave's 'mechanical marvel' justified its name. The 'Marvel' was quickly superseded by the overhead camshaft 'Manxman' a similar overhead camshaft model that was easier to manufacture. The pushrod 250cc 'Norseman', 350cc 'Warrior' and 500cc models proved popular with the motor cycling public in the thirties seeking two-wheel transport at a modest price. In the early days of mopeds, known pre-war as auto-cycles, Excelsior introduced the 'Auto-byk' with a 98cc engine of their own manufacture during 1937.

The 1902 man of small stature would have been more than content with the 'Wellbike' made by Excelsior for the Second World War parachute troops. This miniature motor cycle or scooter could be folded away into a container and dropped alongside airborne troops and thereafter ridden by a paratrooper on operations. This machine was developed for peacetime civilian use as the Brockhouse-built 'Corgi' using the 98cc Excelsior single-speed engine, the 'Spryt' and later the two-speed 'Goblin'. At the same time the 250cc parallel twin two-stroke Talisman was put into production and became popular. With the general trend towards small cc machines in the 1960s Excelsior concentrated their entire resources on production of motor cycle assembly kits for 98cc and 150cc two-stroke engine machines. Now the company makes Britax equipment and accessories for cars and motor cycles.

Bayliss, Thomas and Co. were the first but not the last to make motor cycles with the name Excelsior. The German Excelsior was made in Brandenburg-Havel between the years 1901 and 1906, and from 1927 to 1939 the British-made Excelsior sold in Germany under the name of 'Bayliss-Thomas'. The American Excelsior was made in Chicago, Illinois, between 1908 and 1931 by the well-known bicycle manufacturer Ignaz Schwinn, and from 1917 Schwinn took over production of the Henderson. The American trade name of Excelsior disappeared in 1924 to be replaced by 'Super-X'. Schwinn ceased production of motor cycles altogether in 1931 but continued to make pedal cycles.

16   FRANCIS-BARNETT

Gordon Francis, son of Graham Francis of Lea-Francis fame, combined talents with Arthur Barnett in 1919 to create a new lightweight motor cycle for which they felt there would be a great demand. In the post-war era economical transport was at a premium, and the new motor cycle was developed not only with motor cycle enthusiasts in mind, but also for citizens who had need of reasonably priced personal transport, but were inexperienced with machines. This is not to say that the early Francis-Barnett motor cycles were cheap to purchase, but neither was any form of motorised transport immediately after the war. The policy of motor cycles primarily intended for transport was maintained thereafter.

Gordon Francis and Arthur Barnett were in fact related by marriage. They started their business in Coventry in the Midland area of England, and by coincidence the first Francis-Barnett motor cycle was constructed in the same workshop as the first English motor cycle, the Bayliss-Thomas Excelsior. This was regarded as a good omen. The first 'Fanny Barnett' was a 292cc side valve J.A.P. engined machine with a two-speed Sturmey-Archer gearbox. Since it was being made for transportation rather than sporting purposes, there were valanced mudguards to prevent rainwater or mud splashing the rider, a pannier-holder fitted behind the bicycle-type saddle, footboards with toe-guards for further protection, and a cast-aluminium case housing the primary chain for the chain and belt drive. The petrol tank was painted an attractive red and black making the whole machine a pleasing sight to the prospective purchaser. He or she would only have had cause to hesitate when the price of £84 was mentioned. But the Francis-Barnett found its market and the following years saw modifications to the original and expansion in the range of machines available to the public.

Although not built for sporting purposes the standard model was by no means slow and the 350cc model could quite happily clock fifty miles per hour.

The high purchase price continued to be a problem with the ever-increasing costs of production, and at first seemed insoluble. Happily

Gordon Francis came up with a revolutionary plan which would give the buyer a cheaper but even better machine. The basis for the idea had been conceived during the First World War when he was in charge of motor cycle repairs in the Army. He had observed with alarm the frequency of motor cycle frame fractures and was able to try out his ideas for overcoming this problem when back in the Francis-Barnett workshop. In 1923 he evolved a system of six pairs of straight tubes and one pair specially formed which made up the framework of the motor cycle. In appearance the frame below the tank formed an inverted triangle, the triangular-shaped tank was held by a similarly formed set of tubes and the framework from saddle to rear wheel hub and down to the foot-rest formed yet another triangle. Even persons with elementary geometrical or engineering knowledge will appreciate how much stronger a machine so built will be.

The wheels of the new Francis-Barnett were on spindles which could be easily removed and the whole was driven by a 147cc Villiers two-stroke engine with flywheel magneto and Albion two-speed gearbox, with final belt drive. It could be dismantled and put together again quickly for the makers ensured simplicity by using only two different-sized nuts throughout. Light in weight, easy to strip and re-assemble (one test showed two men could put it together in 20 minutes) it was also light and easy on the pocket, and cost only £25. The reason for the low price was that less costs were incurred in the manufacture of the parts required. Everybody was satisfied with the new little Francis-Barnett which was claimed to be 'built like a bridge' because of its constructional principles. The frames were in fact under guarantee against breakage 'for ever'.

The 147cc was not the only machine to come out of the factory in 1923, as there were also 250cc and 350cc machines with sidecars available. But Francis-Barnetts' interests lay principally with the new 147cc machine which in the next few years was accompanied by a 172cc model. In one of the many tests carried out by enthusiasts in the 1920s, Mrs Meeten rode just over 1,000 miles in five days and averaged 196 miles per gallon. The whole journey cost her less than ten shillings (50 pence) in petrol and oil, a sad reminder of the cheap price of fuel in those by-gone days. Another stunt of the mid-nineteen-twenties was the ride up Mount Snowdon on motor cycles. The Francis-Barnett riders of 1926 were not the first, but were certainly among the speediest in climbing the 3,600 feet in about 22 minutes. A first was recorded in 1927 when Drew McQueen rode his Francis-Barnett 172cc machine up Ben Nevis in just over 2 hours. It was in that year that Francis-Barnett finally dropped the idea of belt drive, having offered the alternatives of chain or belt drive over several preceding years.

The next impact on the motor cycling scene made by Francis-Barnett was the Pullman, a 344cc vertical in-line twin with two-stroke Villiers engine. This became available to the public in 1928 and in the next two years Francis-Barnett followed the fashion which called for cream-coloured machines. The 250cc Cruiser brought out in 1933 typified the Francis-Barnett attitude to the traveller who did not want to dress up to keep clean on his or her motor cycle. This model was virtually wholly enclosed. The front mudguard enveloped the wheel as did the rear mud-guard, casing enveloped the engine and leg shields protected the rider from outside sources of dirt. One could ride the Cruiser in full evening dress and arrive immaculate. Production of this model continued up until the Second World War as did the manufacture of the 'Stag' model, a 248cc Blackburn-engined machine with overhead valves first introduced in 1935.

The other major events of the pre-war period were the manufacture of a 125cc model called the Snipe and an even smaller machine, an autocycle called the 'Powerbike' with 98cc engine, both of which made a return immediately after the end of the war. These models and other two-stroke lightweights were to be the order of the day from that time and con-tinued in production under the name of Francis-Barnett even when the company amalgamated with Associated Motor Cycles Ltd., the Matchless concern, in 1947. In the late fifties production was transferred to the Birmingham-based James Company workshops where they concentrated on making Villiers-engined two-stroke machines under 250cc. The firm, now under its new management, continued to make neat and economical motor cycles and mopeds until A.M.C. Ltd. ceased to operate.

17 GILERA

Guiseppe Gilera was the founder of a motor cycle company that in its heyday was to produce the most powerful engines and most successful racing machines in the world. Guiseppe Gilera's first love of motor cycles came as an enthusiastic young rider and with the aim of making better machines to ride, he started his own factory in 1909 in Milan, Italy. Gilera decided that the only way to improve the quality and performance of the motor cycles he rode would be by making his own engines and from the earliest days his motor cycles used only Gilera-built engines. From the beginning the 500cc was favoured by the young manufacturer and it is in this class that they hit the headlines over the years. The first 500cc models were side valve single-cylinder machines but as time passed and the Gilera became more popular, the range was extended to include 250cc and 600cc models.

It was perhaps not until the late thirties that Gilera came to world-wide attention with the famous 'Four' which took the racing scene by storm, and showed itself to be in a class on its own. This new engine was based on the former Rondine design by Carlo Giannini. The Rondine motor cycle had a fairly chequered career in the hands of its original manufacturers, the Compagnia Nazionale Aeronautica and subsequent owners, before all rights to its design were purchased by Gilera in 1936. The success of the Rondine four-cylinder machine in races had often been thwarted by difficulties in handling experienced by its riders and there was still room for improvement in the engine department. The remedy was swift. Within a couple of years the Gilera Four had made its racing name. It was a 500cc transverse four-cylinder machine, supercharged and water-cooled. The massive engine was held in the duplex cradle frame by webs at each end of the crankcase, and road holding and comfort was improved by the pivoting fork suspension controlled by horizontal units and massive friction dampers. Gilera could point to his first racing machine with pride, since it achieved the world speed record of 154 miles per hour and the world motor cycle speed record of 171 miles per hour. With modifications the same model won the 1939 Ulster Grand Prix at a record average speed of 97·85 miles per hour, with D. Serafini in the saddle. In the same year Gilera won the coveted European 500cc championship.

The greatest racing success was yet to come. In the post-war period Gilera further developed the four-cylinder machine for racing, at the same time manufacturing small single-cylinder overhead valve machines of 150cc and 250cc for public purchase. In 1950 the Dutch and Belgian Grands Prix were added to the list of Gilera 'Four' victories. The factory had not entered the Isle of Man T.T. races prior to the Second World War and their early attempts in the post-war period were thwarted by mechanical failure. But the warning was given by the fast pace set by machines which unhappily 'packed up' before the finish. Reg. Armstrong took third place in the 1953 Senior event and in the following year ace rider Geoff Duke improved that position by one. Duke had changed his allegiance to Gilera from the Norton team by this time and his former colleagues who reigned supreme in the early fifties could feel the hot breath of Gilera on the back of their racing necks. In the following year 1955, Gilera were in front. First and second place in the Senior event were easily taken by Duke and Armstrong, and Duke nearly became the first man to record an average lap speed of 100 m.p.h. when he turned in a speed of 99·97 m.p.h. That honour in fact fell to Bob McIntyre on another Gilera in 1957 when winning the Golden Jubilee Senior race with a fastest lap speed of 101·12 m.p.h. In the same year a 350cc Gilera also took first place in the Junior event, being ridden once again by Bob McIntyre. The difference in the fastest lap speeds between McIntyre's 350cc Gilera and John Surtees' winning 500cc M.V. Augusta in the Senior event the year before was a trivial 4/10 of a mile per hour. In 1957 McIntyre set an incredible 97·2 miles per hour 350cc lap record. Since those heady days when four-cylinder Gileras were the fastest on the racing circuit, other riders to record success on Gilera machines have been John Hartle and Phil Read. When writing of successful road race riders in the Gilera history it would be wrong to omit mention of earlier champions like Piero Taruffi who did so much for Gilera on the track and also assisted in developing early Gilera 'Fours' prior to the Second World War. An example of the quality of Gilera racers, both men and machines, was demonstrated by the exhibition ride of Geoff Duke in the Isle of Man in 1973. In the interval between the Manx Grands Prix races he rode a circuit of the course on a twelve-year-old Gilera racer and recorded an average of 87 m.p.h., which means speeds of over 100 m.p.h. in places. After such a long absence for both machine and rider, this average speed speaks volumes for their joint ability.

Like so many other European manufacturers the latter-day standard production Gileras have largely consisted of lightweight 98cc, 125cc and 175cc single-cylinder models. The racing successes of Gilera have added to the company's prestige, and the sound policy of manufacturing small single-cylinder machines has ensured survival when other equally successful racing motor cycle companies have been obliged to go into liquidation.

18 HARLEY-DAVIDSON

It is almost to be expected that a motor cycle made in the United States of America will acquire slogans eulogising the machine over a period of years, but the Harley-Davidson is perhaps the most famous motor cycle being manufactured in America today, certainly the one with the greatest history. How then did the 'silent gray fellows', 'the motor cycle magnificent', and even 'the bunch of dynamite' begin? The answer is in a Milwaukee basement workshop at the turn of the century when William Harley and Arthur Davidson, a draughtsman and patternmaker respectively, got together to experiment with mechanising a bicycle. They had met working in a motor cycle factory and with the spirit of adventure started their now famous venture. Arthur's brother Walter was called in to assist and he had the pleasure and privilege of road testing their first product, a 3 horsepower single-cylinder machine, and Walter in fact road-tested every new model for the next twenty-five years. Soon afterwards Arthur's oldest brother William joined the organisation making the firm a truly family organisation, which it continued to be through the years, one generation succeeded by the next, until 1969, when the company merged with American Machine and Foundry Co., and 'went public'.

As early as 1907 the police force started using the Harley–Davidson motor cycle as a means of official transport. In the USA the police force is divided into many departments within the various states, but in due time over three thousand departments were using the 'Harley' and for many people the Harley–Davidson became synonymous with the motor cycle cop!

Motor cycles did not catch on in the USA in quite the same way as in Europe and a good reason postulated is the fact that motor cars were very quickly on the scene and selling at remarkably low prices. In Europe there was also the attraction that the motor cycle would ride the road better and possibly be more reliable than the contemporary motor car. The average distance to be covered by the traveller in Britain would be less than for his American counterpart and for that reason alone a car would always prove more comfortable and convenient. Added to this was the unaccountable fact that the European was more enthusiastic about motor cycling as a sport or hobby than the men from across the Atlantic. Today the reverse may well be true.

For one reason or another in the early days of motor cycling the Harley–Davidson really only had one major rival in the USA, the Indian, which unhappily ceased production in 1959.

The early Harley–Davidsons were all high-power models with direct belt drive and twist throttle control. Bill Harley went off to university to get an engineering degree and returned to become the company's chief engineer. Early successes in 'endurance runs' (or trials as we would call them in Europe) did not cause complacency. Harley's aim was to produce a twin-cylinder model, which he achieved in about 1909. Features of the new Harleys were the now familiar low saddle position on a frame which had the front tube vertical and coil or magneto ignition. The wide wheels were to come at a much later date. Chain drive was incorporated about 1912.

Before the First World War found yet another use for the Harley–Davidson, throughout America the machines were being used by police, telephone companies and postal services. In the war the American military men found more use for motor cycles than did the British services. Not only were the Harleys 'conscripted' for construction battalions, the signal corps and medical corps, but also for transporting arms and ammunition. By this time they were known not only for their power and reliability, but also for their speed, having shown this in a hundred-mile test averaging 89 m.p.h. for the distance. Although they rarely sponsored their machines in races Harley–Davidson were able to capitalise on the enthusiasm of racing men with their slogan 'Don't blame us if a Harley–Davidson wins the race!' So when America entered the war it was not unnatural to see that the chosen motor cycle was the big Harley. Whether it was 'army surplus' or to remind the nation of the part they played in the war, Harleys for many years afterwards continued to be painted khaki!

Renewed enthusiasm for motor cycles after the war was encouragement enough for Messrs. Harley and all the Davidsons. The Big Twin model J was introduced to the eager public together with a sporting model which for the first time had a counterweighted crankshaft, enclosed timing gear drive to the generator ignition unit and new exhaust system, leading link forks for the front suspension, the typical foot-boards rather than foot-rests and 3-inch tyres. One of the little exercises undertaken in the early twenties was the Canada to Mexico run, which makes the Lands End to John O'Groats trial seem like a Sunday afternoon outing. On one occasion a Harley-Davidson clipped five hours off the record time for the 1,700 mile run.

Expansion was the main object in the 1920s whether of production or market. Harley-Davidson saw Europe as a prospective market and with that in mind introduced the comparatively small 350s into their production line, which picked up the nickname of the 'peashooter'. This appeared with the unusual bomb-shaped tank, 'hooded' mudguards and wide wheels. The British public at least were already aware of the existence of Harleys, having witnessed another Davidson (no relation to the firm) become the first man to lap Brooklands in excess of 100 m.p.h. in about 1919. The British manufacturers therefore were already on their guard for the prospective invasion. As can be seen elsewhere in this book British machines in the 1920s were more than a match for outside competitors. The 'Depression' also hit production in the Harley-Davidson factory with the result that the challenge never really materialised. The early thirties were a hard time for the company.

An innovation of the thirties was the now familiar 'balloon' tyres, 500×16 Firestones. Another new step was the production of a three-wheeler called a 'Servi-car'. This like the motor cycle was immediately utilised by the police forces of America and also became very popular with delivery services. In 1936 an attempt to open a factory overseas in Japan was not destined to be a success. Another war, another day for Harley's. Nearly 100,000 Harley-Davidson motor cycles were used in this 'world event'. The post-war needs were for economical motor cycling and manoeuvrability, which once again caused the company to bring out a smaller model, this time the 125cc two stroke which, like the B.S.A. Bantam, owed much to the conquered German D.K.W. design.

As mentioned previously, in the early days the directors rather frowned upon the racing fraternity. Over the years the attitude changed, as can be seen from the number of world records achieved by riders on Harley-Davidsons with assistance in some way from the company. For example, in the 1930s Petrali secured the world record with an astonishing average speed of 139·15 m.p.h. But the 'biscuit' was truly taken by the company when in the early 1950s a big Harley won a race over half a mile with a Mustang Aircraft – the latter was obliged then to take off!

The company ceased to be a family business in 1969, but by then they had already expanded into Europe taking over the Aer-Macchi factory in Verese, Italy. Business, as one would expect with anything to do with Harley-Davidson, continues to be big.

19 HENDERSON

William G. Henderson had the distinction of being responsible for two of the most celebrated makes in the history of motor cycling. In a life cut tragically short by a fatal accident in 1922 he was founder and designer of both the Henderson and the Ace four-cylinder motor cycles. In eleven short years Henderson inscribed two names on the motor cycle roll of honour.

Starting the Henderson Motor Cycle Company with his brother Tom in Detroit, Michigan, in the United States of America, William Henderson had his first motor cycle off the production line in 1912. The first model, like all succeeding Henderson motor cycles, was a four-cylinder machine with a distinctive and unusually long wheelbase of 65 inches. Its original method of starting was by way of hand crank, rather similar to that used by most old cars, operated when the machine was up on its stand.

Henderson also finished all his machines in distinctive colours, the first models black with gold stripes, and red stripes on mudguards and tank panels, followed in subsequent models by a basic blue with gold stripes. Part of the reason for the lengthy wheel base was the positioning of the foot-board in front of the engine. Subsequent models were made with a shorter wheel base when two foot-boards were fitted outside the frame on either side of the machine.

The first Henderson seated the rider on the lengthy cylindrical tank just in front of the rear wheel, necessitating rather long handlebars for controlling the machine. Provision was made for possible passengers with a saddle on the tank in front of the driver. This meant that the passenger not only partially obscured his driver's vision of the hazards ahead, but also impeded the free movement of the handlebars and consequently the front wheel. However there were very few other criticisms and Henderson soon abandoned this position for passengers.

Other features of the first model were that it provided a remarkably smooth, quiet ride and a reliable performance. The 1912 model, like its successor in the following year, was single-speed only but this did not prevent a New Yorker, Carl Stevens, from riding one round the world, the first motor cyclist to perform this feat. In 1912 this seven-horsepower motor cycle could be purchased for a mere 325 dollars.

Henderson modified his motor cycle over the next few years. The wheel base was shortened, the riding position was lowered and improvements to the front forks all helped the machine's handling. The shape of the tank was altered and a two-speed gearbox was first introduced in 1914, to be replaced in 1917 by a three-speed version. The Henderson had quickly earned a reputation throughout the United States for reliability and proved its performance in endurance trials. One of the formidable tests was the Coast-to-Coast run across the USA over more than three thousand miles of rough terrain. In those early days the made-up road was confined to the cities and anyone who ventured beyond the city limits did so at his own risk. Motor vehicles found the going particularly hard and their drivers likewise. Allan Bedell, a Henderson enthusiast and a rider with a promising future, made a record-breaking run from Los Angeles to New York City in seven days and sixteen hours, to beat the previous best performance by nearly four days. Tragically that promising future was never realised for young Bedell was one of those who did not return from the First World War.

Another endurance record to fall to the 1917 Henderson was the Canada to Mexico run called the 'Three Flag Route'. Roy Artley on his Henderson Four broke the two-year-old record when riding the seventeen hundred miles in three days and twenty-five minutes. The Americans have always had a flair for publicity stunts – elsewhere in this book the early boasts of Edward Joel Pennington are described – but even he would have been proud to have originated the 'roller coaster run'. This daring feat was performed by one August E. Walter, better known as Blick Walter, who confidently rode his 1917 Henderson Four round a roller coaster track in a Californian fair ground. He presumably still holds the world record for this run!

Whether it was this last feat or the overall performance over a number of years Henderson was brought to the eye of its American rival Excelsior. In 1917 the Excelsior chief Ignaz Schwinn made the Henderson brothers 'an offer they couldn't refuse' and took control of the Henderson Motor Cycle Company in a deal which allowed the brothers themselves to continue work for a short while. The motor cycle produced under the new regime was the Excelsior-Henderson although it is more commonly known as the Henderson X because of the transfer on the petrol tank showing a large red X with the name 'Henderson' emblazoned across it in gold letters.

Both Henderson brothers severed their connection with the Excelsior-Henderson in 1919 and William G. Henderson decided to start again on his own this time without the able support of his brother Tom in a new motor cycle venture. He started his second business in Philadelphia making another four-cylinder motor cycle, this one to be called the Ace. Ace were only in production for three short years until Henderson's death, and the motor cycles manufactured by him were 1168cc and 1229cc air-cooled four-cylinder side valve machines. After Henderson's death the Ace factory was bought up by the Michigan Motor Corporation and later sold to Indian, hence the Indian-Ace produced in the late nineteen-twenties.

But with William Henderson's departure from the Excelsior-Henderson scene, the factory did not cease to thrive. New blood was injected into the design team in the person of Arthur Lemon. Lemon had been with Hendersons from 1915 and transferred with the company in 1917 to Schwinn's organisation. His new design for 1919, the Model K, was a dramatic change from the former Henderson models, with a larger engine and a new type of cylinder and was the first American motor cycle with full pressure lubrication to all bearings. This model was so popular that production of it continued until 1921, while the De Luxe model K continued to be made until 1929. The De Luxe had a guaranteed speed of 80 m.p.h. and an unusual feature, a reverse gear.

Lemon continued at the helm until the fatal accident to Henderson in 1922 caused him to join Ace to assist at their time of crisis. It was in that year that the great American rider Wells Bennett created one of his many records, taking the much-coveted twenty-four hour record previously held by Cannonball Baker on his Indian. Bennett, riding his Henderson X model K de Luxe said to be a standard model, covered 1562·54 miles in the twenty-four hours period and averaged over 65 m.p.h. This record stood for another fifteen years. If this highlighted the reliability of the Excelsior-Henderson K De-Luxe, then Fred Ludlow's 127·1 m.p.h. for the fastest quarter-mile in the world in 1924 proved that endurance was not obtained at the expense of speed. These two qualities always appeal to motor cyclists and to catch the faster men many police forces decided to ride the same machines. There is an American saying 'it takes a Henderson to catch a Henderson'!

Modifications of the De Luxe in the mid-twenties included a change of frame to one which sloped downwards at the rear and allowed for a lower saddle position and the addition of balloon tyres, always popular with American motor cyclists.

A. R. Constantine transferred from the rival Harley-Davidson to take over design of the Henderson X in about 1928. He aimed at a lower riding position and better engine performance and to this end he designed the K.J. model which upon its appearance and performance merited its nickname of the 'Streamline Henderson'. The modified version, the K.L., was reputed to go from a mere ten miles per hour to one hundred and ten miles per hour all in top gear.

During the twenties Henderson engines were also used to power light aircraft and turned in many remarkable performances. But the depression was hovering on the horizon and as it enveloped the country, so it naturally affected the sales of all motor vehicles. Schwinn realised that however good his products were, there would be little market for their sale in the foreseeable future and decided to close down the motor cycle manufacturing side of the business in 1931, while continuing the pedal cycle business. It was therefore no reflection upon the Henderson X as a motor cycle that no more were made after 1931. Happily there are still Henderson motor cycles in existence as constant reminders of their once great presence in the world market of motor cycles.

20 HONDA

The Honda Motor Company was established in 1948. By 1950 their motor cycle production was a mere 9 per cent of the Japanese market with no influence on the outside world. The early 1950s were dominated by the British machines which with years of pedigree behind them were correctly thought to be better, sounder and more reliable motor cycles. Complacency is a dangerous attitude. Soichiro Honda was not a man to shy away from what must have been an awe-inspiring challenge. Nortons, A.J.S., B.S.A., Velocette, and Triumph appeared to have a strangle-hold at least on the British market. By 1958 however Honda had increased output four times over and were looking for a way to catch the buyer's eye. The best advertisement was success in racing, and they scored their first success in the US Catalina Race in that year. 1959 saw the first Honda in the Isle of Man and in 1961 they took both the 125cc and 250cc world championships. Honda was making his impression especially in the low capacity field. His later policy was to make machines to satisfy the requirements of everybody everywhere and he had realised that the small, mobile, easy-to-start 50cc was the machine to meet such a need.

Previous attempts to produce a good 50cc by other manufacturers in most cases had met with conspicuous failure due to the unreliability of the finished product. Most British manufacturers refrained from even trying to make such an animal. Previously it had always been assumed that motor cyclists would only ride a machine that had to be kick-started, was prone to violent vibration during the ride and the introduction of 'gadgets' such as the electric starter, automatic clutch and even automatic transmission seemed unwanted gimmicks. In fact, of course, the motor cyclist is a man of many faces. There are enthusiasts who like nothing better than the machine in parts by the side of the road, or a hard ride in trial or racing conditions, but there is a market for the motor cyclist about town who is not averse to a few luxuries when riding two wheels. Honda, like Scott before him in 1908, introduced his 250cc twin with pistons moving in opposite directions to cut down vibration. The speeds of the small machines was and still is quite remarkable: for example, nearly 100 m.p.h. out of a 250cc. Remembering that second-hand cars could be easily purchased for the price of a new motor cycle, the attraction of two wheels had to be obvious enough to keep a market amongst people who merely wished to travel from home to work or on pleasure drives. Motor cycles had to be more economical to run, but comfort and reliability were the other attractions offered by Honda.

1961 was considered the turning point. Before then, if the man in the street was asked to name a motor cycle, one of the famous British or European makes would have sprung to his lips, but now inevitably the name would be Honda. Although popular in Europe and Asia, nearly a third of the sales were made in the USA. The enthusiasm of the founder is reflected in the attitude of his employees in the factories at Saitama, Hamamatsu and Suyuka. By 1961 these three factories alone were turning out over 3,500 motor cycles per day. Perhaps their success is not surprising. After confining himself initially to the small cc market (250 and less) Honda has now produced four-cylinder models of 350, 500 and 750cc to compete with the best in the world, both on the race track and in market sales. In racing circles the leading Honda exponent has been Mike Hailwood who has electrified spectators all round the world with performances and victories in probably every international race of consequence. Where others have fallen victims to financial problems, Honda's have prospered and the outlook for this Japanese organisation seems as bright as ever.

21 H.R.D.

It is not often that a celebrated racing motor cyclist turns successful manufacturer and in this respect Howard R. Davies was almost unique. Winning the Senior T.T. race is usually regarded as a wonderful achievement and perhaps the crowning glory of the racing motor cyclists' career, but when it was achieved in 1921 by Davies on a 350cc A.J.S. motor cycle in competition naturally with 500cc machines, it truly made history. Indeed Davies' victory should not have been allowed to stand strictly speaking as the tyre dimensions did not accord with those laid down for the Senior race machines, but fortunately sportsmanship counted for something in those days and overwhelmed the professional objections which could have spoilt this race. A further remarkable feature about this combined Davies and A.J.S. success was that the machine was driven by the same engine in the Senior race that had just been used (naturally under heavy stress) in the Junior race. This is a tribute to the A.J.S. reliability and stamina as well as its speed. Davies had in fact already picked up a second place in the Junior which an ill-timed puncture prevented him from winning. By 1921 Howard Davies had already built a good racing reputation with a second in the 1914 Senior T.T. on a Sunbeam to his credit. However subsequent big race success often eluded Davies, due not to lack of skill but to the unreliability of the machines he rode. With a view to changing this situation he decided that 'if you want a job well done, you do it yourself'. Together with the technical assistance of Massey of Massey-Arran fame, Davies went into motor cycle production in 1924 at his new works in Wolverhampton. Howard Davies believed that a rider was a considerable factor in slowing a motor cycle down in a race and therefore lowered the saddle while maintaining the relatively high position of the petrol tank, which was necessary if the long stroke engine was to remain vertical in the frame. He removed the usual impediment of a lower tank rail altogether. The tank itself with the proud gold letters H.R.D. emblazoned on the side was specially adapted by means of careful cutting away to overcome the difficulties created by the valve gear position and size.

The engine chosen to power this new motor cycle was the J.A.P., there being two models of 350cc (sports and racer) and two models of the 500cc (sports and sidecar).

The foot-rests with brake and auxiliary oil pump pedals were adjustable to meet the needs of the individual rider and the whole was set in a rigid cradle frame. Davies wanted a machine to win races as success was the best advertisement. Inevitably the T.T. races represented the big test for him, a way of proving that he had made worthwhile innovations in motor cycle manufacture and that he himself was a great rider of the present and not just the past. He was only a year into production and in competition with the great names in motor cycle manufacturing circles and the equally great names of their riders. Yet Howard Davies rode his own machine to victory in the 1925 Senior T.T. and beat a field that included the great Alec Bennet and Jimmy Simpson, and he took second place in the Junior. Sadly he was not to know personal success like that again, although an H.R.D. and Freddie Dixon won the 1927 Junior T.T.

The General Strike of 1926 greatly affected H.R.D. who like so many motor cycle manufacturers through the ages perpetually walked a financial tight-rope. The H.R.D. motor cycles were sold at 'luxury' prices while other motor cycle prices were becoming more realistic for the would-be purchaser.

H.R.D. went into voluntary liquidation in 1928 and were eventually put back into production by Philip Vincent under the new name 'Vincent-H.R.D.'

Under new management the Vincent-H.R.D. now manufactured at Stevenage showed very little physical resemblance to the H.R.D. which had formerly been on the market. The leading innovation to improve the motor cycle still selling partly under its old name was the Vincent spring frame. This gave the motor cycle an extra diagonal frame tube on each side of the bike running from steering head to a rear pivot supported by Timken taper roller bearings. Phil Vincent later changed the J.A.P. engines for either his own or Blackburne or Villiers.

Howard Davies apparently did not retain any control or have any say in matters after Vincent took over, despite the fact that his name continued to be used on the machine for selling purposes. At no time does it appear that Phil Vincent saw fit to consult with Howard Davies on any design feature or alteration and to all intents and purposes the motor cycles produced after 1928 had no connection with H.R.D. Davies himself reverted to his former occupation as a sales representative for motoring companies.

In 1937 Phil Vincent put his first 1,000cc Vincent H.R.D. with high camshafts into production and it is with these big bikes that Vincent's name will always be connected. It was not until 1950 that Vincent finally dropped the H.R.D. tag and continued production under the sole name of Vincent until 1956. History has a habit of repeating itself. Like the Howard Davies organisation before, Vincents finally succumbed to financial pressures and ceased to be produced. It was a strange quirk of fate that it was only after this that the two men Davies and Vincent should meet for the very first time. A year or so later Howard R. Davies died having contributed so substantially to both the manufacturing and racing history of motor cycles.

22 HUMBER

It was in 1868 that Thomas Humber, later to become one of the greatest names in the world of transport, started production of velocipedes at his workshops in Nottingham. Humber bicycles were of such quality that they were the choice of three generations of British monarchs and the company he established was responsible in the course of time for the production of motorised bicycles, tricycles, quadri-cycles, tricars, motor cars and even aeroplanes. Like Harold James, Thomas Humber had ceased association with his company by the time the motorised transport came into being, but he at least lived to see the motor vehicles bearing his name in popular use. Based at Beeston, Coventry and Wolverhampton in the Midlands of

England, the Humber works by the 1890s were responsible for most reputable bicycles and tricycles. 1892 was a significant year in the life of Humber. It was that year that Humber introduced the supported diamond frame which was adopted as standard by the cycle and motor cycle industry for the next sixty years. The company made its last ordinary or penny-farthing bicycle that year, and also made the most important change of all, when Thomas Humber resigned.

It was not until 1895 that the first experiments with engines were carried out at the Humber factory under the guiding influence of H. J. Lawson. Experiments were at this time also carried out for a short period on an electric tandem cycle. The first Humber experimental motor cycle was ready by 1896 based on the Kane-Pennington design, the patent of which Lawson purchased for £100,000. The experiment was a disaster. Success was to follow, however, with the manufacture of the popular Leon Bollee and De Dion type tricycles for which Lawson again held the patent rights.

1899 saw the introduction of the first four-wheel Humber, a De Dion type quadricycle followed by the M.D. quad with a single-cylinder engine driving the front wheels, while steering was supposedly achieved with the rear wheels.

The company re-formed in 1900 under different management as Humber Ltd., and the manufacture of motor cycles from that time was solely at the Coventry- or Beeston-based works. Humbers were experimenting with motor cars at the same time as motor cycles. The first Humber motor car proper entered the scene in 1901 and production of motor cycles began in 1902 with two models, one of which was belt-driven with a Minerva engine, and the other chain-driven. The latter was made under licence from Phelon and Moore and proved without doubt to be the finest design of its era. One of the most successful Humber motor tricycles was the Olympia Tandem which carried a passenger in a basket chair in front of the rider.

One aspect of the early Humber motor cycle which attracted attention was the use of the free engine clutch. By 1905 Humbers had entered the coach-built tricar scene with another Olympia model. Motor cycle production was suspended for four years between 1905 and 1909 due to the expansion of the motor car side of the business and a general recession in the motor cycle industry. They re-commenced with a $3\frac{1}{2}$ horsepower model followed closely by a 2 horsepower model. Although belt-driven, the $3\frac{1}{2}$ horsepower model had a two-speed Humber Roc epicyclic hub gear with starting handle and substantial band clutches. Its flexibility and reliability played a major part in the acceptance of the light sidecar as a means of sociable transport. That so many machines of the 1911–12 designs are still in existence is a clear testimony of their quality.

In motor cycle racing the greatest Humber success recorded must be P. J. Evans' victory in the 1911 Junior T.T. race in the Isle of Man, when he not only recorded the fastest lap average at 42 miles per hour but also finished over nine minutes ahead of his nearest rival, Harry Collier on the highly esteemed Matchless. Evan's Humber was a 342cc V-twin cylinder machine with belt drive and an Armstrong Triplex hub gear and was kept secret until the race when six such Humbers started and all finished. This model held the Brooklands record for 1911–12 for the 350cc class at 59 miles in the hour. Meanwhile the first regular air-mail service in the world was opened in India using Humber biplanes.

In 1913 an air-cooled motor cycle of 743cc was announced, with two small cylinders to the rear and one large one to the front giving perfect balance. Production difficulties permitted only six to be made, but the design was the forerunner of the 750cc water-cooled flat twin of 1915. This was dropped in 1916 in favour of a $3\frac{1}{2}$ horsepower air-cooled flat-twin as the sole Humber model. Car production ceased to allow the factory to concentrate on the manufacture of the Avro 504K and the BR2 nine-cylinder rotary aeroplane engine. Field kitchens and shells were additional war-time products of the Humber factory.

Motor cycle production re-commenced after the war with a $4\frac{1}{2}$ horse-power air-cooled flat twin which was continued until 1924 and in 1922 the first of a series of conventional $2\frac{3}{4}$ horsepower side-valve machines was introduced and this model continued in production until 1930. An over-head valve model was brought out in 1926 followed by an overhead camshaft 350cc model in 1928.

The latter part of the twenties proved a difficult time for most industries in Britain and financial problems brought several companies to their knees. In 1928 the Hillman factory, close neighbours of Humber, were bought out and it was not long before the directors at Humbers decided to discontinue motor cycles and concentrate on car production. In 1932 Rootes Ltd. took over, and the bicycle interest was sold to Raleigh, the famous Nottingham cycle manufacturers. The wheel had turned full circle.

23 HUSQVARNA

Like many other motorcycle manufacturers, Husqvarna developed from the bicycle trade, the transition occurring in 1903. Indeed the early models were very much like bicycles with the added encumbrance of an engine. The pedals, handlebars, frame, saddle and wheels of the first Husqvarna all had the distinctive appearance of the normal pedal cycle, and since the engine was imported from Belgium, in the beginning Husqvarna could not claim to be pathfinders in the motor cycling world. The first model was powered by the Belgian single-cylinder four-stroke $1\frac{1}{4}$ horsepower F.N. engine with belt drive to the rear wheel. It was claimed that speeds up to 50 kilometres per hour (25 to 30 miles per hour) could be achieved, although (as the instruction manual did warn the rider) there might be certain difficulties in starting the machine from cold. In that event the rider was urged to heat the carburettor 'by holding a burning newspaper under it' and the present day reader may wonder in what proportion machines and riders were lost in that way.

The Belgian engine was used until 1909 when investigation showed that perhaps another foreign manufacturer had a better product, namely Moto-Reve from Switzerland. In fact this change did not prove entirely successful as the Moto-Reve engines were not quite as reliable as the tried and proven F.N. engines. However for about ten years Husqvarna continued an occasionally strained relationship with Moto-Reve. During this period, apart from introducing the twin-cylinder engine, progress at Husqvarna was marked by the introduction of all-chain-drive from as early as 1909 and kick-start mechanism.

Husqvarna's driving force for so long was Gustaf Tham, their managing director from 1911 until 1946, who not only encouraged the development of the machine but also urged the company into motor cycling competition on the basis that success would be the best advertisement to sell the product. At first success was only achieved on a national basis, but this was better than nothing. As early as 1916 Husqvarna were able to produce a sufficiently reliable and tough motor cycle to win the Swedish Novemberkasan (November Trophy) Trial and indeed take second and third places as well. With their growing reputation came an order to supply the Swedish Army with motor cycles, which proved to be a much-needed financial fillip.

It was not until about 1919/1920 that Husqvarna put on the market a motor cycle completely manufactured by themselves. While there had been satisfactory results from the early machines with the Belgian and Swiss engines, Husqvarna naturally wanted to be entirely independent and to put out a motor cycle which could be called Husqvarna through and through. Their first engine was a side valve four-stroke twin-cylinder, and the first model provided the rider with a most comfortable ride, the accent being placed upon springing which was so important in the days when roads were not as smooth as today's. Another innovation on the model was the optional alternative to the lever controlled throttle, the twist grip throttle. The 'complete' Husqvarna was however short-lived because it cost more to make the engines than import them. By the mid-twenties the company reverted to purchasing foreign-made engines and this time looked in the direction of England. Husqvarna considered their 'best buy' to be J.A.P. engines although they toyed with Sturmey Archer (Raleigh) for a short period.

From the beginning of this decade, sidecars had been available as the motor cycle was used not only by the sporting man but also by the family man in Sweden. There were the wickerwork basket-type sidecars and also the most modern aluminium bullet-shaped style to give the rider some choice in the matter.

1936 was a significant year in the life of Husqvarna. The 500cc four-stroke single-cylinder o.h.v. model known as the 112TV was introduced to the public. It was regarded as the epitome of all that Husqvarna motor cycle manufacturing stood for, and it also heralded the end for a long period of time of their 'big bike' production. In 1938 the factory changed its policy to concentrate on production of the lightweight motor cycles which are so popular even today throughout the continent of Europe. In 1938, however, Calle Heimdahl, whose inspiration led to this dramatic change of policy, was setting the trend. His theory that the general public would quickly take to an easy-to-handle light and economical motor cycle proved absolutely correct. Perhaps he anticipated that with another world war such a machine would be worth its weight in gold. The model 301, with its 98cc engine and two-speed gearbox was quickly modified in the next two or three years to eliminate the bicycle pedals and to include foot-rests with a kick-starter. The 'Svartkvarnan' 118cc, a three-speed two-stroke single-cylinder motor cycle, followed in its footsteps and was sufficiently popular to warrant production until 1954. Husqvarna were the European forerunners of Honda and remarkably successful in the small motor cycle field.

On the road race track prior to the Second World War, success had been limited to national level with a few wins in the Swedish Grand Prix in the nineteen thirties and little else, with the result that the works team was disbanded. However it was discovered, as with other makes renowned for reliability, that if racing on the road was not their particular forte, trials and moto-cross could be. The fact that Husqvarna concentrated on the lightweight motor cycle was not necessarily a handicap in these fields and considerable success was achieved at international level, including six first class awards in the 1953 International Six Days Trial on their 175cc machines.

The modified Silverpil (Silver Arrow) 250cc with three-speed gearbox was used with formidable success in moto-cross including making a win possible for Sweden in the 1959 European Championship. Originally the Silverpil was manufactured to meet the market of the sixteen-year-olds in Sweden who were limited by law to riding motor cycles of 75 kilograms or less and the 175cc Silverpil was specially designed for them. Indeed the 'road racing appearance' of the bike was guaranteed to attract the young enthusiast. With these achievements behind them the management at Husqvarna were encouraged to dabble once more with the larger machinery for competition purposes and 'dusted down' their pride and joy of the thirties, the 112TV. This remarkable machine, once modified, immediately helped Bill Nilsson ride off with the 1960 500cc World Moto-Cross Championship and Totte Halman won four individual 500cc Moto-Cross Championships. This if nothing else shows the tough quality, reliability and speed of the machines – 'Husky' by name and it would seem by nature also.

24 INDIAN

At the turn of the century George M. Hendee was a successful manufacturer of pedal cycles and an enthusiast of pedal cycle races. He was the founder of the Hendee Manufacturing Company in Springfield, Massachusetts, in the USA and owned a half-interest in a cycle race track. It was this combination which attracted George Hendee to the idea of making motor cycles. The racing cyclists at this time were in many events paced by motorised tandem cycles of an extremely unreliable nature, with the result that many races were spoiled by the pacing machines which failed at vital moments and left the racers stranded. In 1900, he succeeded in finding a more reliable machine to do this work, made and ridden by one Oscar Hedstrom and it occurred to Hendee that by combining forces they might go successfully into business as motor cycle manufacturers. The contractual formalities were confined simply to one hand-written note and the Indian motor-cycle was conceived in the first month of 1901. George Hendee arranged finances and organised the experimental workshops out in Connecticut, laying down certain principles to which the motor cycles must adhere. Both Hendee and Hedstrom were adamant that any machine built by them must have quality as the foremost consideration, although the purpose of the machine was to provide a motor cycle for the masses. Hedstrom was to be in charge of design and construction and the first Indian motor cycle was on the road later in the year of 1901. From the outset, the machine was christened Indian by Hendee and he insisted that it should be painted red. The spell was cast and the 'magic of the red steed of steel' was about to spread. The prototype Indian was a small $1\frac{3}{4}$ horsepower single-cylinder machine with a basic appearance of a pedal cycle, incorporating pedals and chain-drive. The light high-compression engine formed part of the frame below the saddle and features of the machine were Hedstrom's own special spray-type concentric float carburettor and the battery ignition. From the first the machine was noted for its smooth and quiet performance.

With an eye to future export sales Hendee sent one of the very first Indians to a large motor cycle show in Great Britain in 1901 and set about developing production possibilities. Hendee knew from experience that there is no better advertisement than proving the goods you sell in public and in the first American road race in 1902 at Brooklyn, New York, an Indian was ridden to victory by George Holden in what must have been a record time. While in trials and hill climbs Indians took many 'scalps' including a remarkable first, second and third place in the coveted but gruelling New York to Boston trial covering about 280 miles of difficult terrain, the riders being Hendee, Hedstrom and Holden. By the end of the year demand for Indians far exceeded their output of about 140, but Hendee and Hedstrom were not tempted into making the 'quick buck' by taking short cuts at manufacturing level. The Indian standard motor cycle remained basically the same in design until 1905 when the single-cylinder machine was modified to take twist grip control for carburettor and ignition and spring or cushion forks were introduced. The twist grip system was operated from both hand-grips, the right operating the spark and exhaust valve, while the left operated the throttle. Another model joined the team, a twin-cylinder 490cc machine, making it the first twin-cylinder motor cycle in production in the USA, although it was not marketed for another two years. It was particularly successful in sporting competitions. With greater production came the need for larger premises for the factory and in the same year the Indian motor cycle production commenced in a large old school building in Springfield which was converted into a factory. That school building remained the basis of all future Indian factory expansion although by the time of the last addition in 1931 it would have been difficult to find the original building in the vast estate.

For 1906 the single-cylinder became a $2\frac{1}{4}$ horsepower machine and by 1908 the single-cylinder was alternatively $2\frac{3}{4}$, $3\frac{1}{2}$ or 4 horsepower while 5 or 7 horsepower twin-cylinder models were also obtainable. Other options open to the purchaser were belt- or chain-drive, battery or magneto ignition and automatic or mechanical inlet valves. The little $2\frac{3}{4}$ horsepower model capable of speeds up to about 45 miles per hour was sold at a basic price of two hundred dollars, with the optional extras improving both performance and price. The most expensive model was the seven-horsepower twin-cylinder machine with its racing position for riders including toe clips on the pedals, capable of speeds up to 65 miles per hour. This cost the purchaser a basic three hundred and fifty dollars.

The famous 'red steeds' could in fact be purchased in alternative colours of royal blue or black. The married man or modern Casanova could purchase an Indian Tricar to enable him to take a passenger in comfort. Indians allowed for the addition of a pillion seat behind the rider on standard models, but for the more sedate journey the tricar provided the answer. A single tricar could be purchased for about three hundred and twenty-five dollars while the twin-cylinder model cost an extra fifty. The upholstered passenger chair rode between the two front wheels while the rider sat behind over the solitary rear wheel. Difficulties in manufacture had been experienced at the outset of production of the tricar in 1905 but with the invention of the Indian independent helical spring suspension the solution was found to provide adequate comfort for the passenger and stability to the machine.

For 1909 the major change was the substitution of a loop cradle frame for the twin-cylinder models.

With an eye to overseas markets Hedstrom pushed Indians into European competitions and in 1911 hit the jackpot, when Indian became the first make to capture the top three places in the Isle of Man T.T. races. The Indians were also the first winners of the Senior T.T. since it was only introduced that year. The team of O. C. Godfrey, C. B. Franklin and A. Moorhouse pulverised the opposition with the exception of Charles Collier on his Matchless who was disqualified from second place on a breach of race regulations. The result had the desired result of boosting world sales. The following year an eighth place was the best they could muster. Honour was once more salvaged by A. H. Alexander with a third place in 1913 and O. C. Godfrey's second place (a joint place with the young Howard Davies) in the 1914 event. The major addition to the Indian range of that year was the Hendee Special with its revolutionary electrically operated starter and lighting equipment.

Mention should be made at this stage of the remarkable achievements of two famous Indian riders, C. B. Franklin and 'Cannonball' Baker. Franklin had demonstrated the formidable speed of the Indian two years earlier when he made a record-breaking run of 300 miles in as many minutes over the celebrated Brooklands track in England. Baker demonstrated the endurance and reliability of the Indians on many runs including one which set the Coast-to-Coast record in 1914. This trip of 3,300 miles of unpaved road was a severe test for both man and machine and Baker and his Indian Twin made it in 11 days 11 hours.

A new designer came to the forefront of Indian production in 1914, Charles Gustafson, a former speedway rider. He was responsible for the 'Power-plus' motor which quickly overcame initial scepticism and went into general production in 1916. By that time it had already taken many world records for distance covered in specific times and won many national hill climbs, trials and road races. Again Baker was to prove the worth of the Power-plus in 1917 with his wonderful 'Twenty-four Hours' record run of 1,534 miles, which he held for several years until Wells Bennett came along on a Henderson X in 1922. The Hendee Manufacturing Company were by now concentrating attention on twin-cylinder motor cycles rather than the single-cylinder machines. It was during 1916 that George M. Hendee retired from the company.

The 1917 range prior to the United States entry into the First World War included a 7 horsepower model and a lighter $2\frac{1}{2}$ horsepower model, both with three-speed gearboxes and still featuring the cradle spring frame together with triple-stem front forks. The machine was wanted immediately for the American war effort and over forty thousand olive-drab coloured Indians were used by the American forces during the remainder of the war.

A shot in the arm for post-war Indian production was the arrival of C. B. Franklin hot from the racing stable to assist at the drawing board. His 500cc 'Scout' V-twin-cylinder side valve machine was soon to become, according to Indian advertisements, the 'world's most popular twin solo motor cycle'. Later in the year a bigger 1000cc Powerplus version with rear suspension was added to the range. In road racing circles, Freddie Dixon and Herbert le Vack took second and third places for Indian in the second post-war Senior T.T. The first place was taken by a 350cc A.J.S. ridden by Howard Davies. Two years later in 1923 Freddie Dixon had to be content with third place before he changed his racing stable for succeeding events, and Indian ceased to race in the Isle of Man. The major innovation of the early twenties was the 'Big' Chief, superseding the 1000cc Power plus, a 1200cc V-twin-cylinder side valve monster. In the early twenties balloon tyres were most popular throughout the United States and were naturally featured on Indian models. By the mid-twenties Indian could claim the motor cycle speed record with Paul Anderson's 125 miles per hour down in Australia and this was increased to 132 miles per hour in 1926 at Daytona Beach, Florida, in the USA with John Seymour in the saddle. In the same year Indian brought out another single-cylinder model with three-speed, called the Indian Prince, featuring a new keystone frame in two sections and this model proved itself all over the world in major trials events.

1927 saw the company take over W. G. Henderson's Ace Motor Cycles and put the Indian Ace into production. In the 1928–9 season Indian motor cycles cleared the board in all United States National championship racing events.

The Indian Ace reappeared in the guise of the Indian Four in 1929 and remained in production until the Second World War. The prominent features of the Indian at the start of the 1930s were the touring handlebars with crossbar and heavy spoked wheels on all models. The modifications and improvements made during the next decade did not greatly affect the design or performance of the machines and no new model was offered. The thirties were a hard time economically for people in the USA whether they were manufacturers or prospective purchasers, and to make expensive new models would be money wasted in the design department followed by difficulties in selling the finished product. Once again, Indians produced motor cycles for the troops, in the Second World War, and celebrated the cease-fire with a new single-cylinder model, the 230cc overhead valve 'Arrow'. The 1000cc 'Big Chief' model continued with the ever popular 'Scout'. For 1950 a variation on the Scout model was brought into production for a short time, the Warrior, a 500cc vertical overhead twin-cylinder machine.

However, in the early fifties the Indian Motor Cycle Company was no longer a financially viable proposition and an English-based company, Brockhouse Engineering Company, took over production in 1953. For six years a motor cycle under the name of Indian was manufactured in the north of England, and then this last interest in the Indian motor cycle concern was swallowed up by Associated Motor Cycles Ltd., of London, England, who were basically the Matchless Motor Cycle Company. It was ironical that Indian advertising of 1917 should have referred to its very own Powerplus and light twin-cylinder machines as 'the Team of Matchless Motor Cycles'. Ridden by enthusiasts throughout the world for over fifty years, successfully raced in all the major championships, used extensively by the American armed forces. state police forces and motor cycle fire patrols, used by countless commercial concerns throughout the world for delivery purposes either as solos or with sidecars, Indian motor cycles were a major force in their time and will never be forgotten.

25 JAMES

In one respect at least James must be considered almost unique. The man whose name adorns the motor cycle, Harold James, was not responsible for any motor cycle at all. He had in fact died prior to the manufacture of the first. Harold James was a man whose interest in bicycles began with the 'penny farthing' and the business of their manufacture from about 1880. He was a small one-man, one-room, business in the beginning but developed over the following decade into a prosperous organisation. He was yet one more Midlander involved in the two-wheel transport business, his work-shops being situated in Birmingham. In 1897 the James Cycle Co., was sufficiently large and successful to be turned from a private into a public company, and with the transformation Harold James quietly retired from the scene. When the first James motor cycle was produced in 1902, Harold James had passed away. The man largely responsible for this James motor

ycle was Frederick Kimberley, who, prior to his engagement by the
James Cycle Company, had experience with other pioneer motor cycle
organisations and was able to take the benefit of that knowledge with him.
In the first year of production there were two models of James motor cycles.
Like many of their contemporaries, the basis of the machine was a bicycle
with an engine added to provide the power. However while the model 'A'
had belt drive, the Model 'B' had a slightly less usual device for driving the
rear wheel. This consisted of a small short chain from engine to a friction
roller which was held in contact with the rear tyre. The model 'B' was
powered by a Derby motor and the model 'A' was driven by the popular
Minerva. Either model could be purchased for £55.

The following year only one model James was available for purchase,
the model 'T'. This was a 2½ horsepower Minerva machine, with belt drive
retailing for a slightly lower price of £50. If these prices sound cheap by
today's standards, it should be remembered that at the beginning of the
century a sum like this would constitute the average working man's yearly
income.

In 1904 James first introduced the loop frame to hold the Belgian-
made F.N. engine. It was not original, of course, having been previously
used. In 1908 however James contributed original ideas in motor cycle
construction with the 'Safety' model, the brainchild of P. L. Renouf.
This machine had an open frame with running boards instead of foot-rests
or pedals. The wheels were fitted on spindles so that they could be changed
easily in days when punctures were the everyday occurrence on poor
quality roads. Brake shoes in the hubs expanded to retard the vehicle's
progress. The saddle was long and made more comfortable by leaf springs,
and the machine was powered by the first James engine, a four-stroke,
which had inlet and exhaust valves worked one within the other. The
'Safety' model was to stay for several years and caused changes in the
models produced by many of their rivals. In 1911 James reverted to a
traditional frame but sported a two-speed countershaft gearbox, a multi-
plate clutch, chain-drive, kick-start and shock absorbers.

In 1911 James made their first takeover, swallowing up the Osmond
company who made lightweight motor cycles.

Prior to the First World War, James were successfully producing a
lightweight two-stroke solo machine, a 4½ horsepower single-cylinder
model so popular among sidecar owners especially when used with their
own home-made 'Canoelet' model and a twin-cylinder model for the
speedy rider, called the 'Famous James', a 3½ horsepower 500cc machine.
James contributed to the war effort with motor cycles used by the Belgian
and Russian forces.

Post-war production was interrupted by a fire at the factory which put the company out of action for a couple of years. They resumed with 250cc and 350cc models, both side valve machines in the James tradition, and 500cc side and overhead valve V-twin models later in the twenties. The second takeover made by James came in 1930 when the Baker firm responsible for lightweight motor cycles were hit by the financial difficulties overwhelming so many companies in the motor cycling industry. James lightweight motor cycles were now being powered by Villiers engines, and from about 1930 onwards the company concentrated on the production of two-stroke models in the range 98cc to 250cc.

During the Second World War the factory made munitions and aircraft components and also turned out two-stroke autocycles specially adapted for invasion forces. Post-war production carried on mainly with lightweight models but the company that had taken over other less fortunate motor cycle firms in the past was now overtaken by its own financial misfortunes. In the early fifties it was merged with Associated Motor Cycles Ltd., the Matchless-controlled organisation. From that date machines marketed under the name of James were lightweight models up to 250cc and motor scooters. If Harold James had known about the motor cycles produced under his name, he would have had no cause to be dissatisfied with the contribution they have made to the history of the British motor cycle.

26   KAWASAKI

The first Kawasaki motor cycle was produced in Japan in 1968, making it the most 'junior' make in this book. However the company itself has a considerable history in many other fields of engineering. The Kawasaki company was founded in a dockyard in Tokyo in 1878. The man responsible for the company was Shozo Kawasaki, but the thought of manufacturing motor cycles was not in his mind at this time. Soon after the turn of the century the Kawasaki Dockyard began to diversify its manufacturing interests by building locomotives, freight cars, coaches and bridge trusses, and entered into the marine transportation business. Over the years the company interests continued to expand so that at the present time the company has interests in production of ships and aircraft, rolling stock and commercial vehicles as well as many other products requiring engineering skill and expertise.

The motor cycle division of Kawasaki was started in 1968 at the time of the general regrouping of Kawasaki companies and the founding of Kawasaki Heavy Industries Ltd. At the present time Kawasaki motor cycle are exported to as many as ninety different countries throughout the world and with the increasing demand has come the realisation that assembly plants in countries other than Japan are necessary to satisfy that demand. The company plan such expansion in many countries including Nigeria, the Philippines and the USA, and with the opening of such a plant in America it will be another 'first' for Kawasaki as no other Japanese motor cycle manufacturer will have done this. The main Kawasaki works are at Akashi situated about four hundred miles south-west of Tokyo and alongside the Inland Sea. This plant was established in 1930 originally for the manufacture of aeroplane engines and fuselage components. Now the motor cycle production line there claims to produce a motor cycle every fifty seconds and their popularity world wide is such that over 96 per cent of the motor cycles produced are sold abroad.

The Kawasaki range of motor cycles includes machines of 125, 250, 400, 500, 750 and 900cc. All have five-speed gearboxes with the exception of the 125cc. All machines are two-stroke, for which the Japanese are justly famous, with the exception of the 900cc which is a double overhead camshaft four-stroke.

On the racing scene Kawasaki quickly made the victory rostrum in the Isle of Man T.T. races, with first place going to Dave Simmons on his 125cc machine in the Ultra Lightweight race of 1969. The overwhelming success the company gained on the United States of America road racing tracks in 1973 must have been particularly satisfying for a factory with relatively little experience. The future looks interesting for Kawasaki.

27 LEA-FRANCIS

By the end of the nineteenth century R. H. Lea and his business partner, G. I. Francis, were responsible for one of the most famous pedal cycles in Great Britain. Like so many engineers, their factory was based in Coventry, in the Midlands region of England. The Lea-Francis safety bicycle provided them with a prosperous income and a showroom in the smartest part of Piccadilly in London. The advent of the internal combustion engine interested and intrigued them. Like Thomas Humber and John Marston of Sunbeam, they took the difficult but fascinating step from pedal to motor bicycles. However, Lea and Francis made the transition through experiment with motor cars and subsequent car manufacture from about 1903. This postponed the taking of the step until it was actually negotiated in 1911. The prototype Lea-Francis, designed by Ingle with assistance from the young Norman Lea, was not ready until the following year. The first Lea-Francis motor cycle was a 430cc J.A.P.-engined side valve, twin-cylinder machine, with two-speed gearbox and dummy rim front brake.

The company was determined to maintain the high standard of quality expected of Lea-Francis machines.

By 1914 the motor cycle side of the business was in full production of 430cc, 500cc and 750cc twin-cylinder machines. The engines used were either the home-produced J.A.P. or the Swiss M.A.G., but after the First World War it seems that J.A.P. engines were never used again for the Lea-Francis. The pre-war Lea-Francis 430cc twin-cylinder machine could be purchased for the sum of £69 10s (£69.50) and was generally regarded as value for money. From the beginning Lea-Francis favoured foot-boards rather than foot-rests. For the protection of the rider from mud and water thrown up off the roads, enclosed mudguards with mudshield at the front were fitted together with an under-tray which swung forward to double as a front stand. There was a completely encased chain and easily detachable front and rear wheels enabled rapid repairs. The R.H. Lea patent reflex lamp at the rear provided better illumination.

The First World War brought production to a standstill and with the end of hostilities Lea-Francis resumed where they had left off. G. I. Francis took a close interest in his son's motor cycle company Francis and Barnett Ltd., becoming a director of that company as well. Gordon Francis, the son of G. I. (Graham) Francis was busy at that time with Arthur Barnett in emulating his father's success and the family Francis have certainly earned a niche for themselves in the history of British motor cycles.

The post-war Lea-Francis continued the format as before, with only slight modifications such as the optional improvements to the braking system. The firm, with its spreading reputation, believed that the satisfied customer would repeat his order in due time and would know all about the product he was buying. Its handling in adverse weather and road conditions was proved by the success of the Lea-Francis in trials events. Graham Francis, young Norman Lea with A. J. Sproston all had notable successes on the Lea-Francis in many major events including the Scottish Six Days Trials. Perhaps the great reliability of Lea-Francis precipitated the end of motor cycle production, since satisfied customers had no need to renew their machines.

In 1920 a 592cc model with three-speed gearbox was put on the market for sidecar purposes, and a sporting model costing in the region of £110 was developed for 1922. By 1924 it was decided to close down the motor cycle side of the business and concentrate on the light motor car trade where business was starting to boom. In all forms of wheeled transport Lea and Francis produced quality, class and style and the owners of their pedal cycles, motor cycles and motor cars always appreciated the fact Compared with other motor cycle companies the Lea-Francis output may have been small, but quality counts for more than quantity.

In the annals of British motor cycle history the name Levis is synonymous with two-stroke lightweight machines. The Butterfield brothers aided and abetted by Howard Newey, were pioneers of two-stroke motor cycles and set a standard for others to aim at. Others did eventually pass that standard but this cannot obscure the early achievement of the Butterfield/Newey organisation. Stephenson's steam engine and Ford's idea of the popular motor car were superseded but this does not detract from the importance of their original work.

William and Arthur Hughes Butterfield opened up business in 1906 as engineers, initially with no motor cycle connections other than a natural interest in developments in engineering progress. William started experimenting with engines of his own design and by 1910 had a successful two-stroke engine on the stocks. By 1911 he and his brother were established as motor cycle manufacturers. The name chosen for the motor cycles produced by them came from a classical education – Levis meaning 'light' as in light-weight. The firm's motto from the start was 'levis et celer', and in their day the Levis motor cycle certainly proved to be both light and speedy.

The first Levis set the standard which the Butterfields aimed at maintaining throughout their firm's life. It was a 198cc single-cylinder two-stroke machine with belt-drive and pedalling apparatus, fitted on a bicycle-type frame with bicycle saddle and handlebars. It weighed a mere 85 pounds and was capable of speeds up to about 35 miles per hour.

From the earliest days the Butterfield brothers were given the most able support by Howard (Bob) Newey who is considered by some to be worthy of the title 'Mr Levis', since he contributed so much to the design and development of the Levis motor cycle over the next thirty years or so. He also tuned the racing machines for the works team and in the early days even raced them himself. If William Butterfield was king at Levis, Newey was certainly the Prime Minister. The prototype Levis was modified for sale and the Model Number 1 was a slightly larger 269cc version and the second model to follow in production was the 211cc Baby Levis. The purchase price of each was about £35 10s (£35.50) and £33 10s (£33.50) respectively. Fourteen or fifteen years later, the purchase price of a Levis two-stroke was less than £30. What product of the 1970s will cost less to buy in the 1980s?

1913 was the year of incorporation at Levis, the little firm becoming Butterfields Ltd. The brothers were directors of the company and Howard Newey took the reins as works manager. The models for that year were merely variations on the now popular theme, with relatively minor alterations. These included a lowered riding position and a version of the Model 1 with alternative chain/belt-drive while the Baby Levis and standard Model 1 continued faithfully with belt-drive. The idea of mounting two of their two-stroke engines side by side on one machine with a single common crankcase never really caught on and was quickly dropped.

The business prospered and the company decided to extend their range of machines. For the following year a 349cc De Luxe model was conceived at the De Luxe retail price of £42. For the man with a little less cash to spare, the Popular model, a 211cc, was introduced, while the Baby Levis and the Model 1 with variations continued in harness.

The First World War naturally slowed both production and demand, but the early post-war era showed a healthy demand for lightweight motor cycles. This demand was repeated after the cease-fire of the Second World War, but on that occasion Levis decided not to fulfil it. Rekindling the fires in 1919, the Butterfields made several innovations to attract the customers. Over the early post-war years Levis introduced better gear-boxes mainly of Burman manufacture, internal expanding brakes, kick-starters and mechanical oil pumps. There were now many keen rivals in the two-stroke market as the day of the two-stroke was seen to have arrived, but Levis had experience which counted for much in the early twenties. At that time the competitors were still discovering the difficulties already overcome at Butterfields some eight or nine years before.

If their motto was 'light and quick' they soon changed their sales pro-duction slogan to 'The Master Two-Stroke' and endeavoured to prove this both in production of standard models and also in road racing. Prior to the war the Butterfield concern had dabbled in road racing but the lack of races for machines of 200cc or 250cc was hardly encouraging. There were a few road races in Europe but little on the domestic front, and they had really only been able to show their prowess in Britain in trials, where they had quickly gained a great reputation. Having demonstrated their reliability and endurance, the challenge to prove their speed – and the firm's motto – was irresistible. Fortunately the growing interest in lightweight motor cycles in the early post-war days gave the necessary impetus to the authorities to include a 250cc class in the Junior event of the 1920 Isle of Man T.T. races. Levis were anxious to live up to their new claim of 'The Master Two-Stroke'.

The 250cc trophy was offered for the best performance by a machine of 250cc or less in the Junior T.T., which of course consisted for the most part of 350cc machines. It says something for the Levis 250 that for most of the race R. O. Clark was in contention for first place amongst the 350 machines. In the end he finished in fourth place overall and was the clear winner of the 250cc class, despite the minor handicap of a crash during the last lap. This left his front wheel so buckled that he had to do on-the-spot repairs to make the wheel revolve again on the spindle, allowing him to coast gently round the remainder of the course in order to reach the finishing line. To prove the point Levis took second and third places in the 250cc class with the remarkable veteran rider F. W. (Pa) Applebee in the saddle of the latter. At the age of fifty-eight, it was a formidable task to ride around the $187\frac{1}{2}$-mile course let alone be placed the third rider in his class. He held the record for the oldest competitor in these events when he finally competed in the 1922 Lightweight race, but only for two years until G. Cowley took the 'title' at the age of sixty-one in the Junior race of 1924.

Geoff Davison is an important name in Levis racing history. He took consecutive Grand Prix titles on his Levis in Belgium and France in 1922 and 1923, and won a gold medal in the International Six Days trial on the smallest machine in the field. He also led the first Lightweight race in the Isle of Man T.T. in 1922, coming in thirteen minutes ahead of his nearest rival, after he had narrowly failed to win the year before in the Junior 250cc event. On that occasion a broken belt deprived him of the winning position and left him in a dignified second place. Davison and Levis went hand-in-hand, and loyalty to the company may well have deprived the rider of greater success later in the twenties. As the decade wore on, the rival two-stroke manufacturers rapidly made up lost ground and even if the standard Levis machine was probably more reliable and better value for the customer than the majority of the faster makes, by 1923 it was no longer the swiftest. Levis performances in races rapidly declined. The 1923 model was not up to scratch and in competitions the riders continued on the old 1922 machines. Levis hopes rose when an Ultra-Lightweight class in the Isle of Man T.T. races was introduced in 1924 for machines of under 175cc. The Levis 'Copper-Nob' was developed with great enthusiasm and the fourth place it successfully gained in the race was regarded at Levis as a total failure. The company never seriously competed in the major road races again (with one disastrous exception later in the decade), and concentrated on producing new models to attract the customers in the shops.

The 1924 'K' was an expensive little 250cc model with chain-drive, three-speed gearbox and a top speed of 50 miles per hour. It was a step taken towards chain-driven machines while Levis was still generally adhering to a belt-drive policy. The model M of the following year catered for the man with less money to spend and was just a cheaper version of the model K. Over the next couple of years Levis was able to make sufficient money-saving amendments to bring the purchase price of the machine down even further. By 1927 the model M was re-named the Levisette (not to be confused with the similarly named 1914 model of 175cc) and cost under £29. Both the model K and the Levisette went out of production before the end of the decade, suffering badly in comparison with the earlier Popular which, living up to its name, continued to be manufactured for over eleven years. It only went out of the catalogue when a 'new broom' attitude at management level demanded new models in 1924.

Other new Levis models of the mid-twenties were the Model 'O', a 247cc two-stroke for sporting purposes, and the Model 'A', introduced in 1926 with a distinctive flat tank and three-speed Burman gearbox. The latter was modified before the end of the decade to take a saddle tank, and then a four-speed gearbox and two upswept exhaust pipes to keep in with the common trend. The first 'six port' 250cc two-stroke model was brought out in 1928, yet another to be taken out of production by 1930. During the thirties the accent at Levis was uncharacteristically on four-stroke models. They even made a 500cc and 600cc machine, both overhead valve single-cylinder machines. The Levis policy was never to confuse economy with cheap quality and high standards were always set to the very end. During the thirties a 250cc overhead camshaft model was produced, a swan song for the company. With the arrival of the Second World War, the factory was taken over for the manufacture of aircraft parts. This too was in keeping with Levis tradition as the design and manufacture of aeroplane engines were among the experiments in the pre-First World War era at Butterfield's Birmingham workshops. These happy days of motor cycle pioneering must have seemed a far cry from the life and death battle being waged above them in 1940. For Levis motor cycles, as for so much else, the war heralded the end.

29 MARTINSYDE

Unlike so many other motor cycle collaborators, Helmuth Paul Martin and George Harris Handasyde were not drawn together by their mutual interest in machines on two wheels. Their first love was flying and they joined forces in the first decade of the century solely to make aircraft. Their early ventures were very advanced and successful, for they seriously considered the possibility of a Martinsyde monoplane crossing the Atlantic before the First World War intervened to change their priorities. Naturally the Government looked to Martin and Handasyde for air assistance and found it in their fighter planes. The firm grew in staff and took over new premises for carrying out orders. However, with the cease-fire the demand for aircraft died and Martin and Handasyde looked round for new ways of using their equipment and staff. With the assistance of the motor cycle engine specialist Howard C. Newman (of Ivy fame), Martinsyde metaphorically changed horses (or at least horsepower).

The prototype Martinsyde–Newman was ready by 1919 and the first models left the factory in 1920.¹In the same year Newman also left the factory and the motor cycles produced thereafter were just called Martinsyde. The 1920 machines were 678cc and 500cc models both being two-cylinder V-twin-engined machines with A.J.S.-type gearboxes, and Brampton forks. By 1922 a sports model called the 'Quick Six' was also being produced with a slightly more powerful engine and a distinctive round tank. However, the firm was already beset with problems that eventually proved to be its downfall. Perhaps because of their relative inexperience, machine production was slower than demand with the result that customers grew impatient with waiting. A strike by their suppliers added greatly to the delay. The result was that a large number of customers cancelled their orders, causing the firm heavy financial losses Business picked up to a certain extent in 1921, mainly because those machines which did eventually get off the production line and into the customers' hands proved to be of such good quality that customers were appeased and their reputation grew.

Conveniently situated in their factory near Brooklands, it is not surprising that even in their few years of manufacture Martinsyde machines should have achieved a certain amount of success on the famous circuit, notably in the 500-mile race and in breaking the speed record over one hour. The greatest achievement credited to the machines must be the five gold medals in the 1922 Six Days Trial. Their newly found success was short-lived and the death blow came when a fire started in the workshops and destroyed equipment. The fire in fact did not cause much damage and indeed if it had been more extensive substantial insurance compensation might have helped to turn the tide in the firm's favour.

The 350cc model had no opportunity to prove its worth or save the firm's fortunes, as only six machines ever left the premises. Bankrupt, the company finally ceased production in 1923. Such engines as were usable at the factory were purchased by Bat motor cycles for use in their own machines. For Martinsyde it was a short but worthwhile reign.

30 MATCHLESS

For Matchless, like many other firms, the entry into motor cycle manufacture was a natural progress from the production of bicycles late in the nineteenth century. The Collier brothers, H. A. (Harry) and C. R. (Charlie), made their first motor-powered bicycle in 1899. Indeed in those early years the machines were very much bicycles with the addition of engines placed wherever the maker could find room. The early Matchless motor cycles produced at the turn of the century had the engine placed between the saddle tube and the rear wheel, but by 1903 the engine had been moved forward, in front of and under the front down tube of the frame and behind the front wheel. Pedals were still provided, of course, to assist the engine on steep inclines or when it failed to function. The early Matchless motor cycles were driven by de Dion Bouton, J.A.P. and even M.M.C. engines. The production took place in their small factory in Plumstead, South-East London, and was forward-looking from the start. Pioneers are experimenters by nature, and with the motor cycle still in its infancy, the Collier brothers started to make a tri-car. The principle was that two front wheels replaced the normal single wheel, in order to support the wicker-work or metal carriage for the passenger, while the driver sat on the normal saddle and looked past his passenger at the highway ahead. So he became the original back seat driver.

The 1904 Matchless tri-car was in fact only a follow-up to other machines of quite similar appearance to those which had been manufactured since the beginning of the century under a variety of names. Where the Colliers showed great originality was in their early attempts at rear springing on motor cycles. The 1906 V-twin was equipped with a swinging fork sprung rear frame, the spring unit being placed under the saddle with links to the main frame.

Pioneers in every way, the Colliers entered the first Isle of Man T.T. races in 1907 and won the single-cylinder class with Charlie Collier naturally riding his own marque. In the same race Harry Collier put in the fastest recorded lap by a single-cylinder machine at 41·18 m.p.h. and Charlie's average speed over the 158$\frac{1}{2}$-mile course was 38·22. In the 1908 T.T. event Charlie Collier had to be content with second place, but in that year a Matchless V-twin recorded a shattering 70 m.p.h. at the Brooklands track. In 1909 Harry Collier took over the winning formula from his brother and won the only T.T. event, the two classes having been merged into one. If the motor cycling world thought the Colliers had made their point, in 1910 they emphasised it again in a devastating first and second place, once more in the only T.T. race of the year. While speeds averaged about 50 m.p.h. per lap one must remember that greater skill was needed in those days to keep the machine running (and running smoothly) over 158 miles of poorly surfaced roads. Good fortune did not favour them the following year, and Harry Collier could do no better on his J.A.P.-engined single-cylinder machine than second place in the Junior event. Meanwhile Charlie Collier was disqualified in the Senior for filling his machine with petrol on the road when he ran out, and but for this would have taken another second place. At subsequent top-level road racing events Matchless were not successful although they achieved many trials and moto-cross victories to their credit.

Up to the First World War the Colliers were always anxious to be in at the start of any new motor cycling experiment, and along with many of their rivals they produced a cycle-car. This was a natural successor to the earlier tri-car but resembled the form of a motor car much more closely. The Matchless cycle-car was not so successful as the Morgan, which was generally recognised as reigning supreme in this field, nor as cheap since even then it cost over £100. The most distinctive feature of the Matchless cycle-car was its independent front wheel suspension with separate leaf springs, and a single transverse tube between the front wheels curving down in the centre to form a loop for the crank-case of the J.A.P. V-twin engine. The production of the Matchless cycle-car ceased in the mid-twenties with the arrival of the popular mass-produced small motor car, which gave the family man greater space for his passengers and cost no more than the cycle-car. At the same time as the cycle-car was produced, Matchless sidecar outfits were popular with the public. Although sportsmen themselves, the Colliers did not forget that the motor cycle was a vehicle of transport as well as a competitive machine.

In the 1920s there were as many as eleven models to choose from in the Matchless range, powered from the small 246cc side valve up to the mighty 1000cc V-twin, all of which were now Matchless-made. Like many contemporaries at the end of that decade, the new Matchless machines appeared with white panels on their tanks.

The 1930 Silver Arrow was only in production for three years but during that time it made a remarkable impact. This model was manufactured with the man in the street in mind rather than the racing specialist or trials rider. It was designed strictly for transport purposes with a quiet side valve V-twin 400cc engine. The rider was given a speedy and comfortable journey on the machine's sprung rear frame. Its chromium and white tank was in keeping with the current trend. It was for obvious reasons nicknamed the 'Whispering Wonder'. The Silver Arrow was soon accompanied by a 600cc Silver Hawk. This had a narrow angle V-four engine with overhead camshaft and was obviously aimed at a more sporting public. It retained the Silver Arrow's spring frame and one-piece cylinder casting. At about this time Matchless took over the less fortunate A.J.S. under the new title of Associated Motor Cycles Ltd.

Prior to the Second World War, Matchless not only made their own motor cycles but also built and sold engines to other manufacturers like Brough Superior, Calthorpe and Morgan. During the war Matchless

350cc 63/L overhead valve single-cylinder machines were much in use by the British Army.

The post-war slump in the motor cycle industry did not cause Matchless to cease production. Their models included a 350cc and 500cc single-cylinder, and soon afterwards a complete range of motor cycles was available for the public from 250cc single to 650cc vertical twins. Post-war road racing successes were limited. The G.45, a 500cc push-rod twin racer never fulfilled its early promise, but the 500cc G.50, an overhead camshaft single-cylinder machine based on the 7R A.J.S., proved far more competitive with several seconds in the Senior T.T. The major post-war competitive success has been in trials and moto-cross. Associated Motor Cycles Ltd., took over other rivals who had fallen on hard times in the 1950s, such as James, Francis Barnett and Norton, enabling at least some of the marques to survive. The Collier brothers are remembered equally by enthusiasts for their racing successes and for their technical achievements – their motor cycles, the tri-car, the motor cycle and sidecar and the cycle-car. It is true to say that they were indeed Matchless.

31 MORGAN

H. F. S. Morgan designed and built his first three-wheeler in 1909 in a workshop attached to Malvern College, a well-known British public school. Initially it was constructed for his own personal use but within a year the first Morgan 'cyclecars' were available to the public.

The first Morgan consisted of two wheels and an engine at the front with chain-drive to the solitary rear wheel. There was a body similar to a car but with a single seat for the rider (or driver), on the outside of which there was a right-hand tiller for steering the vehicle. The brake and gear control levers were on the left allowing the driver (or rider) a choice of two speeds. The engine was a J.A.P. air-cooled single-cylinder capable of propelling the machine at a maximum speed of 50 m.p.h.

Three-wheelers were immensely popular in Britain before 1914 with over fifty different makes available. Whether the vehicle constituted a motor car or motor cycle was a much disputed matter and indeed to this day is a matter of opinion. Some three-wheelers were never designed along the lines of a motor cycle and fit comfortably into the motor car category. Those with engines of 1100cc or less and with a maximum vehicle weight of 7cwt, and which were also built on basic motor cycle principles, were classified as 'cyclecars' by the Auto Cycle Union and came under the A.C.U. umbrella for all purposes, including sporting competitions.

Since many of these three-wheelers were inspired by motor cycles rather than motor cars, it is correct to mention at least one make in an anthology of motor cycles. Most historians would agree that Morgans were the most popular and successful of the cyclecars for forty years.

The two-seater cyclecar provided a relatively cheap vehicle for the average married couple compared with motor cars or motor cycle combinations of the day (a pre-First World War Morgan cost under £90). It also provided a certain amount of weather protection with its optional hood and screen, a comparatively reliable engine and a ride which was not uncomfortable – or so the advertisers would have you believe!

A regular magazine was published for the enthusiast called 'The Cyclecar'. Since Morgan came into the field early and had imaginative leadership their machines soon took over as the most popular and successful cyclecar in trials and speed competitions. There was competition in this market from Continental manufacturers. Against such competition a Morgan took a gold medal in the London–Exeter trial of 1911 and won the 1913 Cyclecar Grand Prix in France. After the later success Morgan put a sporting Grand Prix Model into immediate production with a water-cooled V-twin overhead valve J.A.P. engine. By this time Morgan had outgrown the college workshop and were in manufacture at H.F.S. Morgan's newly acquired factory also in Malvern, Worcestershire. The vehicle itself had developed into a two-seater and the tiller control had long since been replaced by a steering wheel.

The major post-war development was the use of Swiss M.A.G. engines as well as the well-tried J.A.P. In the mid-twenties the Aero-Morgan, which superseded the Grand Prix as the sports model, was also available with Anzani or Blackburne engines. By this time the era of the cyclecar had passed and most rival manufacturers either ceased production or turned their whole attention to the mass manufacture of other small, cheap motor cars. For Morgan, however, sporting success at major trials and at Brooklands in speed competitions kept the interest in their particular three-wheeler alive and financially healthy. The factory was now under the general direction of George Goodall who maintained the high standard of Morgan machines by his enthusiasm and ability and encouraged even greater sporting achievements into the thirties.

Just before the Second World War a four-wheeler was put into production at the Morgan factory. Inevitably this signified the end of the cyclecar. At the conclusion of hostilities the factory continued to make the marvellous little three-wheeler but the popularity of the Morgan four-wheeler was such that in about 1950 it was decided to discontinue production of the former. In this way the Morgan cyclecar evolved into the Morgan motor car and so it continues to this day.

32 MOTO GUZZI

Como in Italy is not just famous for its beautiful lake. Among motor cyclists it is equally renowned as the home of perhaps the most popular Italian motor cycle, Moto Guzzi. The Guzzi factory (moto means 'motor, in Italian) was started in 1921 by Carlo Guzzi and has survived many world motor cycle market crises in the intervening years. In the 1920s Carlo Guzzi concentrated on the manufacture of 250cc and 500cc single-cylinder overhead valve and overhead camshaft models. Knowing the value of racing successes as advertisement for his standard road machines, Guzzi quickly entered into competitive road racing. Moto Guzzi were slightly unfortunate and shortsighted in their 1926 Isle of Man T.T. venture, when P. Ghersi rode his Guzzi into second place in the Lightweight race after recording the fastest lap speed, only to be disqualified on a remarkably small technicality – a switch of sparking plugs. The rule was that the machine parts during the races must be identical to the parts which had passed official scrutiny. One sparking plug difference seems a trifle to cause forfeiture of a winning place and could be seen as bad sportsmanship but for the fact that Moto Guzzi had prior warning of the risk they were running. They did not make that mistake again and the following year Archangli repeated the race success, this time without disqualification.

From the start Moto Guzzi have had a reputation in the 250cc class both for the standard product on sale to the public and for their racing models. From the earliest days of the factory the accent has been placed on producing lightweight machines which are fast and easy to handle. The enthusiasts are critical of their past inconsistency. This has certainly shown itself in road racing where a large number of retirements have prevented greater track success.

The Guzzi of the twenties was noted for its horizontal single-cylinder engine with the head facing forward to assist the air cooling. Even in those early days Guzzi combined the gearbox in unit with the crankcase. When certain marques like Matchless were going all out for the narrow angle Vee-cylinders, Guzzi took the opposite course with cylinders set at 120 degrees for their 500cc V-twin. They followed current trends with a low saddle position to improve the handling of their machines and also for streamlining purposes. Enthusiasts will remember that at a later date Guzzi set the trend with other streamlining devices.

Stanley Woods and Omobono Tenni were the works riders for Guzzi in the thirties who achieved great racing success, both claiming victories in the Lightweight T.T. races and Woods also in the Senior. Guzzi prospered in the pre-war years, but did not go under with the reversal of Italy's fortunes. Immediately following the Second World War, Guzzi bounced back with production of their Gambalunga (or 'long leg') 500cc single-cylinder machine designed specially for racing purposes. In Guzzi tradition it was light, a matter of 180 lbs, less than half the usual weight for a 500cc machine. Among its many noteworthy features was the pivoting fork rear suspension.

In post-war years the factory tended to specialise in the smaller production motor cycle and in this field they were very popular. The factory produced two- and four-stroke engines from 49cc to 250cc having particular success with their 98cc 'Zigolo' in the 1950s. In the larger class, the 1954 Guzzi Bialbero twin-camshaft racer and the V-8 water-cooled 500cc model brought out in 1957 for the factory team were regarded as rather special.

Their racing success was greatly assisted by riders of the calibre of Fergus Anderson, Ken Kavanagh and Bill Lomas who ensured victories and high placings in the T.T., Ulster and other Grands Prix of the fifties and sixties.

Moto Guzzi continues to thrive. Although Carlo Guzzi founded the company, the guiding influence for so many years were members of the Parodi family, Giorgio Parodi and Dr Angelo Parodi, who set the high standard of workmanship and skill in the pre-war years and created the internationally famous Moto Guzzi tradition.

The name of Moto Guzzi is now chiefly associated with mighty 750cc and 850cc transverse V-twins with shaft-drive although at the time of writing, 1973, there is talk of additional smaller models being on the way.

33 MOTOSACOCHE

The brothers Henri and Armand Dufaux may be regarded as pioneers of motor cycle progress. They commenced their business of manufacturing motor cycle engines at about the turn of the century in Geneva, Switzerland. They made their name in about 1905 with a development that was most acceptable to the 'man in the street' with little money to spend. The purchase of a motor cycle in those days in Britain cost as much as the equivalent of a year's wages. Their innovation was a power unit that could be attached to the ordinary pedal cycle and so transform it into a motorised cycle. The unit consisted of a double loop sub-frame of two parallel half-inch tubes, approximately 4 inches apart, into which the engine, magneto, petrol tank and belt pulley fitted snugly, giving rise to its name in French, 'moto' (motor or engine) 'sacoche' (tool bag or saddle bag), known in England as the 'Tool Bag Motor'.

This unit with its little four-stroke engine of $2\frac{1}{4}$ horsepower performed creditably in trials, and J. S. Holroyd's exploits in events of the 1908-9 period were quite amazing. He climbed gradients of 1 in 3, completing the course in many long distance trials with distinction and beating many machines of larger capacity.

The unit was manufactured under licence in many European countries and sold well in Great Britain. Several makers, notably Singer, fitted only this engine to their machines. But Motosacoche made other power units apart from their 'tool bag motor', and complete motor cycles as well. For this purpose another factory was opened in France at Lyon. Motosacoche products included single-cylinder and twin-cylinder models, and ranged from the small cycle attachment to a big 1,000cc overhead valve machine. Over the years many manufacturers used Motosacoche power units with the celebrated trademark of M.A.G., including the British firms Lea Francis, Brough Superior, Royal Enfield and Matchless. From 1910 until 1915 there was a particularly close connection with Royal Enfield and the two machines were almost identical.

Just before closing their motor cycle business in the early 1950s, Motosacoche once again caught the public eye with a special utility 200cc side valve model with belt-drive, which also incorporated the unusual brakeless front wheel, a creation of the designer Dougal Marchant, and his own fuel metering device making a carburettor unnecessary. Marchant had made his name with the sterling work put in on the 350cc overhead camshaft Chater-Lea in the 1920s both as designer and rider, and his performances on the Brooklands track are still remembered. The remarkable little Motosacoche was produced in the early post-war years, but gained insufficient support to prevent the directors from closing down the motor cycle department, while continuing the more flourishing business of making power units for industry. But the name Motosacoche is a reminder to all of the time when the firm had something rather special, all in the tool bag.

34 NORTON

In the minds of all motor cycling enthusiasts over the age of 15 the name 'Norton' is synonymous with racing. Like so many, Nortons have had financial crosses to bear, but in the world of motor cycle racing during the course of this century few other machines can claim such long term distinction and success.

In 1898 James Lansdowne (popularly better known later as 'Pa') Norton started up in business on his own to make parts for bicycles. He was 29 years of age and from his formative years had shown great interest in engineering. At the age of ten he was making working models of steam engines and later took an apprenticeship in engineering. The Norton Manufacturing Company produced its first motorised bicycle at Bracebridge Street, Birmingham in 1902, with a 1½ horsepower Clement Garard engine mounted on the front down tube. In the early years of Norton motor cycles, the continental engines produced by Clement, Moto-Reve and Peugeot were fitted, both single and twin with automatic inlet valves, and it was only after the success of the first ever T.T. win in 1907 that Pa Norton put his own engine in the motor cycle bearing his name. The Norton long-stroke 4 horsepower single known as the Big Four was introduced in that year and continued in production, with modifications, until 1954.

The Isle of Man Tourist Trophy was first run in 1907 and at first was more a test of the stamina of both machine and rider than speed (except in the changing of tyres or parts!). A Norton had the distinction of winning the twin-cylinder class of the first T.T., ridden by H. Rem Fowler, who entered the race as a private owner, with active assistance from Pa who was as enthusiastic as the rider. Rem Fowler won the class race on the only Norton in the field, but never actually received the winner's trophy of a silver rose bowl. The happy ending to that story is that in the late 1950s a T.T. 'Replica' trophy was donated by an erstwhile winner and before his death this was duly engraved and presented to the popular pioneer.

Norton started the T.T. races with success, and unlike any other manufacturer can claim to have had entries in every T.T. meeting held.

By 1911 a 490cc engine was in production, the beginning of the models 16 and 16H which were popular with enthusiasts for so many years. Naturally enough Norton entered the first Senior T.T. race run in that year.

In 1913 the Norton Manufacturing Co., was obliged to liquidate, but was re-constituted as Norton Motors Ltd. Under the guidance of Bill Mansell, production continued to provide a contribution to the war effort. Big Fours were sent to Russia, a tribute by the War Office to their well-known reliability. In 1919 chain-drive was introduced in place of the belt and three-speed Sturmey Archer gearboxes were fitted in an effort to improve performance.

The reputation of the Norton motor cycle was summed up in an advertising slogan 'the unapproachable Norton'. A delighted rider had written in gratitude that no other machine on the road could match his own. In later years, with the difficulties of mounting the specially prepared racing models with intricate streamlining, the slogan took on a new meaning! After the Great War came the great boom for motor cycles.

Reliability was still the all-important selling feature of any machine, but speed started to become a bigger factor: Nortons claimed both. A guarantee was issued with each $3\frac{1}{2}$ horsepower belt-driven model BS sold that it had been timed at Brooklands at 75 m.p.h. or more.

Overhead valves were introduced on Norton motor cycles in 1922, and with their arrival came the new mile record speed of 88·39 m.p.h. achieved by Rex Judd, a name closely associated with Nortons for many years. Without stalwarts such as Judd and particularly Mansell, Francis Beart, and Joe Craig with their manufacturing, design and tuning skills, the fame of Norton would have been far less. In the early 1920s the Maudes Trophy was awarded annually for quality in the standard production model of motor cycles. It might be possible to produce one machine out of a factory which could beat all competitors in a race, but this was of no use to the prospective purchaser unless the machine he was going to buy was of the same quality. A team of officials from the Auto Cycle Union deciding the award were given a demonstration of the general high standard of Norton in 1923. They were permitted to select individual parts at random in the factory to be assembled and mounted in a standard frame, which was run in for about eighty miles with minor adjustments and was then run continuously for twelve hours, during which time the speed averaged over 64 m.p.h. and eighteen world records were broken. When dismantled the engine was found to be in perfect condition. The award was instantly given to Norton, who won it for the next three years as well with a variety of stamina-proving tests, such as the journey from Lands End to John O' Groats and back (twice!) and 100 non-engine-stop ascents of Mount Snowdon.

1924 was another landmark in the history of Norton, when Alec Bennett achieved Norton's first Senior victory in the T.T. races at an average of over 60 m.p.h. The Sidecar race was a walkover with more than half an hour separating the first two. Nortons also took first place in the French, Belgian and Spanish Grands Prix. Unhappily 'Pa' Norton died in 1925 leaving others to carry on the manufacturing of machines bearing his name. In the following year an overhead camshaft engine was introduced and with it came another Senior T.T. success.

Between 1931 and 1938 Nortons won every Senior and Junior T.T. race with two exceptions – a quite remarkable achievement. In the production field, the distinctive square-sided bevel box with offside magneto chain arrangement was introduced for 1930 on the overhead camshaft Norton. Other changes included a new lower frame with a shorter wheelbase and certain improvements in the front forks (such as rebound springs). Again a large contribution was made to the Second World War where some 25% of the solo or sidecar motor cycles used by British forces were made by Norton. But after the war only two 500cc models came off the production line: the side valve 16H and the overhead valve model 18, which was first introduced in the 1920s. Although girder forks were still fitted, the 'Roadholder' telescopic type, based on the ones used by the factory racers since 1938, were standardised soon afterwards.

Europe had been conquered by Nortons prior to the Second World War, but America was a new field. Between 1941 and 1953 Nortons won three times in the Daytona 100-mile race and five times in the 200-mile race with numerous 'place' successes.

In 1950 the firm put into production a new pivoted rear fork duplex frame. This was so much more comfortable for the rider than the former 'garden gate' design (with its plunger rear suspension) that it earned yet another nickname, which was to stick, 'the Featherbed'. The Featherbed Norton, brainchild of the McCandless brothers, made a fairy story start in the 1950 T.T. races by taking the first three places in both Senior and Junior, and for the remainder of that decade Nortons made the greatest impression of any make upon the road racing scene.

Norton's Diamond Jubilee in 1958 saw the introduction of the first baby Norton, a 250cc machine, but the end of the Bracebridge Street reign was nigh. In 1962 Norton's were taken over by Associated Motorcycles Ltd., and moved down to London premises. A.M.C. in turn ceased to exist and the name passed to Norton Villiers Ltd. Production continues and perhaps great success lies ahead, but it is unlikely that Norton could now improve on its past record of achievement.

Some of the famous racing riders closely associated with Nortons were Alec Bennett, Jimmy Simpson, Stanley Woods and Jim Guthrie in the 1920s and 1930s. Then Geoff Duke, Ray Amm, Bob McIntyre and Eric Oliver starred in the 1950s, and more recently John Surtees, and Mike Hailwood (who won the 1961 T.T. averaging over 100 m.p.h. on a single-cylinder Norton), Phil Read and Peter Williams. People who know nothing of motor cycle racing are familiar with those names, and even people who know nothing of motor cycles are familiar with the name Norton.

35 N.S.U.

The German name N.S.U. is perhaps best known for its lightweight models and mopeds, which became so popular in the 1950–1965 period before the Japanese made inroads in this field. But the factory at Neckarsulm has been manufacturing motor cycles now for over seventy years, and was originally noted for its V-twins of 500cc, 750cc and 1,000cc. Founded in 1901, the Neckarsulmer Fahrzeugwerke at first used Minerva or Sedel (ZL) engines but it was not long before their own engines were in production. A distinctive feature of the early years was the N.S.U. two-speed epicyclic gear combined with the engine pulley. This successfully overcame the gear problem created by belt-drive encountered by all pioneer motor cycle engineers. As with other gear devices, the consequence was rapid belt wear and frequent replacement. However, subsequent modifications made the gear one of the most popular throughout Europe, and the component was purchased separately by many motor cycle enthusiasts for adaption to their own British machines. It was listed as a factory extra by several manufacturers, notably Bradbury.

Prior to the First World War imported products were not much in demand as there were a number of good quality British motor cycles on the market. However the N.S.U. with its coil springing, was perhaps one of the most popular foreign-made motor cycles. N.S.U. continued to produce V-twin models until the mid-twenties and thereafter concentrated on their new unit construction singles of both side valve and overhead valve in a range of 500cc and below.

It was not until after the Second World War that N.S.U. started to make their very popular lightweight motor cycles and mopeds. The range commenced with the 100cc and 250cc models and subsequently varied between 49cc and 300cc. The N.S.U. 49cc model became very popular in Britain with young persons of both sexes; apart from its inexpensive running costs and minimal weight, it still had a surprising turn of speed. It was a single-cylinder air-cooled two-stroke machine with two- or three-speed gearbox. The 98cc Fox and 247cc Max with overhead camshaft single-cylinder engines were equally popular among persons of all ages.

In the 1950s the factory concentrated much time and money on making successful racing machines and dominated the 125cc and 250cc classes for a few years. They also took the 'world's fastest' with a 'blown' 500cc twin, and added a large number of world records in the 50cc to 500cc classes to their list of achievements. During this time the factory took a batch of machines to Daytona in the USA for world record attempts, and were so confident that the reporting journalists were given typed lists of the existing records to be attacked with spaces left for insertion of the new date and speed to be achieved by the N.S.U. machine! The confidence proved well-founded as N.S.U. took every record attempted.

At the present time the name of N.S.U. is associated mainly with motor cars although the two-wheelers are still produced under licence in countries other than Germany.

36 N.U.T.

The three letters N.U.T., while striking an appropriately mechanical note, were in fact not adopted by the makers of the motor cycle for that reason, but were the initials of the home town of the factory, Newcastle-upon-Tyne. For those readers unfamiliar with Britain, Newcastle-upon-Tyne is set in the heart of the industrial North-East of England, which is perhaps more noted for its beer and football team than for the subject of this history.

The N.U.T. must be one of the least-known makes of motor cycle to have won a T.T. race in the Isle of Man. This victory was recorded in the 1913 Junior T.T. with Hugh Mason in the saddle. Hugh Mason was almost a 'one-man-band' at N.U.T. since he was not only the machine's designer, but also chief test rider and racer. By 1913 many of the big names in motor cycle manufacturing dominated the racing scene, as victories were viewed as the best advertisement for the product. Victory in the T.T. was the highest achievement of all in those days, as it demonstrated a machine's reliability as well as speed over the two hundred miles of its course. Success there meant an immediate increase in sales. The Junior race won by Mason was over a shorter course than the Senior event, but still covered 225 miles of rough roads unlike the tarmacadam in the Island today. Greater credit than ever must therefore be accorded to Mason for his victory in view of the competition he fended off from bigger rival companies. The N.U.T. factory had only been started a couple of years before, and was at this date a very small organisation making a handful of machines a month. Mason and his J.A.P.-engined 350cc twin-cylinder machine recorded the fastest lap speed of the race at over 45 m.p.h., and maintained an average over the whole race of 43·75 m.p.h. to win by just under a minute from his nearest rival, W. F. Newsome on a Douglas. But Mason's victory was no flash in the pan. A warning had been given by the firm's first attempt in the T.T. races the year before, when R. W. Ellis riding the only N.U.T. entry came into a very creditable sixth place, also in the Junior race.

In the three years before the First World War the very few N.U.T. entries in the T.T. races all managed to bring credit to the makers (with the exception of a couple of retirements) but none could equal Mason's achievement of 1913. N.U.T. never entered road racing to the same extent after the war and public interest in the marque waned. Enforced interruption of manufacture caused by the 1914–18 war may have affected the progress and development of the N.U.T. motor cycle. Like so many factories in Britain, the N.U.T. engineering facilities were involved in more important war work and motor cycle production ceased until 1919. A last T.T. fling in 1914 saw N.U.T. in both Senior and Junior races, and with the Spaniard, S. Sorriquieta, riding in both, much was hoped for in the northerners' camp. However, 11th place was the best he could do in the Junior and he failed to finish in the 500cc race.

After the war the factory continued motor cycle production where it had left off, now building their own engines. The machine still had its distinctive low frame, with round tank secured by metal straps in the splendid brown finish. An amusing advertising campaign showed a poster-size walnut to catch public attention. The biggest change came in the next two or three years when Hugh Mason, the architect of N.U.T., severed all connections with the firm.

In the post-war years the majority of the firm's machines were powered by home-produced N.U.T. engines, and the models ranged from the 350cc machine, which had represented the manufacturers so well over the years, up to the 1000cc. Nearly all the models were powered by twin-cylinder engines. N.U.T. had earlier experimented with several engine makes, but generally settled for the reliable J.A.P. The emphasis at N.U.T. was always on quality before utility, and with the quality came expensive prices, such as the 140-guinea tag attached to their 1920 model. The high purchase price did not help sales. Prices were steadily reduced each year for the basic model but the competition was too great, despite the quality offered. In the late 1920s, when unemployment and poverty were the rule rather than the exception, the knowledge that he received good value for money did not help the prospective buyer to find the necessary cash to buy an N.U.T. The price of the product together with internal disputes at the factory and the national crisis combined to ensure that N.U.T. ceased production by the early 1930s – leaving the reputation of Newcastle-upon-Tyne to be maintained solely by the footballers and brewers of that town.

37 P AND M

In 1900 Joah Carver Phelon set to work on the construction of a motor cycle. While others were finding great difficulty in deciding where to put the engine, he made up his mind right away. He removed the front down tube from a cycle frame and inserted the engine in its place, with direct chain-drive to the rear wheel – a far-sighted decision in the days of almost universal belt drive. Harry Rayner was joint patentee of the frame design and his influence was considerable in the machine's development until his untimely death in 1903.

A few machines were made, but since resources were so limited, the design was offered to Humber, who were well established at that time with a vast output of pedal cycles. An arrangement to pay a royalty of 7s. 6d. per machine to Mr Phelon was made. The sloping engine 'Humber' was popular during 1902–3 after which time a fresh model was planned. An associate of Phelon's named Moore realised the potential of the design with a new two-speed gear, and persuaded him to retrieve the licence.

With this fresh venture the Phelon and Moore partnership came into being in May 1904. Their machine had the same sloping engine mounting, two-speed gear and 'free' engine (obtained by two primary chains from the engine sprockets with expanding clutches). This placed the model well ahead of rivals with fixed belt-drive, which necessitated a run-and-bump start after every stop.

A basic change to mechanical inlet valves was made in 1910, all previous machines having had automatic inlet valves. Certain other detail improvements were also made, but the two-speed gear was retained. This enabled the firm to take an interest in competitions, chiefly in reliability trials where these well-made machines excelled. Many successes were also obtained in long-distance events and the A.C.U. Quarterly Trials. The smartness of the models and their riders was a special feature of this period. Attention to appearance was noted by the onlookers, a custom not observed by the majority of riders whose bikes showed the stain of travel on dusty roads.

When war broke out and the Royal Flying Corps was formed the P and M was adopted as the official despatch riders' machine of the Corps, and gave excellent service.

During the twenties racing interests culminated in a creditable 4th place in the Senior T.T. of 1925, with rider T. F. Bullus. Subsequent appearances in the T.T. gave them 10th place in the Senior of 1927 and 9th the following year.

The name Panther had been added to the P and M when up-dating the range in 1926, together with the introduction of saddle tanks.

In 1927 a totally different model was introduced into the range, having an engine-gearbox unit designed by Granville Bradshaw. This little machine, the Panthette, had a 250cc o.h.v. V-twin engine set across the frame. Its unusual construction included a forged channel-type frame and four-speed gearbox which transmitted power to the rear wheel by chain.

The small engine was not a success and production was dropped after two years. In this period the 500cc models had been developed with overhead valves and four-speed gearboxes, again ahead of most rivals, while in 1928 the first of the famous 600s was offered for sidecar work. With modifications this machine was produced until the close-down of the factory.

The depression in 1930 caused much concern with manufacturers and many dropped prices to maintain sales, offering inferior products. P and M continued to offer a quality machine, but the notorious 'Red' Panther, a healthy 250, sold readily at £29 17s. 6d. under the banner of Pride and Clarke, the South London dealers.

Many models were offered from time to time – even a two-stroke powered by a 250 Villiers engine – but the mainstay was the 600cc model. It is a tribute to Phelon's design that his first machine of 1900 should have the engine replacing the front down tube, and that the last one, manufactured sixty-six years later, retained this basic feature.

38 ROYAL ENFIELD

Royal Enfield must be regarded as one of the foremost British motor cycles ever made. The Enfield Cycle Company produced their first motor bicycle at the turn of the century and their last in the mid-sixties, and in between earned a proud reputation for quality and reliability. Motor cycles of various cubic capacities were manufactured during this time under the name of Royal Enfield, but it is perhaps in the lightweight division of 350cc and below that they are best remembered and achieved their greatest success.

An interest in engineering led the Redditch-based company under the guiding influence of Robert Walker Smith to the manufacture of cycles and cycle parts in the 1890s. The natural progress from there was to bring mechanisation to these machines, like so many of their rivals in the Midlands. The first of the Enfield motorised cycles was in fact a quadricycle made in about 1898, and quadricycles and tricycles with de Dion engines were manufactured and sold by the company for several years. Early experiments with two-wheeled machines led to the production of a motor bicycle in 1901, with a small clip-on engine fixed in front of the steering column which drove the rear wheel by means of an elongated crossed belt. The machine was also fitted with pedals for supplementary human drive! The position of the engine was soon changed for later models to the conventional place below the petrol tank. Early Enfields were of $2\frac{3}{4}$ horsepower and $3\frac{1}{2}$ horsepower. During the first decade interest at Enfield had naturally extended to experiments with motorcars and a subsidiary company was soon established for their manufacture.

From the outset the name, symbol and trade-mark of the Royal Enfield motor cycle displayed the firm's close business association with the Royal Small Arms Factory in Enfield, Middlesex. The symbol showed a field gun with the words 'Royal Enfield' pierced by a rifle with bayonet fixed. Early

Enfield colours were two shades of green which persisted throughout their range of models until the late twenties.

By 1910 the company had transferred their allegiance to miniature V-twins of about 350cc based loosely on the Swiss-made Motosacoche design. They developed an expanding clutch two-speed gear similar to that used by the P and M and Scott motor cycles, which involved twin primary chains. The big innovation of the pre-First World War years was the 6 horsepower twin-cylinder model with a passenger chair powered by a J.A.P. engine, an interesting contrast to the MAG 8 horsepower twin used by Matchless. However, the J.A.P. engine was an exception in the house of Enfield, where until the war the connection with Motosacoche had been very marked although not publicised. The range of Motosacoche twins sold in England had components of considerable similarity to Enfield's, including the rubber 'cush' hub in the rear wheel to take the punch out of the chain-drive, a feature that was to be incorporated into all Royal Enfield motor cycles until the very end. In the immediate post-war years the Royal Enfield passenger outfits were powered by Vickers and Wolseley 8 horse-power twins. From those early days Enfield's continued to cater for the sidecar enthusiast. In the twenties the 1000cc J.A.P. twin was superseded by Enfield's own engine, and then supplemented by a 1140cc side valve unit in the thirties. Post-Second World War sidecar models included the 500cc o.h.v. single-cylinder Model J, followed by the 700cc 'Meteor' in the mid-fifties, which was the first of the big parallel overhead valve twins.

The year 1914 marked Enfield's first really successful venture in the Isle of Man T.T. Races. From the earliest days Royal Enfield entered trials and road reliability tests without disgrace, competing as early as 1900 in the 1,000 Miles Trial with their quadricycle, but in the world of racing the marque never, so to speak, made its mark. In the 1914 Junior T.T. however, eight out of nine Royal Enfields finished, with a very creditable five in the first twenty places. The best performance of the day for Enfield ended in tragedy. F. J. Walker was in contention for first place when he crashed on the last lap. Picking his machine up, undoubtedly in great pain, he managed to start his machine again and crossed the finishing line in third place following home the two Williams on their A.J.S. machines. Whether due to concussion suffered in the crash, or for some other unknown reason, he continued to ride down the road and collided fatally with the barriers, which in those days were placed across the road at the conclusion of the race. Post-war racing success for Royal Enfield was mainly confined to the twenties, the Company thereafter preferring to give their support to entries in trials competitions. In the twenties C. S. Barrow rode Enfields with considerable racing success, and among other trophies he helped them to win was the team award in the 1927 Junior T.T. event. The following year

Barrow attained his personal best in T.T. races with a second place on his Enfield in the Lightweight class, coming in behind F. A. Longman on his O.K. Supreme.

For trials the company made the well-loved range of 'Bullet' models starting in the early 1930s. These were light machines usually driven by a 350cc engine. After the Second World War the 'Bullet' was one of the pioneers of the swinging arm rear suspension that is now in universal use, and 350 and 500cc 'Bullets' had a staunch following for many years. The 'Meteor' of the mid-fifties was basically a pair of 350cc Bullets placed side by side. Other innovations of the thirties in the Royal Enfield factory included the 'Cycar' model, a 150cc two-stroke machine, remarkable for its completely enclosed frame and engine and low purchase price of about £20. When it is remembered that the first Royal Enfield cost in the region of £50, this was an advance appreciated by all Enfield enthusiasts. In the sporting field, trials successes were recorded for Royal Enfield in the decade before the Second World War by men like Holdsworth and Booker and the legendary Charlie Rogers.

Royal Enfield's contribution to the war effort of 1939–45 included the supply of 350cc overhead valve models for British dispatch riders (based on their highly successful trials model) and the 'Flying Flea' models, so called because of their compact size and their special purpose. These 125cc two-stroke machines together with the Excelsior-made 'Corgi' provided instant transport for the Allied paratroop divisions landed in Europe. The design of the 'Flying Flea' bore remarkable similarities to the German D.K.W. equivalent and appeared to many people to be a blatant copy. However, as far as Enfields were concerned, they filled a need and continued the factory's history of two-strokes which had begun in 1915. The 'Flea' developed later into the 'Prince' model but this died a natural death.

In the early fifties, apart from the Bullet range, Enfield's most notable contribution was the big parallel twin 'Meteor' mentioned earlier. In the smaller cubic capacity range, Enfield's 250cc 'Clipper' was quite popular. In the later part of the decade another 250cc model, the unit construction 'Crusader', was launched, with a performance better than the same capacity German N.S.U. It was a bold and brave venture, halted mainly by the dying public interest in British-made motor cycles.

Certainly after the war Enfields had continued to prove themselves in trials' competitions, their most successful exponent being Johnny Brittain, but continental two-strokes followed by the Japanese challenge hit the British industry very hard. In a final fling, Enfield's showed a surprising renewed interest in road racing with a 250cc two-stroke single-cylinder machine with great potential. It might well have proved a winner with a little more development. But 'the might-have-beens' litter the world of motor cycling history and for Royal Enfield the history book closed in the mid-sixties when all production ceased.

Thereafter Enfield owners requiring spare parts obtained them from Velocette, until they too ceased production in 1971.

39 RUDGE

Rudge were in the transport business as early as the 1870s, when Dan Rudge made a popular pedal cycle. Rudge started and ended as manufacturers of pedal cycles, sandwiching a thirty-year period of manufacturing very good motor cycles. Dan Rudge hailed from the Midlands, as did the Coventry-born man named Woodcock, initially a lawyer, who took over Rudge and several other cycle companies at the turn of the century to house them all under one roof and the one name of Rudge. After he died the Rudge company joined forces with the Whitworth cycle company of Birmingham to become Rudge Whitworth. The power behind the new company was Charles Pugh, who had been a top man at Whitworth's prior to the merger.

The first Rudge-Whitworth motor cycle was manufactured at their Coventry-based works in 1910. There was nothing remarkable in the design. It had a 499cc single-cylinder engine with the unusual feature of a push-rod operated overhead inlet valve. Like its contemporaries, it used direct belt-drive. However in 1911 the factory introduced a new gear system for machines to be ridden in the Isle of Man T.T. races, which was subsequently incorporated in their standard model on sale to the public. It was known as the Multi gear and, like the Gradua gear designed by Freddie Barnes for Zenith, it provided a variable gear while retaining the smoothness and simplicity of belt-drive. The gear was operated alongside the petrol tank by a lever which opened or closed the engine and rear wheel pulleys together, but in different directions, so that the belt tension was kept constant. By this method an infinitely variable gear could be obtained, over a fairly limited range. The wear and tear on the belt was such that replacements were constantly needed. The gear became both popular and successful and Rudge-Whitworth motor cycles which included this particular gear were known as Rudge-Multis.

Rudges were first entered for the T.T. races in 1912, and their first victory came with Cyril Pullin on his 500cc single-cylinder Rudge-Multi in the 1914 Senior T.T., improving on Ray Abbott's second in the preceding year's event. Pullin recorded a remarkably good race average of 49·5 m.p.h. Cyril Pullin himself re-designed the Rudge-Multi for racing by the inclusion of a long steering head and sloping top tube, making the petrol tank a wedge shape and generally improving the machine's handling.

The new V-twin for 1915 was called the Multwin and still incorporated belt-drive with the ever popular multi-gear. Surprisingly it was also offered with the alternative of a new countershaft three-speed gearbox.

Like other top manufacturers Rudge made motor cycles for the First World War and a large proportion of their output found its way to the Russian front.

Rudge continued to produce their 'Multi' model until the mid-twenties but thereafter only two models were put on the market. These were powered by single-cylinder 499cc and 349cc engines with pent-roof four valve cylinder heads, and incorporated four-speed gearboxes and coupled brakes. The all-black tank was now picked out with gold lines, and the full Rudge-Whitworth name appeared where only the abbreviated version had been seen before. The range was extended later to include 500cc four valve machines in 'Standard', 'Special' and 'Sports' models. Bulbous saddle tanks were a distinctive feature of the Special and Sports models. For 1929 the Sports model was re-named the 'Ulster' in commemoration of Graham Walker's success in the Grand Prix of 1928, the first road race in the world to be won at an average speed of over 80 m.p.h. In the same year Rudge-Whitworth put out their first lightweight 250cc side valve and overhead valve motor cycles, engines courtesy of J.A.P. For 1931 they built their own 250cc overhead valve engine with four valves, which proved very successful in T.T. racing in the 1930s.

The new decade saw the introduction of dry sump lubrication and a new design of the crankcase on the four valve models.

In keeping with the popular trend, the black petrol tank was replaced by a chromium tank with black panels. The new 1930 Rudge could reach 100 m.p.h., or so it was claimed. Certainly it beat all its contemporaries on the T.T. course, taking first, second and fourth in the Senior and first and second in the Junior. Walter Handley, who won the Senior, had intended to ride an F.N. which failed to arrive in time for the race, and so he 'borrowed' a Rudge. Rudges had many successes in the T.T. races of the 1930s, notably in the hands of those most able riders Graham Walker, Ernie Nott, H. G. Tyrell-Smith, Charlie Dodson and Walter Handley. After the Senior-Junior double of 1930, success was limited to the Lightweight class where they eventually achieved first, second and third in 1934. Rudge-Whitworth were also successful in many trials including the Blue Ribbon event, the International Six Days.

In 1938 the factory moved to Hayes in Middlesex. Two years later the company sold out to Sturmey Archer and Norman Motor Cycles and the name Rudge-Whitworth passed into the history books of motor cycling.

40 SCOTT

Alfred Angas Scott, a dyer's technician from Yorkshire, developed twin two-stroke engines to propel bicycles and later his motor boat. By 1908 these experiments bore fruit in the production of the first Scott motor cycle. Like so many pioneers, Alfred Scott had to overcome lack of finance and this was temporarily achieved by allowing another engineering concern to build and sell the machines to his design. He received the handsome royalty of £3 10s 0d (£3.50) on each motor cycle made. The first Scotts were powered by a small parallel twin two-stroke engine, with deflector-type pistons and water-cooled cylinder heads slung extremely low in a wide duplex cradle frame. The straight tube of the frame gave it the appearance of a ladies' bicycle. The duplex-tubed open frames favoured by Scott were reminiscent of those first used in the early experiments of the Hildebrand brothers in Germany in the 1890s. The Scott motor cycle had a rear wheel drive via two chains to a countershaft and a single chain for the final drive.

In 1909, Scott, together with his cousin Frank Philipp and another enthusiast Eric Myers, organised their own Bradford factory for production of Scott motor cycles, backed partly by money from Scott's brothers. Even so it was uneconomic to manufacture frames, and these were supplied by Royal Enfield to Scott's specifications and design. Early advances made by Alfred Scott included internal enclosed spring front forks (forerunners of the telescopic forks of today), the kick-starter, the foot-change two-speed gear pedal, and all-chain-drive.

Scotts were unusual for being two-strokes at a time when most motor cycles were four-strokes. They were renowned for their quiet engines, fast acceleration, low centre of gravity and their lightness and ease of handling. From the very beginning, Alfred Scott had caused jealousy among rival manufacturers, and when in 1908 he had swept the board with three gold medals in an important hill climbing event, there were complaints that on a two-stroke machine he had an unfair advantage over the other competitors. The Auto Cycle Union ordered him to alter his engine to deprive himself of the advantage. In time this apparently absurd penalty was removed. However, it did not interfere with Scott's plans for the Isle of Man Senior Tourist Trophy Races, and in 1912 Frank Applebee rode his Scott to victory in the Senior T.T., recording an average speed over the 187½-mile course of 48·69 miles per hour. In the 1913 Senior T.T. this Scott success was repeated by H. O. Wood. In 1912 business had improved and another factory was opened, this time in nearby Shipley, Yorkshire. Success in the Isle of Man T.T. was guaranteed to boost sales.

For the First World War Scott developed a sidecar-outfit-style, shaft-drive 'gun-car'. Soon after the war Alfred Scott with his colleagues decided to sell their interest in Scott motor cycles. Scott considered he had made as much progress in the development of the two-wheeler as he could hope to make in the foreseeable future, and felt he could more usefully apply his talents to the manufacture of a unique side-car combination, the 'Sociable'. With his departure went some of the inspiration behind the progress of Scott's, and despite the comparative success of the Squirrel series and the boom in popularity at the end of the twenties, Scott's were never pacemakers in motor cycling again.

The Squirrel series started in 1922 with a sports model of 486cc with light mudguards and dropped handlebars. H. Langman boosted the Scott 'Squirrel' with a third in the Senior T.T. and Scotts also took the Team Prize, finishing in fourth and ninth places.

By 1925 the 'Super Squirrel' was on the scene in 498cc and 596cc forms with water-cooled cylinder heads. The 596cc was specially built with sidecars in mind. In 1926 Scott produced their 'Flying Squirrel', a newly tuned twin watercooled two-stroke, still on the duplex open frame with the optional extra of the elongated tank used on their T.T. machines.

In the thirties there was a significant change from the duplex frame to a frame with a single down tube. The detachable cylinder head was introduced and the short-stroke engine was retired. The Scott factory also made a three-cylinder water-cooled luxury machine. Like many British motor cycle manufacturers, financial clouds continuously hovered on the horizon and the Second World War added greatly to Scott's difficulties. Soon after the war in 1950, Matthew Holder's Aerco Jig and Tool factory in Birmingham bought Scott's and from that time on, under new management, Scott motor cycles were built to order in Birmingham. But for all the various hands that have controlled the destiny of Scott motor cycles, the touch of Alfred Angas Scott is still very much in evidence to this day, since the design of his original motor cycle remained basically unchanged through some sixty years.

41   SINGER

Singer and Company of Coventry drew considerable attention with the 'motor wheel' used to propel their motor bicycles and tricycles at the turn of the century. Messrs. Perks and Birch, also of Coventry, patented the device in 1899. The 'motor wheel' was a wheel with engine, petrol tank and complete motorising works within its perimeter, which could be fitted to a perfectly ordinary pedal bicycle or tricycle. Perks and Birch were intending to put their invention out to the public under the appropriate name of the 'Compact', but in 1900 Singer put the machine on the market with a 2 horsepower four-stroke engine mounted in the middle of an aluminium spoked wheel. The 'motor wheel' was usually the rear wheel in the bicycle and the front wheel of the tricycle. It was probably the first motor cycle fitted with a magneto, a low tension type with make and break inside the combustion chamber, for which the credit must go to F. R. Simms. The speed of the machine was controlled by a lever which operated by a form of throttle control to the carburettor. The 'motor wheel' proved very popular indeed in the first few years of the century and Singer earned a reputation, despite the obvious awkward positioning of the petrol tank and the engine. By 1904 the wheel was re-designed with the spokes of the wheel all placed on one side to improve access. Singer also catered for the lady rider with their dropped frame model. Both ladies and men were given the opportunity to assist their motorised cycles with pedalling equipment, a common feature of nearly all motor cycles at the beginning of the century.

After 1904 Singer motor cycles were re-designed. A central vertical engine was fitted between a split front down tube of the cycle frame, and the machine was fitted with a new high tension magneto fixed in front of the engine, protected from the grit and grime by the valanced front mudguard.

It was not long before Singer were experimenting with a three-wheeler (as opposed to the tricycle which had always been popular with them). From there it was but a short step to the four-wheel motor car. The Singer car was available by the end of the first decade of the century, and motor cars eventually dominated motor cycle production in the Company.

Singer's always made their own engines and after the 'motor wheel' produced both two-stroke and four-stroke machines, the early models being air-cooled and the later models water-cooled. One of their most popular machines just prior to the First World War was the 500cc four-stroke single-cylinder model. This model was often used with sidecars, enabling the enthusiast to be accompanied by a fellow enthusiast or even his wife! Never a great success in racing competitions (fifth in the 1913 Junior T.T. was the high spot in their short career) and at first disdaining to enter trials (such as the first Auto Cycle Club 1,000-miles Trial in 1903), Singers were undoubtedly popular with the 'everyday' motor cyclist. However, the company's decision to concentrate on motor car production meant the end of the motor cycle department in 1915. It was a short but illustrious life that made a worthwhile contribution to the development of motor cycles.

John Marston and Co. were an old-established Midlands firm which manufactured saucepans and other metal items until they turned their attention to bicycles in 1890. They were immediately successful in this venture. In 1912 their first motor cycle was produced almost entirely in their works, and was a neat little $2\frac{3}{4}$ horsepower (350cc) side valve machine with a two-speed gearbox and an attractively painted green tank with silver panels. As the quality was high, so was the price and only a few were sold. In 1913, in addition to the $2\frac{3}{4}$ (now fitted with the famous black tank with gold line), a $3\frac{1}{2}$ horsepower single and 6 horsepower J.A.P.-engined twin were offered principally for sidecar use. Unfortunately, the 500cc machine had many teething troubles, resulting in a redesigned engine for 1915, when military orders were secured from the French and Russian governments. Since both preferred final belt-drive, the only belt-drive machines made by this firm were produced. All the $3\frac{1}{2}$ horsepower machines had three-speed countershaft gearboxes, and all civilian models primary and final drive in oil bath chain cases. The V-twin machine was powered by various engines including the Swiss M.A.G., but from 1917 until 1923 the 8 horsepower J.A.P. was fitted.

After the war modification and improvements were made to the $3\frac{1}{2}$ horsepower model, but the $2\frac{3}{4}$ horsepower machine was discontinued. The decision to re-enter racing to back up the considerable success already achieved in reliability trials was taken as soon as events were organised. In 1920 T. C. De La Hay had a handsome victory in the Senior T.T. race in the Isle of Man. Two years later Alec Bennett scored another victory for the marque in the same event. They were obliged to wait until 1928 for Charlie Dodson to win another Senior T.T. for them, but he repeated the performance the following year with Alec Bennett pursuing him home in second place. Sunbeams were not to experience T.T. success like this again.

In the mid-twenties an overhead camshaft engine of 600cc was designed with a view to competing in the sidecar T.T. races, but this was never used and an experimental 500cc version proved equally unsuccessful.

In the thirties Sunbeam standard models with 250, 350, 500 and 600cc side valve and overhead valve single-cylinder engines were marketed with moderate success. Any lack of success can be attributed fairly to the high purchase price, beyond the reach of so many purses. The make retained such a reputation for quality and handsome finish through its entire production, that it was often referred to as the gentleman's motor cycle.

John Marston's were taken over in 1937 by Associated Motor Cycles and the design continued as before until the war. After hostilities the name Sunbeam passed to the B.S.A. Group, and was used on an entirely new range of luxury mount models, the S.7 and S.8. These were notable for their huge tyres and overhead camshaft vertical twin engines with shaft-drive, the frames being fully sprung. Unhappily these did not prove a financial success and were discontinued in the mid-fifties. The final appearance of the name was on the ill-fated B.S.A. group's scooter. A sad end to a famous British marque.

43 SUZUKI

Suzuki is now probably one of the most popular makes of motor cycle in the world. But it was not until the mid-fifties that this Japanese company even considered making such machines, having previously made its name and money on specialised engineering directed at the textile trade. The company was founded in 1909 by Michio Suzuki and the first factory was opened for production at Hamamatsu. In 1952, following a drastic recession in textiles, the company looked for another outlet for their engineering knowledge, experience and craftsmen. It was quite a step to enter the world of motor cycle production.

In 1953 the first Suzuki motor cycle was produced in Japan and like all that were to follow, it was a two-stroke. At the time of deciding company policy, the two-stroke machine was not considered by most manufacturers to be a profitable or worthwhile field, but like other Japanese manufacturers, Suzuki proved the fallacy of this theory. The first ever Suzuki motor cycle was a 60cc model and so great an impact did it make, that production was almost immediately increased to a remarkable 4,400 power units per month, approximately equivalent to the total number of power units produced by all the British manufacturers at that point in time.

In 1954 the company changed its name to Suzuki Motor Company Ltd. 1955 saw the first Suzuki 125cc and at the same time Suzuki produced their first Mini motor car, again powered by a two-stroke engine. With the increasing demand for their motor cycles, the company expanded gradually over the years until at the time of writing there are five factories set up in Japan concentrating on production of Suzuki machines. Suzuki in fact manufacture boats and outboard motors for boats, and Snowcats which are better known in colder climates where mobility is still required even when the snow lies thickly upon the ground.

The range of Suzuki motor cycles has also increased over the years and there is now available to the enthusiast a choice of any size machine from the 50cc single cylinder five-speed gearbox model up to the 750cc water cooled three cylinder Super Bike, all two-stroke machines. Suzuki can fairly be described as the motor cycle of today and tomorrow, and their 'history' is still to be made. The company have, however, in the few short years of their motor cycling existence managed to stake a claim to fame in both 'tourist' and 'competition' worlds. Suzuki have always aimed at making their machines attractive to the prospective purchaser, the man in the street, and have placed the emphasis on the facility of starting, the smooth running of the engine, the comfortable seats, bright paintwork and chrome. But pretty colours alone do not sell motor cycles, and the true credit for the success of Suzuki must rest with the engineers. Even now with an eye to the future and the ever increasing world wide pollution problem, Suzuki have obtained the world manufacturing rights for the production of the re-volutionary Wankel rotory engine. This, however, is still in the future.

Suzuki sales since production began have been remarkable, and have been particularly high in the USA. In Great Britain the Suzuki franchise came under the management of the Lambretta/Trojan Group and established the company firmly in the market.

Suzuki have also had considerable success in motor cycle competition, be it racing or trials. The factory's first entry in the Isle of Man T.T. races was in 1960 but it was not until the innovation of the 50cc event that Suzuki had their first T.T. success. Suzuki had the distinction of being the first winners of the 50cc T.T. race in 1962, Ernst Degner managing to average over 75 m.p.h. round the $75\frac{1}{2}$ mile course, a quite astonishing performance. Suzuki emphasised its superiority in this class by winning again in 1963 and 1964. 1963 was indeed a successful T.T. year for Suzuki as the factory took the coveted 1, 2, 3 placings in the Lightweight 125cc event in addition to the 50cc trophy. Road racing success has continued since that time with much credit due to riders like Hugh Anderson and Barry Sheene. Other notable racing successes have been achieved in moto-cross grands prix and in 1971 their riders won all four of the manufacturers' and individuals' titles in the 250cc and 500cc events giving them complete victory in the 1971 World Moto-cross Grand Prix. In 1972 they again won the 250cc and 500cc world championships.

It is small wonder that the name Suzuki is associated the world over more with motor cycles than with engineering in the textile industry. For Suzuki motor cycles, the story is only just beginning.

44 TRIUMPH

The founder of the Triumph pedal cycle business chose a name that was easily identifiable on the continent as in Britain, since he himself was a German living in London, Siegfried Bettmann. The cycle business was started in 1885 and Bettmann soon joined forces with another German, Schulte at their Coventry premises in the midland area of England. In 1897 the 'New Triumph Cycle Co., Ltd.', was formed but the title was soon shortened. Schulte, the chief engineer, was naturally interested in the new developments in engine-propelled bicycles and in the German-made Hildebrand and Wolfmüller. But Triumph did not rush into a venture ill-prepared. It was not until 1902 that the world saw the first Triumph motor cycle. This was a single-geared, single-cylinder motor bicycle, with a Minerva engine fitted below the front down tube of the frame and with the petrol tank clipped to the crossbar. This was followed by a similar machine with a J.A.P. engine in 1903. Schulte introduced the first Triumph motor cycle engine in 1905 and it soon gained popularity. In the first Isle of Man Tourist Trophy events, Triumphs came second and third in the single-cylinder class, and improved on that performance the following year by winning the event with Jack Marshall in the saddle. Triumph motor cycles featured high in the honours list of motor cycle sporting competitions from the start. Triumph's designed their own carburettor and fitted magneto ignition to improve the reliability of their $3\frac{1}{2}$ horsepower machine in performance, so much so that the nickname 'Trusty Triumph' was quickly applied and stuck fast for evermore.

Triumph's contribution to the British war effort consisted of about 30,000 motor cycles used by despatch riders. The model chosen was the famous Model H, a 550cc single-cylinder side valve with a three-speed gearbox and final belt-drive. For such important work the forces had need of 'trusty' motor cycles and Triumph maintained their reputation.

In the immediate post-war period Lt.-Col. C. V. Holbrook, C.B.E., took over as managing director of the company in the place of the retiring M. J. Schulte, and motor cycle production continued as before. After declining the opportunity to compete in the 1920 Isle of Man T.T. races publicly on a point of principle (the reason being the tendency of manufacturers to make 'specials', which were not representative of their products), Triumph's returned to the fray in 1922. In that year came the first Triumph overhead four valve engine created by Sir Henry Ricardo. A Triumph won second place in the Senior race with Walter Brandish in the saddle, only seven seconds behind the great Alec Bennett on his Sunbeam. The 'Ricardo' also won several speed records at Brooklands and other famous tracks.

During the twenties the Triumph range increased to include a side valve 350cc model, a model P 500cc and a colour change from grey and green paintwork to black with blue panels. It was also during this decade that Triumph motor cars first came into production.

The thirties were a period of change at Triumph's. In the early part of the decade the world financial crisis took its toll and by the middle years it was obvious that Triumph motor cycles would no longer be made unless there was drastic re-organisation. As a result J. Y. Sangster set up the Triumph Engineering Co. Ltd. With Edward Turner, formerly of Ariel, as managing director and chief designer in control, Triumph's continued with renewed zest. The influence of Turner was immediately felt by his introduction of the 'Tiger' range of 250cc, 350cc and 500cc singles, called respectively the Tiger 70, the Tiger 80 and the Tiger 90. In 1938 a 500cc vertical twin-cylinder engined machine called the Speed Twin was introduced, which was so successful that it altered the whole trend of motor cycle engine design throughout the world. It was widely copied and in updated form is still in production by Triumph today, thirty-five years later – a record surely equalled only by Volkswagen. For 1939 a sports version of the 'Speed Twin' was put into production called the Tiger 100.

With the start of the Second World War, the factory immediately turned its machinery to war work, but the German air 'blitz' on Coventry reduced the factory to rubble. The company transferred activities to premises in Warwick and started making spare parts for service machines, gradually progressing to making complete motor cycles again. The Meriden works were ready by 1942 and these premises have continued to be the home of Triumph's since that date. One war development was the adoption of the vertical twin-cylinder engine for use in driving a 6 K.W. (D.C.) auxiliary generator set for the Air Ministry, and many were manufactured for this purpose before the end of hostilities.

After the war Triumph's continued with a policy of twin-cylinder models, and the company prospered with orders rushing in from both home and abroad. Motor cycle demand in both Europe and the United States was high in early post-war years and Triumph's were particularly popular. In the United States Triumph success mainly centred round the Speed Twin with its high mobility compared with American motor cycles in production at that time.

The great innovation of early post-war years was the 650cc Thunderbird, brought into production in 1950. It was renowned for speed and high performance from the beginning, proved by the 214 m.p.h. run of Johnnie Allen on the Utah Salt Flats in the USA in 1956.

In between these years there had been further re-organisation with the Triumph Engineering Company being taken over by B.S.A. in 1951, but continuing to produce motor cycles under its own marque. Examples of new Triumph models in the new era were the 150cc overhead valve single-cylinder Terrier produced from about 1954 and the little 200cc Tiger Cub. The feminine touch was applied with the introduction in the mid-fifties of the 'Tigress' motor scooter.

The 224·57 m.p.h. world speed record was claimed by Triumph's in the early sixties at Bonneville Salt Flats in Utah, USA. Bill Johnson achieved this remarkable speed on a 650cc Triumph Bonneville in 1962. By 1969 the Bonneville became the first production machine to lap the Isle of Man T.T. course at more than 100 m.p.h., and during the same season was awarded the F.I.M. Coupe d'Endurance for production machine racing.

The year before, in 1968, an important Triumph model had been announced, the Triumph Trident 750cc, setting the pace again with an original three-cylinder motor cycle. The Trident has performed with considerable success both on the roads and in competition. Triumphs over the years have also made their name in the trials world. For the man in the street Triumph motor cycles have been daily brought to his attention as the mounts of the British police and of other police forces elsewhere, which indicates their reliability and performance. By the time of publication it is hoped that Triumph production will have moved its base to Birmingham under the umbrella company of Norton Villiers Triumph. Only time will reveal the success or failure of this venture, but the name Triumph will be remembered as long as motor cycles are made and ridden.

45 TRUMP

The Trump motor cycle had a comparatively short life between the years 1906 and 1923. It was originally built by Angus Maitland (a man who also had a close interest in the manufacturing of motor cars and cyclecars) and his cousin Frank A. McNab. Maitland and McNab's first factory, later called Trump Motors Ltd., was opened in Surrey, in South-East England, and produced the Trump-J.A.P. cycle with J.A.P. engines. The Trump-J.A.P.s were mainly single-cylinder machines ranging from 250cc to 500cc, but a few big twins were also built. Since the young founders were keenly interested in racing, the early Trump-J.A.P.s were designed for speed. In the first decade of this century, the maximum limit for racing motor cycles was 1000cc, although the reason for this limit is still a mystery. The standard was certainly not set by the Isle of Man T.T. races which were first classified by whether a machine was a single- or twin-cylinder. Trump-J.A.P.s were most successful in road races, especially in the hands of McNab who had many race successes at Brooklands. In a stunt race against an aeroplane the finish was so close that the record books are divided as to who was the winner. Earlier in 1909, a 500cc Trump-J.A.P. created a track record when covering forty-eight miles in an hour. Their road racing successes did not stretch to the T.T. races where on the only occasion Trumps were entered, namely in the solitary 1910 event, both machines were forced to retire.

The early Trumps were characterised by their braced steering-heads and the 'big tube' situated just behind the engine. The long, narrow petrol tank was specially designed for racing purposes. In order to ensure minimum loss of time in refuelling. the petrol cap was closed by a coil spring fixed to the tank floor. The oil tank, as on many racing machines of that period, was fixed on top of the petrol tank. The '90 bore' overhead valve engine introduced in about 1910 proved the most successful. Another significant Trump feature was their comparative lightness since the 1000cc model weighed in at an almost insignificant 220 pounds.

Maitland left Trumps in 1911 to carry on his own business elsewhere, while the organisation continued making motor cycles for another twelve years, latterly in a factory based in Birmingham.

Despite a relatively short existence Trumps could claim royal support, for in 1922 the Duke of York owned a Trump-Anzani which was ridden in competitive events by S. E. Wood, including races at the famous Brooklands track. In fact, the Essex Motor Club ran a charity meeting at Brooklands in that same year and the Duke was present to watch his machine perform.

46 VAUXHALL

The name Vauxhall is mainly associated with the famous motor car, and indeed the firm, which dabbled with two-wheelers in the 1920s, never came to satisfactory terms with motor cycle production. Major Halford, who was responsible for the celebrated Napier 'Sabre' engine used in the Hawker 'Tempest' fighter aircraft, was the designer for the first Vauxhall motor cycle. It was an ambitious project and the machine would have been perhaps the most technically advanced motor cycle on the road, but the fact that it would also have been the most expensive may well have prompted the decision not to go into production. With only twelve engines and less than half that number of frames ready the company decided to sell off the only two completed machines, which were made in 1922, and cut their losses. Both were sold to employees for about £45. The net result was that the purchasers were in the happy position of owning rare motor cycles, and, in the not-so-happy position of having to find the rare spare parts when some mechanical failure occurred. The answer was that if a spare could not be found, it had to be made by the owner. It is therefore all the more remarkable that a Vauxhall motor cycle is still being ridden on the roads today. The credit must go to R. D. (Bob) Thomas, a Vintage Motor Cycle Club enthusiast, who obtained possession of a Vauxhall motor cycle in about 1950 when it had lain stripped and in boxes for over twenty years.

Many parts were missing, others needed repair, and all needed cleaning and painting. Undaunted, Mr Thomas set about the task, which included the manufacture of the main frame, petrol tank, handlebars, exhaust system and clutch. It took over twelve years of his life to renovate this machine but he considers it all worth while. He still rides it today having passed the thousand-mile mark. The top speed recorded is about 82 m.p.h. but he claims the machine will cruise at 50 m.p.h.

The Vauxhall was certainly different from its British contemporaries. It was the first British four-cylinder shaft-driven motor cycle and had the remarkable feature of fully interchangeable wheels. The engine has four separate cast-iron cylinders with fixed heads and parallel push-rod operated overhead valves giving 30 b.h.p. The engine, gearbox and clutch are housed in one complete unit and the clutch is operated with a foot control. There are three gears with two selectors, again an unusual feature. The frame carrying the large engine unit is of duplex cradle type with a detachable tube to allow the gearbox and clutch to be taken out for repairs and maintenance. The silencer is a casting under the left foot-board and the tool box is another casting of similar shape under the right one.

A propeller shaft transmits power to the wheel. There are indeed many features more common to motor cars than motor cycles, including flutes on the fuel tank, but the only Vauxhall motor cycle now known to be in existence still gives much pleasure to its owner and rider.

47 VELOCETTE

The firm of Veloce Ltd., formed in 1905 by Johann Goodman, was a family concern, which included his sons Percy, Eugene and daughter Ethel and grandsons Bertram and Peter, and made history in the motor cycle world by producing exceedingly high-grade machines.

Veloce were always a leading design force, and the famous overhead camshaft engine produced in 1924 was to win innumerable races between then and 1950.

The first machines of note were lightweights to satisfy the demand which existed in the years prior to the First World War. After that the 250 two-stroke models were highly competitive and in the top-grade lightweight class.

The Goodmans always concentrated on sound engineering principles and the little pre-war lightweights demonstrated this clearly. The two-speed gear, chain-drive machines were very advanced. When production re-commenced in 1919 the two-speed two-stroke first incorporated the characteristic de-saxe offset crankshaft. It is interesting to note that a ladies' model was offered, with provision in the dropped tube frame for the adequate skirts worn in this period. One-piece crankcases were used with a single bearing crankshaft until 1926, after which the more conventional split crankcases were adopted with bearings at both ends of the crankshaft. The sports two-strokes were developed to exceed 70 miles per hour, and performed admirably in the T.T. races in this immediate post-war period. In 1921 they finished 3rd, 5th and 7th in the 250cc class of the Junior and again 3rd in the first Lightweight race.

In 1924, Percy Goodman started work on one of the most famous motor cycle engines of all time, a 350cc overhead camshaft model K, destined to win many T.T.s, Grand Prix races, and innumerable races in the hands of private owners.

This new machine was on exhibition at the 1924 show at Olympia as a Veloce and attracted much attention. Since it was common practice in pre-war days to add 'ette' to lightweight machines, such as Levisette, Zenette, etc., dealers insisted on the name Velocette being used.

As the prototype went through major development in the winter of 1924 and early 1925, the production models which first left the factory in July of that year differed substantially from the show version. To cope with the demand for the new model, as well as for the popular two-strokes, a new factory was necessary and the move was made to the Humphries and Dawes works, home of O.K. motor cycles. The winning of the 1926 Junior T.T. and seven subsequent T.T. races and Grands Prix have endeared the make to motor cyclists the world over. The first 'K's were fitted with Druid forks, but a year later Webbs products replaced them. A small batch of roadster models with Dowty telescopic forks was built in about 1948.

The Velocette policy of offering their successful racing products to the public was popular, particularly in 1929 when the replica race winning model was available as a 'KTT' to private owners. They made full use of these excellent machines in all types of speed events.

Apart from the Goodman family, one name stands out more than others in the development of the machines, the late Harold Willis, whose keen sense of humour is still remembered. Possibly his most important single unit was the excellent positive stop foot-change device, devised when hand change was the order of the day.

Alec Bennet became the first famous rider to win a T.T. on a Velocette, other riders being Frank Longman, Freddie Frith, and Stanley Woods. At Brooklands in 1928, F. G. Hicks won the 350 sidecar class in the 200-mile race at 70·84 m.p.h., and a solo took the hour record at 100·39 with Harold Willis in the saddle. This was the first 350cc motor cycle to break the hundred barrier for the coveted 'hour'.

Speedway was catered for in a year when most manufacturers offered a 'dirt track model' at the show of 1929. The new model offered a modified frame with lateral strengthening, special forks, countershaft only and a 'bored' out (82mm) 350, with a standard stroke of 81 and high compression piston for use with methanol, giving a capacity of 411cc. This did not prove successful as most manufacturers discovered, with the exception of Rudge and Douglas who for a spell were supreme in this type of racing.

Many are confused by the engine prefix on Velocettes. All the OHC models are K. The following letters denote the model, for example, KSS meant Super Sports model or variations in specification, while KTT indicated T.T. Replicas, KTS-Touring Sports, and so on. All 'M's' are push-rod overhead valve models.

The depression demanded an economy model in 1930. This was a modified K with coil ignition, full equipment and a two-port head, all popular items but, even at a competitive price, this was not the answer. The model was therefore dropped in favour of a high camshaft 250 o.h.v. in 1934, starting the 'M' range – the 'MOV', to be followed by a larger version a little later, the 350, which became the MAC. Three-speed gearboxes were used up to 1932 on the 'K' models; thereafter the four-speed boxes of similar basic design were fitted to all models.

The late 1930s brought more interesting designs in prototype form, such as the model O, an overhead valve vertical twin built as a super touring machine, while for racing a supercharged 500cc twin appeared nicknamed 'The Roarer'. Development of both these models was stopped by the war.

The machine adopted by the War Office was a modified MAC, designated MAF and many of these models gave useful service under the difficult conditions of war.

After hostilities, production was resumed with both K and M ranges but by 1949 the Ks were discontinued – a wonderful span of twenty-four years for a design still successful in races to the end.

Modified 'M' types brought up to date with short-stroke motors as Venom and Vipers proved popular until production ceased.

The LE (little engine) was a winner from the start, despite many teething troubles. This was a horizontally-opposed side valve and water-cooled, shaft-drive twin of 150cc, enlarged almost immediately to 200cc. There was full protection for the rider, and also the great asset of easy starting by hand lever, which could not fail to attract utility riders.

This machine was almost universally adopted by police forces throughout the country and overseas, and enjoyed a production run of some sixteen years.

A 200cc sports version was offered in 1956 and was produced until about

1961, basically consisting of the unit construction crankcase gearbox unit and shaft-drive of the LE, but with overhead valves and air-cooled cylinders in a tubular frame. It was certainly a delightful little bike to ride, but, owing to its small 200cc engine, it was on the whole over-driven and suffered extinction.

The last impressive proof of performance was in March, 1961, when a 500 Venom Clubman, the push-rod o.h.v., successfully attacked the 24-hour record at Montlhery, averaging 100·05 m.p.h. which included the 12-hour record at the astonishing average speed of 104·66 m.p.h. This was the first machine to top 'the ton' for a day and at the time of writing it still holds the 24-hours record in the 500cc class.

The factory closed down in 1971 with the family of Goodmans still in charge, a wonderful record of production of high-class motor cycles, bettered by none.

48 WOOLER

The 'Flying Banana' was a Wooler motor cycle of the early 1920s. John Wooler made his first motor cycle in 1911 and quickly gained a reputation for originality and advanced ideas. His first was a 344cc two-stroke machine with a double-ended piston for the horizontal single cylinder, which eliminated crankcase compression. Even the first Wooler motor cycle was a pioneer of spring frame design. He used a special type of variable pulley gear, where the front pulley swung radially on a quadrant, inside of which one gear was fixed to the crankshaft driving a gear fixed to the variable pulley. This was operated by two pedals and the device reduced belt slip and generally facilitated gear changing.

In the post-war period up to 1926, only 350cc and 500cc models were produced, these being flat twin-cylinder machines. The 350cc models had side exhaust and overhead inlet valves, the 500 had an overhead camshaft. The nickname of 'Flying Banana' was given by Graham Walker to the Wooler after a creditable performance in the Isle of Man T.T. Junior Race of 1921, when it finished in thirty-fourth place. As the elongated bright yellow petrol tank flashed past it drew this analogy from the lips of the enthusiastic observer. The tank was further distinguished by the fact that, unlike most others, it enveloped the steering head at the front of the machine. This particular aspect of the tank was changed by the mid-twenties. An advertising gimmick to emphasise the economy of the Wooler was the claim that the 350cc machine had attained the phenomenal consumption of 311 miles per gallon, a feat that was actually achieved during a special test. Another innovation at Wooler's at this time was a 511cc overhead camshaft single-cylinder model, but very few were made.

It was not often that a Midlands-based motor cycle company was uprooted and brought to London, but this happened when Wooler took over the Packmann and Poppe motor cycle company in the late twenties. The latter were renowned for their clean and quiet motor cycles, as the engines used were the sleeve valve Barr and Stroud, and the machine was called the 'silent three'. Production was continued in Wembley until 1930. That was also the year when Wooler's stopped production for seventeen years as the demand for motor cycles had drastically decreased and the production costs had just as drastically increased. Wooler's put up the shutters until after the Second World War when production started up again for a short period of time. In 1948 Wooler showed a prototype 500cc flat four-cylinder with a complicated crank arrangement based on a Beam engine, which unfortunately was never put into production and not more than two engines were actually made.

The Company continued in business until 1955 making a handful of completely redesigned prototypes, with a more conventional flat four-cylinder overhead valve engine and swinging arm spring frame. Unfortunately only two of these machines have survived.

John Wooler died in 1952 having experimented with motor cycles since 1909 and having complete control of the firm until his death. He was a brilliant engineer with original ideas and worthy of a place in any history of motor cycle pioneers.

49 YAMAHA

This is another Japanese company who in a comparatively short period of time have earned a world-wide reputation for production of high quality two-stroke motor cycles. The first Yamaha motor cycle was in production in 1954 and at the present date the two-stroke range includes machines of 50, 75, 125, 200, 250 and 350cc, whilst the factory is introducing the concept of four-stroke machines of higher cubic capacity. The company claims the first rotary engined motor cycle prototype ever built in the world, the Yamaha Rotary RZ201 which was first shown to the general public at the 1972 Tokyo Motor Show. The motor cycle of the future is being developed at present by the Yamaha engineers. Yamaha were quick to export their machines and have met with particular popularity in Canada and the USA. Apart from success in the streets, Yamaha have also had considerable success on the race tracks, in moto-cross and trials events around the world. Much of their road racing success has been due to riders of the calibre of Phil Read, who in fact collected the first T.T. winners trophy for the company in 1965 in the Lightweight 125cc event. Road racing success has steadily improved at Yamaha and in the early 1970s the factory won the 250cc world road racing championship three years running.

Yamaha have also earned a reputation in another less well-known racing event, ice racing, which is so popular in Scandinavian countries. Certainly Yahama is popular in the cold climates as the Yamaha snowmobile is to be used in the mountain rescue service in Norway. With this knowledge and expertise being applied to the production of motor cycles perhaps Yamaha riders apply their brakes in winter with a little more confidence than other motor cyclists! The reliability of Yamaha was put to the test by S. Shoji of Japan who followed in the tracks of other men before him making the lonely motor cycle trip around the world, starting in 1971 and finishing the trip in twenty-two months covering 73,000 kilometres on his Yamaha 250 DT1. The Yamaha motor cycles appear to have passed these gruelling tests unscarred, and the future seems to offer even more opportunities and challenge for them. No doubt Yamaha will rise to the occasion.

50 ZENITH

Zenith motor cycles were in production from about 1904 until 1950, the machines being manufactured at a variety of factories in or around London. The driving force behind Zenith was their chief designer F. W. (Freddie) Barnes who, apart from being the man responsible for manufacture of frames (which were used in conjunction with the big J.A.P. 1000cc engines for many high speed events), was responsible for the 'Gradua' gear. This gear was devised at the time when motor cycles were belt-driven. The mechanics of the Gradua gear were a variable engine pulley with adjustable effective diameter worked by a handle, with simultaneous correction of the belt length made by sliding the rear wheel backwards or forwards in the rear fork slots. As a solution to gear problems it was very much a 'curate's egg'. Its disadvantage was that in the higher ratio range it was of no use, except to the big twin-cylinder machines when travelling exclusively on the level, which in the early years of this century was comparatively rare. Its advantage showed itself most effectively in speed hill climbs, where other machines found themselves limited to a single choice of gear ratio before commencing their ascent. The Zenith rider could change during the journey up, which in the minds of rival riders (and manufacturers) eager for success, was an unfair advantage. The net result was that the Zenith motor cycle with its Gradua gear was barred from entering single-gear classes in speed hill climbs by about fifteen or sixteen leading motor cycle clubs of the day. Quick to spot the publicity value in this unfavoured attribute, the firm took the word *barred* as their trade-mark.

Throughout their production life Zenith used engines made by other companies, chiefly Fafnir and J.A.P. The Zenith 'Bi-Car', propelled by a Fafnir engine, first caused the public to pay attention to the firm. A whole range of Zenith motor cycles from 147cc to 1100cc were manufactured over the years, the small ones powered by Villiers engines, the larger by Bradshaw, Fafnir, Precision and J.A.P. engines. The range of models followed the standard patterns, and eventually in 1950 the lack of independence in engines for their machines finally told. Finding it impossible to obtain suitable engines from outside sources, the firm ceased production.

The name of Zenith was prominent in the results of hill climbs, but the marque will more probably be remembered for its many successes on Brooklands race track. Captain O. M. Baldwin, Joe Wright, G. W. Patchett, T. R. Allchin and H. J. Knight were all notable riders on this make and holders of the Gold Star for lapping Brooklands at over 100 m.p.h. Among his many successes, C. T. Ashby included a victory in the 200-mile sidecar race of 1925, and Joe Wright in the same year took the lap record to 109·9 m.p.h. Both Baldwin and Wright held the Brooklands lap record on many occasions as well as the maximum speed record.

MODERN MOTOR BIKES
IN COLOUR

MODERN
MOTOR BIKES
IN COLOUR

by

Laurie Caddell

CONTENTS

ACKNOWLEDGEMENTS

Laurie Caddell and Jasper Spencer-Smith wish to thank the following companies for making available motor cycles from their stock for photography:

Boscombe Motor Cycle Centre, Bournemouth, Dorset;
Etna Motor Cycles, Parkstone, Dorset;
Horswill Motor Cycles, Bournemouth, Dorset;
Ray Fisher Motor Cycles, Christchurch, Dorset;
Motor Cycle City, Farnborough, Hampshire;
Station Garage, Taplow, Buckinghamshire;
Rye's Motor Cycles, Southampton;
Three Cross Motor Cycles, Verwood, Dorset;
Peter Williams Motor Cycles, Southampton, and
Quasar Motor Cycles, Staple Hill, Bristol.

TOWARDS THE MODERN BIKE AND BEYOND

We are in the late 1970s enjoying a boom period in motor cycling with companies offering a bewildering array of machines in all shapes and sizes with as much or as little advanced technology built in as you could wish. You could want a push-button monster with a sewing-machine-smooth multi-cylinder engine producing a seemingly endless supply of power and speed, or be more content with a big single or twin on which you can feel each and every power stroke and which needs to be given constant attention just to be kept in running order. Whatever, the choice is there, and you can rest happy in the knowledge that running a bike is a whole lot more than having a cheap form of transport at hand, for being out there with the elements and having consciously to be aware of and make allowances for other more forgetful road users gives an almost primeval pioneering spirit to the rider. Instead of getting in a car and locking yourself away, you are almost starting on a new adventure each time you ride off, and you are right there with the delights, and sometimes dangers, just a few engine revolutions away. It is something which has not changed and, indeed, will never change no matter how advanced motor cycles become.

Far from being advanced, man's first attempts at powered two-wheelers were very sorry affairs, aided not at all by the only power system available at the time, namely the steam engine. It is hard to imagine what it was like travelling over the rutted and rock-strewn tracks on a solid-wheeled, solid-framed bike with a fiery boiler bubbling and ready to explode at any moment tucked behind the motor cyclist's back. Luckily, these monsters, which were envisaged around the 1850s and which, it was claimed, ran a few years later, did not catch on and it was not until the arrival of the internal-combustion engine that man had the chance to increase his mortality rate on two wheels on the road.

As with most things automotive, there is a great deal of conjecture as to who actually built the first petrol-powered cycle, although it would be fair to say that the two main contenders are Gottlieb Daimler and Edward Butler, whose designs saw the light of day in 1885 and 1884, respectively. What is true is that their initial designs sparked off many ideas around the 'motor cycle' and, although diversified at times, a pattern was to appear. Hilderbrand & Wolfmüller first put a bike into production, in 1894, while Werner in 1901 set the style for its design with a machine of push-bike proportions with the engine and power take-off point where the pedals would normally be. Just to make sure that nobody would lay claim to the idea in later years, Holden built several four-cylinder bikes, the first of which appeared in 1897. To help the cycle manufacturer who could not run to the expense of building his own motors, Comte Albert de Dion and Georges Bouton offered for sale the first proprietary engines to clip on to frames. So, the stage was set and the industry had established designs, a power unit that was becoming ever more powerful and reliable and a world wanting to experience the self-propelled machine. The car was there, too, but that would soon become too complex and even further out of the reach of the pockets of the ordinary man.

In the years to come, the motor cycle industry would survive two world wars, countless slumps and market depressions to arrive in the 1970s as one of the growing and more prosperous industries. Indeed, with the car being the prime target of attack for conservationalists and environmentalists, the bike with its inherent economy advantages was to become ever more popular.

The main reason for the biking renaissance of the 1960s and '70s has been the growth of the Japanese industry since World War II and its ability in making drawing-room dreams a production reality. Considering Japan's position in 1946, it is quite remarkable that by the early 1970s their bike exports would be several million units. In the year after the war, there was a grand total of 1603 civilian motor cycles registered there and the companies that survived mostly relied on imported engines or cribbed designs at best. Why did the revolution start in Japan which had previously had such a low standard of living? It is said that necessity is the mother of invention and, although they didn't invent the motor cycle, they did have the necessity for cheap transport when their rail systems and bus services were in tatters. The ordinary man could fit a suitable power unit to his push bike and, if it worked, could do another for a friend; so, from nowhere, small factories started to spring up. Many, of course, would sink without trace, but others would soldier on, and in a five-year period from 1949, production in Japan increased from around 1500 units to well over 100,000 with some 80 manufacturers involved. Import blocks on foreign machinery made sure that the industry would survive, while a desire to wage war on western bikes from both the showroom and racetrack impassioned the Japanese by no small amount.

However many machines they produced it did not matter to the rest of the world, for the quality did not match up to the quantity, as most were little more than dated autocyles. It was obvious that only the fittest were to survive if the country was to be a threat to Italy, Great Gritain, Germany and America. Racing was to improve the breed, as a series of events at a circuit called Asama attracted the interests of the major manufacturers, many of whom are long forgotten in Japan and have hardly even been heard of outside: Cabton, DSK, Marusho, Tsubasa and Rikuo are examples. Others had more ingenuity, were more successful and so succeeded: Meguro were bought up by Kawasaki Aircraft in 1964, as the aviation company decided to jump on the bike bandwagon; SJK renamed as Suzuki; musical instrument maker Yamaha tried bikes, too, and indeed still use their three-tuning-fork emblem on their machines; Honda were most successful at Asama and even debuted a four-cylinder there in 1959. They had a reason for being the best : Sochiro Honda himself had been to Europe and seen the British and Italian machinery lapping at phenomenal speeds on the Isle of Man; he just had to go back and prove that he could do better.

By the early 1960s, the feelers had been put out and soon everybody was to take notice of the now exotic machinery that boasted such funny Oriental names and which sounded like nothing on earth. It just needed a little money to tempt the best European riders on to the bikes and the battle would be won, for the ordinary biker would relate to it all and want to be part of it. He could afford the mopeds and small bikes that shared the name with the race winners, where a few years earlier the purchase of a Gilera, Moto Guzzi, MV Agusta or even Norton might have been out of the question.

How did other countries react to the invasion? Germany, who had built some 200,000 bikes in the year just before the war, was in the same position as Japan, but somehow did not have the passion or the absolute need to be so inventive, and so carried on almost

3

from where they left off. Their major manufacturer, BMW, picked up its old design, modified it and carried on, right to where they are today with basically the same bike. The great Depression had killed most of America's industry years before the war, anyway, leaving Indian and Harley-Davidson as the major suppliers. Their bikes were also in a different class. A Harley owner would consider no other bike and, although no-one in America would try and stem the rush of imports, no-one would stop buying their own great American freedom machine, either.

Italy suffered at the hands of Japan, but the glory on the race tracks in the 1950s would be enough to see the manufacturers through into the late 1960s and early 1970s, and even if there was to be a further crisis, there would still be enthusiasm and money ready to bail out. The major figure in the Italian industry has been the Argentinian Alejandro de Tomaso. One time Vice President of Ford in America, he travelled to Italy and almost single handed got things running when times looked bleak. He may have made enemies and, indeed, the country is split down the middle with people for and against him, but he has kept many names alive and more importantly made them prosperous. Benelli and Moto Guzzi were taken over and, when MV were about to transfer production to the Ducati factory who themselves were in danger of folding, it was de Tomaso who expressed interest in offering a helping hand. Italy cannot compete with Japan with production of full size motor cycles, so they build cheap mopeds for the masses (just like France who prosper in this field, too) and make primarily sporting bikes which are as charismatic as they are nimble.

The true casualty is, of course, Great Britain who at one time produced bikes the envy of the world. Its industries' death, however, is as much suicide as murder for it did not adapt when the need arose. By the time the world was beginning to accept the multi-cylinder bike as a road machine and not just a freak racer, the British industry was still quite content with resting on its parallel-twin laurels. Vincent, whose machines were legends even before they left the production line, were forced out when the late 1950s dictated a move to smaller less grandiose bikes, and if they could go down anybody could. By the time that BSA-Triumph decided to tack on an extra cylinder to their 500 twin it was too late. Precede the big 750 Honda it may have done, but the Trident was for its ingenuity still no more than one-and-a-half 500 twins in the eyes of most. The industry in Britain even at this time was perhaps starry eyed because the Americans who couldn't afford Harleys might just accept a Bonny or Commando instead, but what was the point of a few enthusiastic exports to the USA when the home market was crying out for something British that would compete with the ever-growing Japanese tide? By the time NVT was producing Easy-Rider mopeds to make a basis for their more advanced projects, it may have been too late. Small specialist manufacturers continued to prove that it was not lack of sound design that was to blame, while even NVT had a range of machines on the drawing board that in metal would have had few peers. That was where the difference lay, however, between Britain and Japan.

The future may hold few surprises and will surely see the Japanese dominance remain if not increase. Unlike the car industry where everyone can offer opposition, the bikes have few rivals and so a block on that country's exports is out of the question, for there would be nothing with which to fill the void. It is left to the rest of the world to catch up slowly if at all possible, while the companies involved might just decide that status quo has been reached and that they are all happy producing their separate wares. The burden then falls on the Japanese industry to keep the potential buyers' attention and continue to build bikes that grow in specification and standards of equipment each and every year.

A great deal of racing-bike technology goes into the road machines of today, a far greater amount than the car industry can boast. For example, strip the body off an MV Agusta and it will take a trained eye to tell the difference between a racing and road version. Inside the engine, too, there is a great deal of similarity. Yamahas have dominated the 250 and 350cc classes of Grand Prix racing for many years now with bikes that are strikingly similar to their roadsters in the engine department, with the main modification being the adoption of water cooling. The GT750 Suzuki was identical almost to that company's superbike racers and the latest 650, 750, 900 and 1000cc Hondas have engines which were developed from their Formula One and Endurance Racer machines. More generally, the disc brake since its appearance on the circuits has prompted a braking revolution on road bikes, pioneered by Bridgstone and mass produced by Honda; gas dampers and forks are becoming increasingly popular, with the GS1000 Suzuki the first to exploit the system developed on Grand Prix bikes; alloy wheels which offer the advantages of lighter weight and greater strength than the spoked variety transformed racing and are now transforming the appearance and roadworthiness of our street machines; and tyres are perhaps the most forgotten components in the motor cycle make up. However, the tyre technician is the man on whom the greatest responsibility falls, and his lessons learnt on the racing circuits with different mixes and compounds, sizes and tread patterns will be passed on to the road rider who can be sure that his tyres will work well in conditions wet or dry and will last longer and be more resistant to punctures and blow outs.

It is surprising that in all the advanced technology that goes into engine, brake and tyre design, few people seem particularly bothered with the modern motor bike's biggest drawback: its frame. Even the best GP machinery to grace the tracks in the late 1970s can boast little more than a mangled conglomeration of tubing that would make car designers, aircraft engineers and metallurgists alike shudder in disbelief. These high-performance racers are running around with frames that are little more than sturdy push-bike designs and, indeed, not far removed from that first Werner. The race engineers seem content to increase their bikes' performances by having stickier tyres and more powerful engines with that old standby of welding some bracing struts to the chassis if the power or roadholding gets too much and affects handling.

There are, of course, exceptions to this general trend, but it is left up to the individuals who go endurance racing to dabble with ideas like hub-centre or kingpin steering, low-mounted fuel tanks and scientific frame design. There have been many attempts at the monocoque bike, the Norton racer being a major example, while Bimota have at least proved that a sound spine design can give a standard racer a leading edge, Cecotto's Yamahas and Villa's Harley-Davidsons being proof of this. Bimota do build road bikes but only in such small numbers as to cater for the rich enthusiast, while the rest of roadster production relies mainly on chassis inferior to the not-so-great race bikes. Certain Japanese bikes of the late 1960s and early 1970s ably demonstrated that having a great deal of power in a weak frame is only acceptable if you have the flat surface and open spaces of a track to experiment and perhaps a set of tyres that would hold the plot together. If you had a 'stroker' Kawasaki or the like and tried to use its performance on the swings and roundabouts of the country you could find that under certain conditions the bike felt strangely articulated or spongy. You may have realised this after a nasty 'tank slapper' which sent you cursing or sent you tumbling. Either way, you would have had first-hand experience of antiquated frame design. A case of modern motor bikes being not so modern.

So in the end a manufacturer will come up with an acceptable mix for a bike they wish to market: the engine will be there, so will the frame (however good) and all the running gear. That will be only the start, however, for the appearance of a machine is these days just as important.

Firstly, alloy wheels must be considered because the public has decided that spokes are old fashioned and out. If alloy wheels are going to be too expensive be like Honda and produce a Comstar with an alloy rim and steel spokes that look the part; or be like Yamaha with their XS1100 and have a complete cast iron wheel. Disc brakes are a must of course because they look so much neater than drums, even if few disc-braked roadsters have come near to matching the performance of the drum units fitted to the Vincent Black Shadow, for example. The drum fitted at the back of the CX500 Honda in its Comstar wheel looks attractive as does the conical brake set up used by Campagnolo in their alloy wheel and seen on the race tracks with certain Harley-Davidsons, but the disc is here to stay, with slots, cross drillings, sintered steel pads, anti-lock devices and all. Then there are the instruments that have to be there even if they are given little attention when the bike is in motion. The more gauges, dials and idiot lights the better. Of course, they are useful, but the designer has to cater more for aesthetics than practicality.

The bike's bodywork is probably the biggest headache of all for from a time when machines were virtually identical, the last few years has seen clever design staff jiggle around with the admittedly small components to produce finished machines which look different from one another, with some good and some bad. Even Kawasaki who added a little tail-fairing cum cubby hole to their bikes of the late 1960s could not have foreseen that virtually every bike produced a few years later would have a similar design of tail piece as a matter of course.

Honda were to learn the biggest lesson with their Dream series 250 and 400 models that were met with the greatest apathy when presented to an unsuspecting market. The bike that hastily replaced it, the Super Dream, was basically the same underneath the new clothes, but the different tank, side panels and tail was enough to make a great deal of difference.

Even with the eager buyer apparently catered for, there is still much to be done, for a bike that suits the builder and the buyer had these days to cater for somebody else: the man who works out the regulations covering lighting; specifications for different ages of rider; noise; and, most importantly, exhaust emissions. The lights are the least of his problems for a powerful and correctly adjusted system will suffice except in the few areas where 'daylight headlights' are compulsory. Now that Great Britain does not require its moped riders to be able to give their machines pedal assistance, restrictors to make them travel at 30mph or less are the only worry. A decent exhaust that is not too restrictive will make sure that noise isn't a great problem, but the emission regulations and controls could take as much time sorting out as the rest of the bike altogether.

Environmentalists and ecologists have all but killed off the two-stroke machine and even though it continues to dominate on the race tracks and has no competitor to oust it, its days on the road are all but numbered except for the smallest of bikes which use so little fuel that they hardly matter. Not that the four-stroke engine has escaped completely, although it is not frowned upon as much as similar units in cars. The effect of catalytic converters, stratified-charge engines and using low-octane fuel has drastically cut the performance of cars sold in America, for example, and the road performance of machines there will never ever reach the peak that was achieved in the mid 1960s. The motor cycle industry has been able to cope with the small demands imposed on them and, roughly speaking, power has dropped on larger bikes by just a couple of horsepower since emission controls were brought in. Kawasaki, for example, have on all their four-strokes a positive crankcase breathing system which recycles blow-by gases and reduces hydrocarbon exhaust emission by, they say, up to 40%. The toll on power is minor, and the engineers can get back what has been taken away by steady development of combustion chamber design. 5mph bumpers and energy-absorbing structures and steering columns have yet to be specified for motor cycles, so there at least with a bit of common sense the designer is allowed free rein.

There it is: the new bike is on the road where it can join the countless others and all that has to be done is for a salesman to attract the customer, which if the sums have been done correctly, should be as simple as can be. What does the rider choose, though, and what sort of bike does he want? Engine size ranges from around 50cc to almost 1400cc; top speed ranges from 25mph to around 150mph; while fuel consumption varies from about 300mpg for a 'powered push bike' to under 30mpg for a multi-cylinder sports machine.

Obviously, the first place to look if you want a good performer with lots of reliability is the Japanese manufacturers. Bikes that do better than them cost a lot more and the differences will probably only be noticeable in the uppermost ranges of performance where even the quickest of riders will be for just a few per cent of the time he is in the saddle. Firstly, decide how much or little performance you want and whether your bike will be used mostly for commuting a few miles to work, touring across continents or purely for fun at the weekend. Even learner machines of up to 250cc can be placed in those three categories, so the choice is very large indeed. A two-stroke bike for a given capacity will usually have more power and so a greater performance than a four-stroke; will be more sensitive to the throttle; have a narrower power band (which will make it necessary to keep the motor running quicker for the extra zip) and be thirstier and more temperamental in traffic with its fouling sparking plugs.

It will also be easier to maintain due to its simple construction, and will be smoother than a four-stroke of the same configuration, although will be tiresome on long journeys. Having decided what type of engine is most suitable, you can then figure out how many

9

cylinders you need. A small single will be adequate for mopeds and lightweight but further up the scale the choice will usually be 'two cylinders or more'? The latest batch of counter-balanced twins are quite smooth indeed and unless used at the top of their rev ranges will not cause too many vibration and hence fatigue problems . . . for bike or rider. There is a considerable weight saving with just two cylinders while a bike thus equipped will be narrower and therefore feel easier to manoeuvre than a multi. Next up is the three-cylinder machine which is the least popular configuration of all. Balance of the engine, either primary or secondary, is in between that of a two- or four-cylinder, so the 'three' is something of a compromise unit altogether. A four-cylinder is the most popular design for larger bikes where balance, and therefore vibration, is a big problem. These engines offer great smoothness and power and are usually so understressed that reliability is a problem that rarely crops up. The next, and so far final, step up is the six-cylinder engine which is the smoothest of all and the most powerful, but the problem arises of their enormous width. Not only does it hinder cornering (as the crankcase is likely to touch the ground first), but a mass of engine offered to penetrate air at anything up to 140mph does not do the job that efficiently.

Once you have decided what power unit is needed it is only left to the extras on top that one manufacturer produces that another doesn't and vice versa. Touring or racing style does not matter a great deal, for most of what is offered from Japan is a compromise that will suit no rider perfectly but every rider adequately.

Maybe something common and even bland to a degree is not for you, and you may need something more expensive but a little more sporting. Then the obvious market to turn to is the Italian. Obviously, their output is much smaller than Japan's but they have machines as varied and in all cases have an edge in performance on the road if not on paper. Also in all cases, reliability will be a little less and the finish will be a little or a lot poorer, but a hand-made machine may have a little more character for you than one rolling off a production line. Apart from Japan and Italy, few other countries market their machines on a wide basis, and few bikes are available to the mass market. The exceptions are the German BMW and the American Harley-Davidsons, although these bikes are unique and unlikely to have no competitors in their respective owners' eyes. The communist bloc countries market machines like Cossacks, Jawas, CZs and MZs, but it would be fair to say more at the economy end of the range. Generally speaking, though, the other countries' manufacturers bother little with exports and make their way selling machines specifically suited to the needs of the local populous. In the past ten years or so, road bikes have reached Britain from places like Mexico, Portugal, India and Spain, but never to such an extent that they have greatly affected sales of bikes imported in larger quantities.

The smaller competition bike market knows no such boundaries, though, and one can readily buy a Swedish Husqvarna, Spanish Bultaco, Austrian KTM or American Rokon, for example.

Nowadays, modern bikes are very reliable and makers are able to offer warranties on them without risking a great deal of money. Although for off-road competition bikes it is really a matter of personal discussion regarding specific complaints and whether the bike has gone wrong on its own or been maltreated in any way, a guarantee will generally include free parts and labour for six months to a year, sometimes with a specified mileage or sometimes unlimited.

The choice of bikes is enormous, the quality with very few exceptions is excellent, but what can be expected in years to come and how will the motor bike develop from here?

One may think that engine design has just about reached a peak with bikes like the XS1100 Yamaha, CBX Honda and Z1300 Kawasaki around, but you can guarantee that development of more complex and even faster machines will continue for some time. As far as new concepts of power unit are concerned, the bike industry will follow a few steps behind that of the car. Suzuki and DKW/Hercules got their fingers burnt with the Wankel, while Yamaha opted out of their plans for rotary bikes just in time. NVT seem convinced that the idea is still worthy of time and money, but their bike is meant to be a no-compromise low-volume production sportster aimed at those to whom fuel consumption will be of little consequence. For the mass market, however, the Wankel as yet is not a practical proposition and, until a breakthrough with rotor-tip reliability and fuel consumption problems have been achieved in cars, there will be no revolution of the sort with two wheelers.

Across-the-frame engines, too, have gone as far as is practical with the Benelli Sei, Z1300 Kawasaki and Honda CBX, and even Honda had to pull out all the stops with their design ingenuity to make their six narrow enough not to furrow the tarmac every time it was laid over in a corner. It will be a brave and foolish man who presents his superiors with plans for a straight-eight, however extravagant and publicity magnetising it will be. The future is based on the vee-configuration unit in multiple-cylinder guise, longitudinal for shaft drive, as is sensible, or across the frame, which is better suited for sports bikes that cannot afford the complication or added weight of the shaft. An across the frame vee engine canted forwards may be adequately cooled by air, but the chances are that liquid cooling will be increasingly utilised, for as well as leaving the designer a free hand at its location, it will allow higher combustion chamber temperatures to be attained without the added problem of heat dissipation at lower speeds and allow cylinders to be closer together. That such an engine will seem smoother and be quieter are added bonuses.

The turbocharger is another key to the future for, although it has been used in racing now on and off since the 1930s, only recently has it been thought necessary for roadsters. In recent years, various small tuning companies have been experimenting with turbocharged 750s and 1000s, while Kawasaki took the major step of introducing a turbo bike through their 1000-odd dealerships in America to be an intermediary until they could launch their competitor to the CBX. Making the quickest of bikes quicker is of more novelty value than anything else when it comes to supercharging, for the real future lies with the smaller bikes. For example, a 350 or 500cc machine with a turbo could rival present-day 750s or 1000s when the need arises, while still being economical and tractable for town use, The necessarily lower compression ratio would ensure better fuel consumption than a normally aspirated competitor (although at the loss of performance bite), while being much quicker when the performance is needed. Dropping down a couple of gears and opening the throttle wide would ensure the complete transformation. A move to fuel injection would be advisable with turbos.

As far as the transmission is concerned, the simple and efficient manual unit is likely to be with us as long as the bike itself. The automatic box is useful for touring and about-town work and most riders will find them strangely addictive, but bikes so equipped with their higher fuel consumption and lower performance are completely opposite to what motor cycling is about for most people. The 750 Hondamatic and 1000cc Convert Moto Guzzi have adequate performances and are passable, but for anything smaller like the 400cc Honda Dream which has trouble keeping up with small cars in a straight line, the future must seem bleak. The shaft drive system is becoming more and more popular as bikes get bigger and put greater demands on chains. Nowadays, as Yamaha, Honda and MV have proved, such a system does not have to be too ponderous and cumbersome in operation, even though it can never be as smooth and as slick as the chain.

Braking is an area where there has recently been a lot of development with Moto Guzzi pioneering the way with their integral system, whereby the front and rear systems are linked mechancially. Kawasaki were next to join the fray with their range being transformed with the adoption of sintered-steel pads. Anti-lock systems will start to be seen on bikes in the near future, too. Having disc brakes which work in the wet is only now becoming something for the everyday rider and not just a luxury for those who could afford machines with cast-iron discs.

It has taken the Japanese industry a long time to discover that their frames leave a lot to be desired in terms of structural rigidity, but slowly they are making them adequate if not brilliant. Having a chassis made of straight tubing with triangulated joints is an ideal which cannot be achieved on a bike with a large engine, but development on those lines is taking place, with the specialist manufacturers leading the way. A move to any radical form of frame or chassis is, if at all, a long way away off unless again someone can show in practical terms that the efforts to new goals are that significant, or more importantly in this commercial world, to be appreciated by every rider. Some companies are considering monocoques, but are loath to be the first to try one out with the public.

The one other major advancement of the future will be in the area of bodywork, for the rider of today who wishes to travel great distances demands some form of protection from the elements that special clothing alone cannot ensure.

Things will develop along the lines of the immaculate fairing fitted to the RS BMW which has proved so popular. Yamaha have a full fairing as an option on their XS1100 which is interesting in that the top half swivels with the bars, while the lower part, armed with extra lighting, is rigidly mounted. Soon, manufacturers will realise that they can break in on the specialist manufacturers who make a living out of building fairings and produce their own, specifically designed for each model. A full roof, like that of the revolutionary Quasar, may be seen on an ordinary roadster, but the trend will probably stop at efficient dolphin or even dustbin designs.

In the course of less than a hundred years, the motor bike has advanced from a slow and fragile push-bike design that could be outrun by even the unfittest of men to the modern motor bike of today that has the pace of a missile being fired. The future may bring a lot more advancement but, even if one day there will be offered a turbocharged twin-rotor Wankel bike with automatic transmission, shaft drive, gyroscopic balancers, to ensure the bike stayed upright at rest, and a full fairing with built-in heater and sound system, you can still bet your last penny that somewhere there will still be a single-cylinder bike with kickstarter on offer with people queuing up to buy it just to sample the basic pleasures motor biking can give.

1   BENELLI 250CE

The Italian firm of Benelli produce two completely different 250 motor cycles, the cheaper and less glamorous one being their 250CE. The 250CE is a two-stroke, twin-cylinder bike which follows the layout of the popular Japanese bikes in the quarter litre class. With a 56mm bore and 47mm stroke, the engine actually displaces 231cc from which is extracted 30bhp at 8000rpm. This power gives the small Benelli a top speed of 90mph and a fuel consumption of 45mpg. Again, as is usual with Japanese machines, a five-speed gearbox with left-foot change is utilised. The frame of the bike is of duplex design and the suspension is conventional in every sense. However, the whole outfit is very taut and well designed, so that the handling and roadholding are of the highest order. One failing of the machine is that it still needs to be fed with petroil mixture instead of the more usual self-mixing set up with separate tanks for petrol and oil.

The finish and appearance is not quite up to the example set by Japanese manufacturers, so the bike misses on this score also. Interestingly, two models of the Benelli 250CE are manufactured, one with drum brakes front and rear and one with a front disc. Although the disc version is considerably more expensive, it is not as effective as the drum in the wet.

Also, if you are not keen on the Benelli name, you can have an identical bike with the Moto Guzzi badges on, as they are made at the same factory.

2   BENELLI 250/4

In a completely different sector of the market to its two-stroke stablemate is the Benelli 250/4 which is, as its name suggests, a four-cylinder bike of approximately 250cc. Like the larger six-cylinder 750 Sei, the 250/4 is an undeniably extravagant bike and that is something which is reflected in its astronomical price, a figure which is almost twice that asked for the CE Benelli. It is not in performance where the four-stroke four has an advantage for, with 26.5bhp and a top speed of just on 90mph, the CE gives nothing away at all. What is interesting is that the four-cylinder 250 is almost 50lb lighter than the CE and in every dimension is a very small bike indeed. The heart of the bike is an overhead-camshaft engine which looks something like a miniature 500 Honda unit and is, in fact, of basically the same design. Maximum power is produced at 10,500rpm but the engine is safe to over 11,000 where it makes a sound like a noisy sewing machine. If the engine is not revved to its full potential, the fuel economy is excellent and far better than anything possible with an engine of two-stroke design.

Apart from the engine, most other parts of the bike are of conventional design with a front disc, rear drum and standard oil fork dampers and swinging arm. The designers have, however, made the small Benelli appear as modern as possible with a one-piece tank/seat/rear fairing unit. Set in a panel in the front of the tank unit is the instrument nacelle with a tachometer and speedometer. Unfortunately, however neat it looks, the dials are hard to see and take ones attention away from the road. To finish the modern appearance there are cast-alloy three-spoke wheels which look a little odd but are strong and easy to clean. As with the CE, a Moto Guzzi version of this bike is available, called the 254. Its styling is a little different but again is merely badge engineering.

The company did experiment with a bike powered by two of the little 'fours' mounted together to make a 500 V8, but the costs were prohibitive, while a 125cc 'four' developed at the same time as the 250 was thought to be just too extravagant.

3 BENELLI 500

The most striking thing about the 500 Benelli is that it bears more than a passing resemblance to another four-stroke, four-cylinder half-litre machine, the 500 Honda. The similarity centres on the engine which not only looks like the Japanese bike's unit, but also sports the same cylinder dimensions: 56×50.6mm. However, with a 10.2:1 compression ratio, the Benelli produces slightly more power with 55bhp available at 9800rpm. The single-overhead-camshaft engine, which is fed by four Dell'Orto carburettors, can push the 440lb bike to a top speed of 112mph. Because of the bike's relatively low weight, fuel consumption is good and 50mpg is easily possible. Although initially available with two powerful drum brakes, the 500 is now equipped with a two disc front and single disc rear layout, a move dictated by the public's reaction to the many disc-braked Japanese bikes. Styling is typically Italian with wide flat handlebars and boxy panels, tank and instruments.

Incidentally, the bike's engine is manufactured at the Moto Guzzi factory in Mandello del Lario, as are all the Benelli four-stroke engines, while the two-stroke units of the two companies are built at Benelli's Pesaro works. This has been the case since motor magnate Alejandro de Tomaso bought out the ailing companies a few years ago. Since that time, the single-cam Honda lookalike engine has been the basis for most of the companies' four-stroke range.

4   BENELLI 750 Sei

When the 750 Benelli was announced it caused no small sensation, for it sported no less than six cylinders. Mounted across the frame, the engine is an impressive sight, although it must be admitted that such a layout has its problems. For example, if the bike had straight tracts for the inlet manifolds, the carburettors would stick into the riders knees. So, the pipes for the three Dell'Orto carburettors are mounted on twisted pipes which bend in under the tank. The other problems encountered with such a layout are the large frontal area offered to the wind and that the bike is very wide and thus difficult to wield in and out of traffic. Apart from those detractions, everything else about the Sei's engine is excellent. The natural balance afforded by such a layout means that the engine is very smooth and the fact that, because the power take off from the crankshaft is at its middle, there is no chance of crankshaft whip as is sometimes possible with other automotive engines of the same configuration.

The Sei is not a highly tuned machine but nevertheless produces 71bhp at 8900rpm and there is a wide and flat torque band which makes high-speed cruising an easy affair. The top speed of the 485lb machine is 115mph and fuel consumption usually stays on the good side of 40mpg.

The Sei has a very sturdy frame and so handling is as good as one would expect for a thoroughbred Italian machine. One criticism was levelled at the machine when it appeared and that was that it was not as powerful as had been expected. One European distributor for the marque produced a 900cc version, while the company itself tried a few twin-overhead-camshaft prototypes. In the end, Benelli exhibited their own 900 in early 1978 which would put Benelli back in the ever-growing race for bigger and more powerful motor cycles.

5   BMW R45

From being in a desperate financial position in the late 1950s, BMW have now turned the tide in the opposite direction and are now enjoying a large share of the top-range-bike market. The success of the company was built around large touring models of 500cc or over and it was not until the middle of 1978 that a new range appeared, the R45 and R65 series, which replaced the larger and older 500 and 600cc models. Much neater and smaller than its predecessors, the R45 nevertheless still weighs a hefty 425lb, the same as its larger stablemate. Two stages of tune are offered on the R45's oversquare engine, 26bhp for the German market, where it gets into a lower insurance bracket, and 35bhp for the rest of the world. On the export version, peak power is reached at 7250rpm, while maximum torque is 27.5lb ft attained at 5500rpm. As is now legendary with these Berlin-built bikes, the engine is of flat-twin configuration with valves operated by pushrods and rockers. It may not be the most modern layout available on a motor cycle but, over many years, it has been improved and developed so that it is reliable, efficient and very smooth. Performance is not a strong point of the R45 but it will reach a top speed of just on 95mph. Fuel consumption on the other hand is excellent, with an average figure of 55 to 60mpg being possible. The bike has a 4.8 gallon fuel tank, so it is obvious that it was made with touring in mind.

Transmission is by five-speed gearbox and shaft drive, while braking is by a single cross-drilled disc at the front and a powerful drum at the rear. Standard fittings on the bike include cast-alloy wheels, audible warnings for the indicators, twin mirrors, electric starter and a plug for fitting an intercom device. The standard of finish is about as good as can be found on a motor cycle, but there is a price to pay for that: the price itself, for the smallest BMW produced is more expensive than many 750s on the market.

6   BMW R80/7

BMWs have never been competitive with machines of similar capacity in recent years, because straight-line performance has not been of prime importance to the company nor it would seem to the riders of its bikes. However, BMW thought it would not be right to be left a long way behind in power, so they replaced their R75 750 with the R80 which actually displaces 785cc. Going a little way up the capacity scale means that tractability and economy are not lost in the quest for extra acceleration and top speed as would happen if a smaller engine had been uprated.

Displacing 785cc, the flat-twin engine produces 55bhp at 7000rpm, which gives the bike a top speed of 115mph. Drive is via a car-type single-plate dry clutch, five-speed gearbox and shaft drive and, although BMW have done a lot to remedy it, the transmission suffers a lot from a clunking effect as gears are changed. The change itself is smooth but it is very positive and slow due to the inertia in the system. Great care has to be taken on slippery roads when changing down as the rear wheel can break traction momentarily, for a shaft layout is not as forgiving as a chain. That apart, the middleweight BMW is safe and predictable in all weathers, a fact which is helped by a powerful cross-drilled disc on the front wheel.

A feature of all BMWs is the long travel of the suspension which makes for a very comfortable ride over all surfaces and this, along with good tyres, keeps the whole smooth and running in a straight line, even over white lines and ridges which would keep other machines weaving. Extra equipment for the bike is available, including large custom-built panniers for the rear which hold as much luggage as many a two-seater sports car, and either of the fairings for the larger bikes from the company, the dolphin 'S' type or full 'RS' type.

7 BIMOTA SB2

Bimota is a company which was formed by messrs BIanchi, MOrri and TAmburini, and is situated in the Italian Adriatic resort of Rimini. They supplied the frames for the Harley-Davidsons with which Walter Villa secured 250 and 350cc World Championships several times and the frame for his only serious rival, the Yamaha of Johnny Cecotto, a combination which won the 1975 350 title. Since then the company have decided to build roadster frames too, and their results are among the most efficient sculptures of metal ever to grace the engine of a motor cycle.

The SB2 is their second design (Suzuki Bimota 2), the first being for a Kawasaki, the KB1 (Kawasaki Bimota 1). The Suzuki design will take either the 750 or 1000cc GS straight-four engine in standard or modified form, although the weight saving over a standard frame is a performance boost in itself. Under the bike's bodywork is a mass of bright-red large-diameter tubing which cocoons the engine, itself a stressed part of the whole set-up. Unlike a normal frame which features a loop cradle and a roughly horizontal top tube, the Bimota has a sharply angled design with the top tubes running from the steering head almost down to the level of the rear suspension pivot. There is no need for a high mounting point for the rear suspension as the Bimota is an intriguing monoshock design.

Strong the massive frame may be, but it would seem at first glance to be a nightmare for any major power unit maintenance. That is where the Bimota's famous split frame comes in. Right in the middle of the top tubes on either side are conical couplings fastened by three socket bolts. Undo these and the frame can be taken away from the engine in around 20 minutes. The secret is that the coupling is male to female so perfect alignment and rigidity is assured.

An hour glass shaped (narrow in the middle to allow for narrower pegs and so more ground clearance) box-section swinging arm is attached to an unusually small vertically mounted spring/damper unit of car design at the bottom of the sloping top tubes. The arm widens around the back of the transmission to pivot exactly where the secondary drive gear emerges, so that suspension movement does not alter chain tension and so give the rear wheel fluctuating torque outputs. It is a simple idea, but something quite rare on a chain drive bike. Front fork design is novel, too, with the fork angle different to the rake of the steering axis, so that trail is kept more constant under suspension travel than is normal.

Clothing the bike is superbly contoured and quickly detachable glassfibre bodywork, comprising a nose fairing, under fairing and an elaborate tank/seat/rear fairing moulding which hold an alloy 3.5 gallon fuel tank and a suede cushion. In all, the bike looks very futuristic, and this accentuated by the standard red, black and white colour scheme. A weight of 21lb for the standard frame helps give the bike an overall weight of just 433lb, which is a saving of around 70lb on the standard GS Suzuki.

The Kawasaki version is different in that it does not have or need the split frame design, it has a normal horizontally mounted monoshock spring/damper rear suspension and is clothed in smoother bodywork virtually identical to the 1977–78 OW-31 and OW-35 racing Yamahas as used by Agostini, Baker, Cecotto and Roberts.

8   BMW R100RS

When the BMW R100RS was announced in September 1976, it was seen as one of the most innovative motor cycles in recent years. Underneath, it was little more than a larger-engined successor to the R90S 900cc bike, but what was different from any other machine was the large fairing. It was clear that there was a great deal more to the bike's bodywork than just appearance and, in fact, there was, for BMW spent a great deal of time in the wind tunnel of the Italian automotive design studio of Pininfarina perfecting the shape.

The fairing increases the frontal area of the machine by quite a large amount which does have a detrimental effect on top speed and performance at high speeds, but there is the advantage that, with the rider's head bobbed down behind the screen, a great deal of weather protection is afforded. One problem with fairings usually is that stability at high speed is sometimes suspect, but this is remedied with the BMW by a lip around the centre of the body which increases downthrust. Incidentally, the lip is in roughly the same position as the downthrust tabs on the faired Moto Guzzi V1000, so obviously the two manufacturers who have had wind-tunnel facilities have come up with the same and right answer.

With the larger engine, now of 980cc, performance is more than adequate with a top speed of just over 121mph. However, one unfortunate BMW trait is exaggerated with such a large engine and that is the bike's tendency to tip to the right if the throttle is blipped at standstill due to the torque reaction of the longitudinal-mounted-crankshaft engine. In fact, the bike is decidedly lumpy at low speeds and much more at home when running at higher revolutions.

Since the R100RS has been in production, the rear drum brake has given way to a cross-drilled disc to match the two at the front, alloy wheels are fitted as standard and a proper dual seat is standard equipment rather than the rear-faired single which was neither a true racing saddle nor proper twin. As is now famous with BMWs, the switchgear is excellent as are the instruments, including the quartz clock which adequately sums up the company's attention to detail.

9   COSSACK DNIEPER MT-9

The Cossack Dnieper side-car outfit is a very rugged and reliable machine, and that has a lot to do with its being an old design. The origins of the bike are a little unclear but it seems as though plans for BMW machines got into Russian hands after the war and subsequently found their way to the Cossack factory, albeit some time afterwards.

Today, the outfit is obviously outdated but to someone who wants a practical form of transport and who is willing to put up with having something which is totally non-sporting in character, the Cossack works. The bike's power unit is the venerable pushrod flat twin which, in this guise, displaces 650cc and produces 32bhp at 5200rpm. Running with a low 7:1 compression ratio means that the cheapest grade of fuel can be used and that fuel consumption will be good. A figure of over 56 miles per gallon can be achieved which is good for a 650 and excellent for an outfit of any kind. The penalty one pays for this is the performance, for a little over 60mph is all that can be reached in the top ratio of the four-speed box; incidentally, the Dnieper in side-car form also has the luxury of a reverse gear which comes in handy as the combination weighs just under 700lb and is too heavy to push out of kerbs, for example.

Apart from the inherent handling difficulties side-cars present, the Cossack has one other fault and that is that it comes with the bike mounted on the left of the chair, the opposite to normal practice.

Seating is available for three people with one in the chair and one each on the single rubber saddles of the bike, the pillion unit being mounted on top of the rear mudguard with a grab handle bolted on to the seat base. The Cossack can be made into a complete touring outfit for the options available make it a very well equipped machine. There are leg guards for the rider, a stereo for the chair and a trailer which can be hitched on the back which can also take a tent unit.

10   CZ 250

Although the Czechoslovakian Jawa and CZ companies are separate entities, they are both state owned and geared together to help each other rather than take each others' potential markets. In fact, just about all the main parts of the Jawas, apart from frame and electrics are made at the CZ works. The CZ 250 is very near the top of that company's range, with only a motocross-type Enduro more expensive and powerful.

The basis of this Eastern bloc 250 is a twin-cylinder, two-stroke engine which, although not a high-speed unit, nevertheless produces a respectable 17.5bhp at 5250rpm. This gives it a top speed of just on 70mph, while standing start quarter mile acceleration takes 19.5 secs; fuel consumption is not exceptional as it consumes petroil mixture at the rate of 50mpg. Unlike some other small CZs and the Jawa 350 (which is very much a stretched 250

CZ), the bike does not have the companies' Posilube or Oilmaster automatic lubrication which, these days, is something of a sad omission.

Power from the engine drives through a four-speed gearbox which is the most unusual and ingenious feature of the CZ. Firstly, the left-foot gear-change pedal is pressed in towards the crankcase and swung back where it acts as a kickstart. After the motor fires up, the pedal is put back into its original position where it acts like the slick-shift units fitted to Triumph bikes a few years back. To change gear, the hand clutch is not needed, for slight pressure on the gear pedal releases the drive so that a new ratio can be chosen. In operation, it needs a positive yet smooth foot to control it, but after practice it is even possible to select first gear while stationary and pull away.

Where the CZ loses out to the opposition is in the braking, for the drum unit at the front is rather spongy in operation and not too effective, while the pedal for the rear is too far away from the footpeg. The handling of the 350lb bike, on the other hand, is excellent and trouble free, although the tyres do not grip too well in the wet.

Just like most from the Eastern European countries, it is well equipped with a rear-view mirror and large toolkit, including hand-pump, as standard.

11   DKW WANKEL 2000

Due to a British bicycle factory's having the rights to the name, the motor cycles of Nurnberger Hercules Werke AG are sold as DKWs in Great Britain. The company's most interesting bike is the Wankel 2000, which was the first ever motor cycle to feature the rotary engine designed by Dr Felix Wankel. The 2000's power unit is a derivative of a snowmobile engine manufactured by proprietary unit builders Fitchel & Sachs, and differs from it by the adoption of an electric starter to replace the rewinding pull cord of the winter sports device. The single-rotor unit is cradled underneath the frame and mounted longitudinally, although the rotor itself sits across the bike which makes for interesting gyroscopic effects when cornering.

After driving through a six-speed gearbox, the power has to be 'turned' for the chain drive, although this was not a problem with the prototypes as they were housed in shaft-drive BMW frames. However, with 32bhp and 24.5lb ft of torque at hand, the bike had to make do with something smaller than a large BMW type chassis. All together, the production 2000s weigh 350lb, so performance from the 294cc engine is brisk, with a 100mph top speed possible. The capacity of a Wankel is a very interesting point, with varying views on whether it should be classed according to the capacity of one, two or three chambers of three-lobed rotor. Unfortunately, it seems that most people regard the bike as being of 588cc, twice the stated amount, while the bike has the performance of a good 300 and the fuel consumption of a 900, at around 34mpg. This is not praising the Wankel at all but it must be remembered that the engine is in its infancy of development and that cars built by NSU in the 1960s were not very fast or frugal machines. However, automotive engineers seem to have overcome that obstacle on four wheels now, and it remains to be seen whether the same can be done for bikes. In operation, the Wankel 2000 two-stroke is noisy and not as smooth as one would expect, but its ability to rev freely and quickly gives it an urgency that is unmatched by reciprocating piston engines.

After substituting the petroil system for direct injection and adding other refinements to the bike, Hercules decided to drop the Wankel as it was not competitive on a cost/performance basis with conventional bikes, but given time and money that could be rectified.

12   DUCATI 500 SPORT DESMO

The Ducati 500 Sport Desmo is one of the new breed of increasingly popular half-litre sporting bikes which most of the important manufacturers are now making. This 500 is a 180° parallel-twin four-stroke which like the Darmah and 900SS features desmodromic valve operation. The practicality of such a system is debatable on road bikes for, although the mechanical opening and closing of the valves means that valve bounce is eliminated, something has to be done to modify the rest of the engine before it is

able to rev to limits where conventional engines would run out o
breath. Further, some form of spring is usually advisable to mak
sure that the valve is shut when starting and such a system is ver
difficult to design and worse to keep running satisfactorily, wit
service intervals measured in hundreds instead of thousands o
miles. However, the layout works well enough in the Ducati and
even if the company is shy about disclosing power outputs, the bik
is well able to match its rivals, with a top speed of over 110mph an
the ability to cover a quarter mile from start in 13.5 secs. Fue
consumption is only barely as good as its larger stablemates a
45–50mpg so with a 2.6gal tank fuel stops have to be very frequen
on long runs.

The Desmo is a very nimble bike on the open road and the rear se
pedals and clip-on style bars make sports style riding easy an
enjoyable. With three disc brakes to take care of just on 400lb o
bike, stopping is easy and fuss free in all weathers with n
premature locking or fade. The fact that the 500 is aimed at th
rider who enjoys riding fast is accentuated by the saddle being larg
enough for one person and a very close friend and no more; also, rea
foot pegs are not a standard fitting. Were a passenger accom
modated, the rider would find that sitting forward would mak
things very uncomfortable with the controls.

Switchgear and instruments, although adequate are not of th
same quality as larger Ducatis, but Italian bike enthusiasts are use
to that.

Although the middleweight Ducati has been available for only
few years, it is likely to be replaced by a small version of the famou
Taglioni vee-twin which will give an even greater impression tha
the 500 Desmo Sport is a Darmah shrunk in the wash.

13/14 DUCATI DARMAH

The Ducati Darmah is in all respects a thoroughbred motor cycle ir
the best tradition of the great Italian manufacturers. Named after
fictional tiger, the Darmah does have something of a tiger qualit
with its effortless power and agility. The power unit of the bike is
90° vee-twin engine mounted longitudinally in the frame with th

1. BENELLI. The two-stroke Benelli 250 which had all the performance of a Japanese bike with the handling qualities and price of an Italian thoroughbred.

2. **BENELLI.** Sister to the two-stroke quarter-litre Benelli is the extravagant and wildly expensive four-cylinder 250/4.

3. BENELLI. The Quattro is an unashamed copy of the Honda 500.

4. BENELLI. The six-cylinder Sei was the pioneer 'six' bike.

5. BMW. The R45 is the first of a new generation of smaller and neater BMWs.

6. BMW. The middleweight BMWs, like the R80/7, are popular for touring.

7. **BIMOTA.** Undoubtedly, the SB2 Bimota Suzuki is the best café racer around.

8. BMW. The R100RS was the pioneer of the aero-dynamcally designed fairing for large roadsters.

9. COSSACK. The Dnieper MT-9 sidecar outfit offers cheap transport for three people.

10. **CZ.** The 250 CZ does not have a great performance, but is cheap, reliable and safe.

11. **DKW.** The DKW/Hercules W2000 was a brave but expensive attempt at enticing the public to the revolutionary Wankel.

12. DUCATI.The 500 parallel-twin configuration Desmo.

13. DUCATI. The desmodromic-valve superbike from Bologna is the updated 900SS, complete with massive 40mm carburettors.

14. **DUCATI** desmodromic-valve superbike engine.

15. FANTIC. The lightweight Fantic with their Chopper 125.

16. HARLEY-DAVIDSON. A 75th Anniversary 1200cc Electra Glide.

17. Harley-Davidson 1200cc engine.

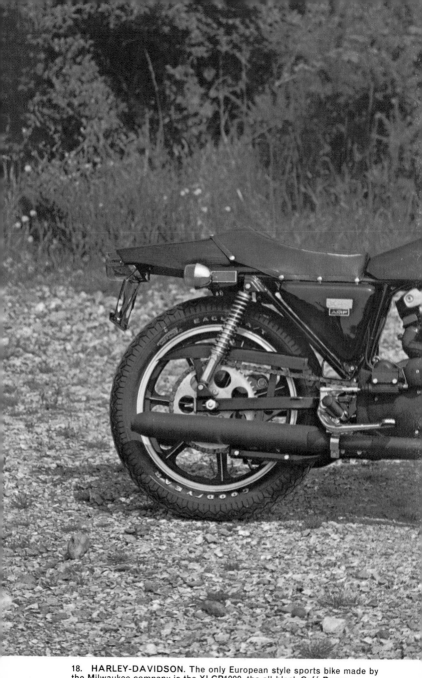

18. HARLEY-DAVIDSON. The only European style sports bike made by the Milwaukee company is the XLCR1000, the all-black Café Racer.

19. **HONDA.** The CB250N is now designated the 'Super Dream' after the apathetical response to the Americanised styling of its 'Dream' predecessor.

20.　**HONDA.** The powerful little 125 twin from Honda.

21.　**HONDA.** The single-cylinder XL250S.

22. **HONDA.** The 400 Auto Honda stays as a Dream for the time being.

23. **HONDA.** The much mourned four-cylinder 400.

24. HONDA. The 750 was one of the first Honda superbikes and the F2 was the culmination of its development.

25. HONDA. Everything about the popular CX500 is unconventional.

26. Honda **CBX** 6-cylinder engine.

27. HONDA. Sporting more than 100 bhp, the CBX is shatteringly quick in a straight line with a top speed approaching 140 mph.

28. HONDA. The GL1000 Gold Wing Honda is a very refined motorbike.

29. INDIAN. This ME-125 is an attractive and well finished machine.

30. **KAWASAKI.** The KH125 is surprisingly sporty.

31. **KAWASAKI.** The KH250 was one of the last three-cylinder strokes from Kawasaki.

32. KAWASAKI. The 400cc class is quite popular these days and the Kawasaki version follows the classic four-stroke parallel-twin layout.

33.   KAWASAKI. The Z1R is the sports version of the famous Z1000 which held the Kawasaki title of 'King', being the fastest bike of its time.

34. KAWASAKI. The Custom 650 is easy to ride fast.

35. KAWASAKI. The Z750 is a Japanese version of a typical British design.

36. LAVERDA. The 175 uses a Zündapp power unit.

37. LAVERDA. The 2TR multi-purpose off-roader.

38. LAVERDA. The Jota is still the sportiest machine built by the Braganze Company, but is only legal in Britain, largely due to its throaty exhaust.

39.   LAVERDA. The 500S Alpino is a well bred sports machine.

40.   LAVERDA. The 1200 Mirage is almost a 'Jotarised' 1200.

41. MORINI. A competitive bike in the Italian half-litre category.

42. MOTO MERIDEN. The Co-Uno 125.

43. MORINI. The 3½ Morini is available in single or twin seat form, the Sport and Strada.

44. MOTO GUZZI. The 850 Le Mans is now available with a Spada-style fairing and bodywork.

45. MOTO GUZZI. The V50 is just like a scaled-down 850 in appearance.

46. MOTO GUZZI. The automatic V1000 Convert.

47.   **MV AGUSTA.** The 350S manages nicely as a twin-cylinder.

48. MV AGUSTA. The single-cylinder 125.

49. MV AGUSTA. The Monza developed from the 750 America.

50. MZ. The East German MZ has a very respectable turn of speed.

51. NORTON. The famous Commando.

52. QUASAR. The Reliant-engined Quasar is like nothing else
in motor cycling.

53. RICKMAN. The Rickman brothers keep their hand in with some excellent café racer and touring chassis to take either Honda or Kawasaki power units.

54. ROYAL ENFIELD. Although the name is dead in Britain, the Royal Enfield lives on as a 350 manufactured in Madras, India.

55. SEELEY. Colin Seeley builds bikes like the Rickman brothers, but his are exclusively Honda powered and have very short wheelbases.

56. SUZUKI. The TS185 is the middle range machine in the off-road class built by the Company.

57. SILK. Although the British bike industry as a major part of the economy no longer exists, small Companies still thrive. Silk have a long waiting
list for their two-stroke 700S.

58. SUZUKI. The X7 has revived for Suzuki the glories they captured with their 1960s version of the 100mph 250cc bike.

59. SUZUKI. The GS400 is a dual purpose (sports and commuter) middleweight roadster.

60. SUZUKI. The GS550 Suzuki gives superbike performance.

61. SUZUKI. The bike on which Barry Sheene's 750 triple racer was based, the GT750. This bike's accent was on touring.

62. SUZUKI. The RE5 was Suzuki's attempt at manufacturing a popular Wankel-engined bike.

63. Suzuki RE5 Wankel engine.

64. SUZUKI. The GS1000 can handle and corner as well as a lightweight.

65. TRIUMPH. The Triumph range carries on with electronic ignition and revised switchgear. The single-carb version is the Tiger.

66.   TRIUMPH. A British bike with a famous name is the twin-carb version
of the Tiger, the Bonneville.

67. Triumph 500cc single-cylinder engine.

68. YAMAHA. The Yamaha RD250 has a reputation for quick acceleration and fine handling.

69. YAMAHA. The DT250 is fitted with monoshock rear suspension.

70. **YAMAHA.** The SR500 is a single-cylinder sports roadster that typifies the big British 'thumper'.

71. Yamaha 500cc single-cylinder engine.

72. YAMAHA. The XS400 is a four-stroke machine in
the popular 400 class.

73. YAMAHA. The XS500 is a parallel-twin four-stroke machine.

74. YAMAHA. The XS1100 is an XS750 with an extra cylinder and a 'bit more capacity'. It is blisteringly quick in a straight line.

rear cylinder offset to the right of the front. Like the other large Ducatis, it has a capacity of 863.9cc but only the 900SS shares the same desmodromic valve system, as designed by famous race-engine builder Fabio Taglioni. Although not as well endowed with horsepower as some Japanese bikes, the 65–70bhp put out by the engine has to power considerably less weight than the competitors, so performance is not that far behind. Top speed is just on 115mph, while a standing start quarter mile takes just over 13secs. As with all big Ducatis, fuel consumption is excellent, being between 45–50mpg most of the time. Where the bike does score over opponents is in the handling and road-holding sector of performance for, with light weight, good balance and a sturdy frame, this bike is just about *the* quickest on a twisty road. Like Vincent, Ducati use the engine as an integral part of the frame with the front downtubes bolting on to the bottom of the crankcase, having the cylinders one behind the other makes the bike narrow so that the handling and roadholding can be exploited to the full. Other now almost standard Italian chassis parts include Brembo discs all round, Ceriani forks at the front and good-looking but expensive Campagnolo wheels.

Ducatis have never been the most attractive bikes (except in an engineer's eyes, perhaps), but with Leo Tartarini taking a hand in styling, they have gained a new image. The Darmah features neat tank and tail bodywork which, with subtle striping, look neat and racy. Also, Nippon Denso instruments have been put on to replace the suspect items of older models and an electric starter is there to save the aggravation of kicking the plot into life.

The Darmah is the touring version of the famous 900SS which has a 9.5:1 instead of 9.4:1 compression ratio and the option of 40mm instead of 32mm carburettors. With a dolphin fairing less weight by virtue of a manual starter and more power (80bhp is claimed), the 900SS is an unashamed road racer and top of the Ducati range.

15 FANTIC CHOPPER 125

The word chopper when connected with motor cycles conjures up visions of outlaw gangs of bikers with their Triumph and Honda-powered custom bikes, but to the Italian Fantic company it means a neat 125cc bike on sale to the general public. Their Chopper comes with a 125cc Minarelli engine which is hardly enough for a bike gang to terrorise a neighbourhood, but enough to make an unusual-looking lightweight a spirited performer.

The lower half of the bike's frame is fairly conventional, but the duplex cradle rises up at the front way past the engine to the steering head where it meets the long outstretched front forks which angle away from the bike one way and join on to large 'high-rise' handlebars the other. To go with the image is a thin 16in tyre at the front and a large almost car-type 5in wide × 16in cover at the rear which, with just 15bhp to transmit to the road, should last a long while. In spite of the bike's unaerodynamic appearance, performance is good with a top speed of 70mph possible; fuel consumption is good, too, with the bike using approximately one gallon of petroil mix per sixty miles. However, as the bike uses a 'peanut' tank of just over a gallon capacity, fuel stops should be frequent. Behind the 'peanut' tank is the 'king and queen' seat (another spin-off from outlaw jargon) which is surprisingly comfortable, although the low-slung rider squab will present problems for those riders who are over six feet tall. The pillion is altogether better catered for, with a higher seat and a large comfortable back rest. On the rear of the rest as well as in between the handlebars there is lattice work bracing which makes the bike just a little bit too gimmicky.

Handling the bike is not the nightmare one would expect a chopper to be and, in fact, once used to the somewhat awkward riding position with the footrests almost in front of the engine and the downward pointing bars, cornering is brisk and trouble free. Although only sporting small drum brakes front and rear, stopping is no problem as the bike weighs a mere 230lb.

What the little Fantic does best, of course, is attract a great deal of attention and not many bikes, let alone 125s, do that. If you live in Italy and want the looks, but less power, the company also does a 50cc version, which must make it the ultimate moped.

The Electra Glide Harley-Davidson is probably the most famous motor cycle ever, and certainly the machine that made Milwaukee famous is the one bike which just about anyone in the street can identify readily.

For 1978, the familiar 45° vee-twin engine of the Glide was uprated from its famous 1200cc to a full 80cubic inches, which is 1338.8cc, making it the largest capacity bike ever built by the American company and one of the largest built by anyone anywhere.

With 722lb of weight to carry, the Glide needs all the power it can get and is still only just able to reach the magic 100mph in its latest guise. Just to save the Glide owner from any nightmares, a centre stand is not fitted, and the bike has to be rolled on to its massive crash bars for any repairs or wheel changes. The company boasts that the bike has the widest tyres available for its flagship and they really do grip the road in the dry, even to the point of screeching when they start to break traction. In the wet, however, the beast deserves the upmost respect for they are quite willing to break away even at low speed. The single disc units mounted at either end are not nearly as effective as the drum units of older models, and this is one point where Harley-Davidson would have done better sticking to their famous traditions.

The rider tucked behind the large fairing has a beautifully contoured fully sprung seat to sit on which easily compensates for any harshness in the suspension, while there are neat foot boards instead of the usual pegs. The footboards are necessary as trying to pivot one's right foot on to the car-like rear brake pedal would be impossible if you tried to keep the ball of your foot in touch with the bike. Just to emphasise the car-like style of the Glide, a foot-operated clutch pedal is available to special order; this would rule out even further any pretentions one might have to sports riding. The Electra Glide is purely a tourer, though, and the makers even believe that the rider will have plenty of time to look down at the tank-mounted speedometer and operate the tank-mounted light switch, such is the lazy style of the machine. Mounted as standard at the rear is a large top box and colour matched side panniers, each with its own chrome-plated crash bars.

On the road, most 250cc machines will romp away from it from a standstill but there is no better machine made for travelling two-up with as much luggage as you would want in supreme comfort over as many continents as you would have time for.

18   HARLEY-DAVIDSON XLCR1000

Aside from the Aermacchi manufactured two-stroke lightweight motor cycles of the early 1970s, the Café Racer Harley-Davidson is one of the more unique variations of the famous American concern. What the bike is and what it appears to be (a road-going lookalike of the company's XR-750 road racer), may not be that much alike, but the Café Racer name tag is an admission that this Harley really wins the most points in the cosmetic stakes. Underneath the looks, however, is a powerful and manageable sports bike which, although only as sophisticated as the other ancient vee-twins in the range, competes favourably with many other machines of later ancestry. As enthusiasts would say, the Harley-Davidson *is* the engine, and the Café Racer uses a high-compression version of the redoubtable overhead-valve narrow-angle vertical vee-twin, which has very undersquare dimensions of 81mm × 96.8mm, giving a capacity of 997.5cc. Maximum power of the bike is 68bhp at 6200rpm while the torque is, to quote the manufacturers, at 3500rpm more than any other machine available. Top speed of the Café Racer is limited by its low gearing, for it rushes up to the red-line speed of 106mph with apparent ease. The sprint like quality of performance is accentuated by its 13secs dead time for the quarter mile. A five-speed gearbox would raise the top-end performance, but just as with the venerable vee-twin, a four-ratio unit is part of the company's tradition.

With a long wheelbase and large grippy tyres on alloy rims, the Harley corners and handles well, and this is helped by its deceptively low weight of 485lb. The performance of the twin Kelsey Hayes discs at the front and single unit at the rear are, however, not up to the task of stopping the beast adequately, while wet conditions will make them barely noticeable at all.

94

The Café Racer's most distinctive feature is its colour which is black virtually all over, something which might make safety conscious environmentalists shudder, but which to an enthusiast is mouth watering. The screen of the small fairing is dark-grey tinted, the wheels are black, 90% of the engine is black; and even the contorted snake-like siamese exhausts are black; it would probably be wise of the rider to wear a dayglo orange suit to compensate. One bad design of this and all Harley-Davidsons is the indicator system which consists of push buttons on either side of the bars. The indicators operate only while the button is depressed which, to say the least, is hazardous when trying at the same time to operate the main controls.

19   HONDA CB250N

When the CB400F2 four-cylinder was decided to be unsuitable for the American market, and therefore the world, Honda had to produce a twin-cylinder bike with at least as much performance, and came up with the Dream, or Hawk as it was known in the USA. It was also decided that a smaller version could be made for the quarter-litre class and this would also help make their four-stroke 250 quicker and more in keeping in touch with the opposition's quicker two-stroke machinery.

Thus, the 250 Dream was introduced but, after the Europeans said that the styling was too American, it was dropped in favour of the 'N' series, better known as the Super Dreams. At that time, Honda hoped they had finally got their mix right!

The engine of the 250 is a four-stroke air-cooled twin which features three valves per cylinder, two inlet and single exhaust driven from the single overhead camshaft. They allow better breathing and therefore more performance and economy. To keep the engine smooth, the motor has the now almost universal contra-rotating balance shafts. Power output of the engine is 27bhp at 10,000rpm, just a couple of horsepower down on the admittedly lighter 'strokers'. This power is fed through a six-speed gearbox and performance is to the order of a 90mph top speed and 16.5 secs standing start quarter mile time. Fuel consumption is 65mpg.

The CB250N weighs around 350lb so is quite heavy, but this does not affect the handling unduly, and the bike remains well balanced and easy to ride. The wheels on the bike are the famous Comstars which unlike the earlier Dreams which had alloy rims and pressed-steel spokes are now all alloy and a lot lighter.

The styling is the most obvious change of the Super Dream and it has a simulated one-piece tank/seat/tail unit to replace the earlier bike's more touring look. The modern sports look of the replacement model is probably overdone with its tank stripe a rich colour by the saddle only to fade out as the paintwork reaches the steering head and the computer-age-digit numerology on the side panels.

20   HONDA CB125T

While the competition finds it more economical and easier to build their lightweight motor cycles with two-stroke power units, Honda has persisted with motors of four-stroke design to the detriment of weight and performance. Honda had two 125s in production: a pushrod single with an amazing economy, the CG125, and a sports version with an overhead camshaft engine, disc brake and more performance, the CB125J (which, incidentally sported a CB125S badge on the side panel).

However, even the J model was not quick enough to rival other manufacturer's wares, so Honda decided to build a completely different bike in the same class, and so came up with the twin-cylinder, overhead camshaft CB125T. The bike's engine features just oversquare dimensions of 44 × 41mm, displacing 124cc, and breathes through two quite large 22mm carburettors. With its compression ratio of 9.4:1, the engine produces 16.5bhp at 11,500rpm, while the red line is just on 12,000rpm. Performance is brisk with a top speed of 75mph, while fuel consumption is good, too, averaging out at 75mpg. Not surprisingly, the engine's torque output is not great at low engine speed, and the motor has to be kept spinning above 7000rpm before it pushes the bike's 251lb weight with verve. For more performance, a six-speed gearbox would be better than the five-ratio unit fitted.

The CB125T has a single down tube frame which bolts to the engine making it a stressed member, while steel pressings are used for the other attachment to the steering head. Braking is by a cable-operated disc at the front and drum at the rear.

The Honda is a comfortable machine, and with a seat height of 30ins (as tall as many larger bikes) it should suit tall riders who find many lightweights difficult to ride. The pillion rider is well catered for, too, with the rear footrests mounted on the frame and not like so many small bikes on the swinging arm, where the passenger's legs go up and down with the road undulations.

Honda have paid a lot of attention to styling recently and the CB125T is a particularly attractive model with its one-piece-look tank and side panels, grab handle at the rear and stylish upswept twin exhaust pipes.

21   HONDA XL250S

Honda's XL250 trail bike was at one time rather outclassed by its competitors as it was a great deal heavier and not nearly as potent. However, the XL250S is a much better machine with a lot less weight and an innovative new engine.

The power unit of the 250 is an all-alloy single-overhead-camshaft single which features four valves, making its breathing easy and efficient. Power from the oversquare unit peaks at 20.2bhp at 8500rpm which gives the bike a top speed of almost 80mph, yet a fuel consumption which is decidedly frugal at 70mpg; on the road, of course. An interesting feature of the engine is its exhaust system which features twin pipes, claimed by the manufacturers to be superior to a larger-bore single unit for low-speed torque. Power is fed via a wet-multi-plate clutch and five-speed gearbox to the 18in rear wheel, which looks rather odd considering that the front is a massive 23in diameter. However, as has been found in motocross, larger front wheels make things a lot easier on really tough ground. The performance of the XL off the road is excellent and the bike is a lot more than just a trail/fun bike for it could well be a competitive club racer.

Many trail bikes are hard to ride on tarmac purely because their knobbly tyres just don't grip. However, the Honda uses Yokohama covers which are of specially developed dual purpose type and so make road work a little less of a nightmare experience. In fact, with such light weight (260lb), the off road Honda makes many pukka roadsters seem clumsy.

The bike is liberally scattered with good ideas like an engine decompressor which works automatically when the kickstart is used, which takes all the strain out of that. There is a neat instrument cluster which houses the speedometer with a place set on the side for milometer and reset trip meter, which makes things just about ideal for the enduro competitor.

All in all, the XL250S should suit anyone interested in doing anything off road, except perhaps GP motocrossing, for the bike is a superb performer, and a smooth one at that. For this machine has a single-cylinder engine with a balance shaft to cancel out vibrations at high revs, which makes it one of the most well engineered bikes available.

22 HONDA CB400 AUTO

Automatic transmissions may seem somewhat unnecessary on motor cycles, but they are very popular in the United States and, as theirs is such a large market, it dictates that more should be made. The Honda 400 Auto is unique in that it is the first of the new-generation autos as a middleweight roadster rather than superbike, like the 1000cc Convert Guzzi and 750 Hondamatic.

The 400 is the CB400 Dream and, like the manual version, is a four-stroke, twin-cylinder machine. The Auto's engine differs in tune from the manual and has 30bhp at 8000rpm compared to 43bhp at 9500rpm. Torque is down just a little to 20.25lb ft at 6000,which is 2000rpm lower down the rev range than its sister bike and much more useful for its semi-automatic gearbox which has just two gears. The modifications are by way of smaller carburettors, smaller ports and milder camshaft. The three-valves-per-cylinder (two inlet, one exhaust) twin with chain-driven contra-rotating balance shafts in auto guise is a very smooth and well-mannered machine indeed, even if performance is not a strong point.

The bike's gearbox is not truly automatic in the car sense, being a two speed unit with torque converter and manual change. First gear is for up to 50mph, while second will take the machine to its top speed of 95mph.

Riding the 400 requires a new technique. The bike will only start if the gear selector is in neutral and the gearchange order is neutral at the bottom, with the two gears 'up', second above first. Should you forget to take the bike out of gear and put the side stand down, a failsafe switch will cut-out the ignition, thus preventing the bike from taking off without the rider.

The bike works remarkably well if just left in the higher of its two ratios and will pull away, albeit fairly slowly, from second gear. As can be expected, even using both gears, acceleration is not startling, with a standing start quarter mile time of 17.2 secs. Fuel consumption is good, however, and can average out at just on 60mpg.

With the exception of the gear-position indicator replacing the unnecessary tachometer, and a parking brake replacing the clutch lever, the CB400 Auto is just like the pre-Super Dream manual version with its 'Americanised' styling and attractive Comstar wheels.

23   HONDA CB400F2

The 750 Honda four-cylinder, which appeared in 1969, was the first in a vast range of fours from the giant Japanese company. Although most were upwards of 500cc, one model was marketed using an engine of 350cc mounted in a chassis that gave it an appearance similar to that of the 360 twin. More successful than that early 'small-four' venture, however, was the CB400 which was granted Super Sport nomenclature by the company. Like its larger stablemates, the 400's power unit is an across-the-frame, single-overhead-camshaft, four-stroke engine which, in its later modified F2 guise, produces 37bhp at 8500rpm. In fact, breathing through four Keihin carburettors, the engine will rev freely right up to its 10,000rpm red line with no fuss, and a formula one car like shriek replacing the usual smooth clock like whirr of the motor. The power is transmitted through a six-speed gearbox which may seem rather extravagant, but which in reality is very necessary, for the bike thrives on revs and is not that powerful lower down the engine speed scale. For instance, if the bike is cruising at 70–75mph in sixth gear and the rider runs into a strong headwind or starts to climb a motorway hill, the bike will lose pace fairly easily, thus necessitating a change of gear. This is even more pronounced when riding with a pillion aboard.

However, if the engine is kept spinning at a high rate, the 400 is turned into a very quick machine with a top speed of 103mph and a standing start quarter mile time of 15secs dead. With such an efficient little engine, fuel consumption is excellent with over 50mpg being attainable under most conditions.

The frame of the 400 is an interesting design with a single downtube running from the steering head through the centre exhausts where it is split into a cradle that winds round under the crankcase. It looks and is very sturdy and gives the bike very taut handling qualities. This is helped by the fact that all the considerable 395lb weight is kept low. Smaller riders will find that the little machine is very easy to handle in traffic and to put on and off the centre stand.

Unlike most other Japanese bikes, the CB400F2 has not been overburdened with unnecessary braking and retains just a single disc at the front and a drum at the rear; the front disc has a neat cover incidentally which keeps out a great deal of water in the wet.

Unfortunately, Honda decided to stop production of the 400 four, as the buyers in the large American market really wanted easy-to-maintain twins. The European market thought that this would be a retrogressive step, so the fours were snapped up from dealers in the hope that they would be collectors items when the twin Dream series arrived. However, sources in 1978 suggested that a completely new range of small fours would be built along with the twins, using twin-overhead-camshaft engines and ranging right down to 250cc.

24   HONDA 750F2

The 750 Honda was arguably the first of the new range of superbikes when it was announced in 1969, and even the rival, the earlier-announced Triumph Trident, had one less cylinder than the Japanese bike's four. Steadily, the Honda was developed from its initial K1 guise until in 1978 it was available in K7 form. During that time, what was the incredible performance of the early bike had dissolved, as the power unit was modified to suit pollution regulations. In a bid to resurrect the performance to meet the ever-growing competition, a Super Sport F1 version was announced, which featured sportier looks, if not a lot else. The F2 was an altogether different proposition, however, with a completely revised engine which was hoped to keep customers happy until Honda's sixteen-valve twin-cam range was ready.

The F2's engine is a 736cc single-overhead-camshaft four which, with larger inlet and exhaust valves than the F1, produces 6bhp more at 73bhp at 9000rpm; torque peaks at 46lb ft at 7500rpm. Although not as sophisticated as other Japanese fours, the Honda unit is nevertheless powerful and very smooth and able to give the bike a top speed of just over 120mph. Cosmetically, the F2 is far removed from its predecessors and its looks bear more than a hint of the famous Honda Formula One racers. The matt-black engine has an air of quality about it as do the steel Comstar wheels. The original Honda 750 was the first mass-produced bike to be fitted with a disc brake as standard, and since that time every manufacturer has adopted them. This sporting Honda has three: twin front and single rear, with floating calipers and slotted brake pads.

Handling has never been the 750's best point, but the F2 is an improvement over the rest with its revised suspension. The Japanese tyres are not as safe as European covers, however, on this particular bike.

The standard of finish on Hondas is high, and the F2 is no exception, with the chrome on the four-into-one exhaust, which finishes at the tail of the bike with a width of no less than five inches, standing out in particular. Night time riding on the F2 should be easy with a powerful quartz halogen headlamp cutting a path.

More like the endurance racers is a limited edition F2 which features a 'Phil Read' twin headlamp endurance style fairing, finished in Honda Great Britain colours. That, until the sixteen-valve series comes along, should keep the road racers happy.

25 HONDA CX500

Honda's offering in the increasingly popular half-litre class is unlike any of its competitors, and unlike any other Honda before, being a water-cooled vee-twin, with a longitudinally seated crankshaft.

Unlike most other vees, the CX500 has its cylinders mounted at an odd 80° with the cylinders then twisted by 22° so that the mixture goes straight from the hidden carburettors into the combustion chamber and out of the exhaust without any power-consuming twists. Having that set-up also means that the carburettors are conveniently out of the way of the rider's legs. Of course, the main problem with the twist of the cylinders is that it rules out the possibility of employing overhead camshafts, so the CX has instead a central cam operating lengthy pushrods. These, in turn, operate rockers on either head which are connected to the four valves per cylinder. Not only does the engine rev freely with such efficient breathing, but it is also powerful, producing a maximum 50bhp at 9000rpm with its 10:1 compression ratio.

The engineers at Honda thought that air-cooling would not be efficient enough to dissipate so much engine-generated head, so a liquid-cooled system was built on to the bike. This has the added bonus of making the bike a lot quieter than it would normally be.

The CX500 has a contra-rotating clutch which helps negate the inherent torque twist which pulls the bike to one side, and it transmits the power through a five-speed gearbox to a shaft final drive. The engine and transmission unit hangs from a stiff spine frame and, although it is rigid and helps the handling, it does add even more weight to an already heavy machine which, in all, tips the scales at 450lb. With this bike, Honda decided to keep a drum rear brake, along with twin front discs, just to make sure that the bike can be stopped adequately whatever the weather. In reality, they are well able to stop the machine from its top speed of 108mph. Not only is the CX500 technically different from all other bikes, but it looks different, too, with its wide saddle, large black radiator and odd casing around the instruments which looks rather like a small nose fairing with the screen removed.

Considering that Honda had a 500cc four-cylinder machine at one time, the CX500 may seem a backward step, but underneath is an advanced technology which makes the middleweight bike one of the most interesting available.

26/27   HONDA CBX

Honda were the last of the Japanese manufacturers to build a sports 1000cc bike, although they already had a one-litre machine with the touring-style Gold Wing. Instead of tuning that bike, they decided to build a roadster on the lines of their endurance racers, of straight engine configuration, with twin camshafts and four valves per cylinder. Two models were tried: one a four-cylinder not unlike their CB750 machine and the other a six-cylinder model. In testing the six was found to have around 5bhp more than the smaller version and it was thought that this along with the obvious sales charm of a bike with more cylinders would be enough to keep the customers satisfied. 1978 saw the arrival of the Honda CBX which was received with mixed blessings: some thought it was fantastic, while others saw it as the superbike war escalated out of all proportion.

A lot has been done to try to keep the across-the-frame straight-six narrow and co-designer Masahuri Tsuboi managed to keep the crankcase from being little broader than the Honda fours; above that, the cylinders are obviously wider. The engine is very much an oversquare unit with dimensions of 64.5×53.4mm, giving a capacity of 1047cc. Six Keihin carburettors are mounted in a broad vee fashion so as not to obstruct the riders knees and help give the engine a maximum power output of 105bhp at 9000rpm, maximum torque of 62.2lb ft at 8000rpm and a red-line figure of 9500rpm. Top speed of the 548lb bike, with its large frontal area to penetrate the wind, is 140mph, while it will accelerate over a quarter mile from a standing start in a little over 11.5secs. Fuel consumption is around 35mpg, depending on how hard the bike is used.

There seems to be something odd about the bike when first seen and it seems hard to say just what, that is until it is realised that there are no down tubes on the frame. In fact, the engine hangs from a large spine structure, with the wheel thus closer to the engine and so offering a shorter wheelbase for better handling. In fact, that is handy for the bike would have been even more ponderous in its road manners had the wheelbase been longer. Quite safe on smooth roads, the CBX can be tricky when the going gets rough. Three disc brakes (twin 11in units at the front and a 12in at the rear), mounted on Comstar wheels, cope surprisingly well with stopping the big bike from high speeds. Like the CX500, tubeless tyres are fitted.

With a curious mixture of styling curves and angles, the CBX may not be to everyone's taste, but one glimpse at the remarkable engine would bring to mind that oft-quoted phrase 'racing improves the breed'.

The four-cylinder prototype later saw the light of day as the 900cc CBFZ.

28   HONDA GOLD WING

The Honda GL1000 K2 Gold Wing, built to rival the BMW and Moto Guzzis, is the flagship of the Japanese giant's touring fleet. This bike, more than any other, has a great deal of motor car technology built into it and that accounts for its weight which, at 584lb, is in the super heavyweight class. The heart of the machine is a flat-four (or Boxer) configuration engine of 999cc set low in the frame; this feeds through four carburettors to the valves which are actuated by a single rubber-belt-driven camshaft for each cylinder bank. With water jacketing around the cylinders, the size of the unit is accentuated even more.

Drive is via a five-speed gearbox and shaft, another example of car technology. Chain drive on such a heavy and powerful machine would need adjustment every one hundred and fifty miles or so and on a long-distance tourer like the Wing that could mean stopping during a journey to carry out the task. Honda decided to adopt the shaft-drive principle at the expense of the inherent clunking gearchange of such a system.

Although smooth and extremely quiet, the bike's engine produces no less than 80bhp which gives the Gold Wing a more than respectable performance with a top speed of 123mph and the ability to cover a quarter mile from rest in 13.2secs. Fuel consumption can be heavy if the bike is pressed too hard, but with normal use petrol will be consumed at the rate of approximately 35–40mpg.

The big Honda is quite deceptive in appearance, for the fuel tank is under the seat and not above the engine where it appears to be. In fact, the 'tank' is a dummy which has a cover which lifts to reveal a neat little oddments tray; also inside are catches which open panels on either side of the 'tank'. The left reveals all the electrics, while the right houses a lever, which acts as a kickstarter when inserted in the engine, and the header tank for the radiator, which is housed behind the front wheel. Having the fuel tank under the seat helps lower the centre of gravity which enhances the handling which, in itself, is good rather than great. However, the Honda Gold Wing is a tourer and never happier than with a large fairing and panniers, making it the nearest thing to a two-wheeled car ... albeit with a true motor cycle performance.

29   INDIAN ME-125

Indian is a name from the history of motor cycling which is synonymous with large touring motor cycles like Harley-Davidson, some of which were of four-cylinder configuration.

More recently, the Indian name and, indeed, the famous logo, have appeared on completely different motor cycles from a company based in Beverly Hills, California. In fact, since the demise of the great company, there have been many attempts to revive the name, although the present one is the only one which seems to have succeeded.

The present Indian company markets a range of small roadster and trail machines, the most potent of which, although not the largest, is the ME-125. The little 125 trail bike is quite a mixture for, although the Indian headquarters are on the West Coast of America, the bikes themselves are manufactured in Taiwan with engines from the proprietary unit firm of Minarelli in Italy.

The bike's engine is a conventionally ported two-stroke single of 123.48cc which produces 16bhp at 7200rpm and drive is via a five-speed gearbox. What alters the performance of the engine on this Minarelli-powered bike is the exhaust system, two-strokes being very sensitive to exhaust design. The elaborate plumbing of the

Indian seems efficient, though, as it produces 1bhp more than the similarly equipped Fantic and 2bhp more than the Barron. Top speed of the bike is just on 75mph, while it will return upwards of 60mpg. The ME-125 is very much a dual-purpose vehicle for, while it has a lot of ground clearance and the off-road norm of 17in rear and 19in front wheels, the rest of the machine is aimed at the commuter-type motor cyclist, with mirror, indicators and a rear carrier as standard, something very few roadster manufacturers think of.

Performance on the rough is something of a compromise, too, for not only are the tyres not that grippy, but the whole bike is not really sturdy enough for the enthusiastic mud-plugger who enjoys leaping bikes and generally 'giving his bike stick'. As a part-time trail machine, the Indian is useful and fun, however.

One small criticism is the exhaust, though. Efficient it may be and attractive it certainly is as it sweeps out, round and over the engine but, even with a guard, it gets terribly hot and tends to make the rider sit bow-legged when the machine is still in traffic.

30   KAWASAKI KH125

With many companies turning their attentions away from two-stroke bikes, because of their pollution problems, it was surprising to see Kawasaki pursue them with a small range of commuter 'strokers'.

The KH125 is typical of the line being a tiny but very nippy motor cycle. The heart of the bike is its single-cylinder engine which is canted forwards in the frame. The oversquare unit uses a disc valve which makes it more powerful, economical and cleaner than normal piston-ported units, and this is exemplified in its power output which is 14.5bhp produced at 7500rpm; this is combined with a torque output of 10.5lb ft. Top speed in the highest of its six gears is 72mph, while standing start quarter mile acceleration takes 18.2secs. Obviously, the bike's miniscule weight of just over 209lb is a contributing factor here. Fuel consumption of the self-mixing variety is around 70mpg which is not far away from that of the slower four-stroke machines in the same category.

Braking is taken care of by a disc at the front and drum at the rear which are easily up to the task. The front disc is one of the very few on the market which is cable operated, but on such a small bike it is hardly noticeable.

Although not intended as such, the KH125 is rather sporty in appearance and this is further accentuated on the bike as the rider leans forward quite a lot to the bars, making the whole plot look like a mini racer. This does not mean that it is uncomfortable, however, and even two up you will find that long trips are well within the bounds of possibility before you start aching. The KH125 is well equipped with a fuel tank that will give the lightweight bike a range of over 170 miles, a neat tool compartment in the rear fairing and a mirror. Earlier bikes had mirrors either side, but the manufacturers later thought that the second one was unnecessary.

31 KAWASAKI KH250

The KH250 Kawasaki is an air-cooled two-stroke three-cylinder bike, the only triple in its capacity class and, like its larger sister machine the KH400, the last of a famous breed of fast strokers from the Kawasaki Heavy Industries Group. In the late 1960s and early '70s, Kawasaki's triples had a reputation for being difficult to handle, very dirty (with their two-stroke smoke following at all times), uneconomical and very very fast; so fast, indeed, that the larger models could be somersaulted backwards from a standing start with little difficulty. With environmentalists forcing manufacturers to build cleaner and more frugal machines, Kawasakis lost a lot of their famous edge in performance until by the late 1970s they were docile and very maneagable machines indeed.

The KH250 has its three cylinders set across the frame which displace 249cc and, with a compression ratio of 7.5:1, produces 28bhp at 7500rpm and 19.5lb ft of torque at 7000rpm. Top speed of the machine is around 95mph, while it will cover a standing start quarter mile in 16secs. The performance is accompanied by a high-pitched whine which is more in keeping with a bike of half its size. If all the performance is used, the KH250 can still be a very thirsty machine and return less than 30mpg. However, if treated with restraint, a figure of well over 40mpg should be possible. Although the KH250 still emits a great deal of smoke under hard acceleration, oil consumption is quite comparable to many seemingly cleaner machines.

The Kawasaki frames have never had the best of reputations, but that of the KH250 copes remarkably well, the bike not having an excessive amount of power (unlike its predecessors) helping this no end. A single disc brake is fitted at the front while a drum is mounted at the rear.

As is typical with Kawasakis, the instruments and switchgear are excellent and a nice touch is the handlebar-mounted choke lever which is a boon, as the little bike is sensitive to it on cold mornings and would present problems fiddling around for the device by the carburettors.

Unlike its competitors, Kawasaki do not have comparable four-stroke machines in their range, but that time cannot be far off, because although the KH250 and the much faster KH400 are among the most exciting machines in their classes, there will be no place for them in the conservation-minded 1980s.

32 KAWASAKI Z400

The Kawasaki Z400 is an air-cooled four-stroke twin, like most of its competitors and, by its specification, a touring/commuter machine rather than a sports bike. However, again like its competitors, it does have a fair turn of speed and is not quite the bland machine that the '400' tag implies.

Although just a twin cylinder, the Kawasaki is a smooth and well developed bike with its balancer-shaft 360° engine. Valve actuation is by a single camshaft mounted overhead, while breathing is via two Keihin carburettors. The engine is red lined at 9000rpm, while maximum power is developed at 8500 (35.7bhp) and maximum torque (23.7lb ft) at 7000rpm. This means that to extract the most performance, the engine has to be revved quite hard, but as the unit is well balanced and smooth, it doesn't make things too tiresome. The engine is coupled to a six-speed gearbox with the ratios well spaced. The top speed is 102mph which is just on the red line and, as the maximum speed in fifth is a fraction over 90mph, the top ratio could be a bit longer for more relaxed high-speed cruising.

Fuel consumption is one of the Z400's stronger points and it can average over 55mpg, while being able to cover over 85mpg if the speed is kept down. The fuel tank holds 3.1gals which should enable a touring range of over 180 miles.

The middleweight Kawasaki has quite high bars which make it extremely comfortable around town, although they do make high-speed travel tiresome after a while. As 75–80mph is the bike's limit before it sounds fussed and stressed, this should not be too much of a problem.

The bike uses a broad duplex frame with conventional springing which is well able to cope with the demands of the average rider. The same can be said for the tyres which, with a softer compound than the notorious covers used some time ago by the Japanese industry, work well in all weather conditions. Braking by a single disc at the front and a drum rear is adequate rather than exceptional.

The Z400 perhaps gets forgotten among the famous machines from the same stable and its less than sporty image does not help it at all, but as a practical and well engineered bike with a surprisingly good performance, the Kawasaki does its job well.

33 KAWASAKI Z1R

In the late 1960s, Kawasaki was planning to produce a 750cc version of its four-cylinder 650W, but were taken aback when Honda beat them to it with their CB750. Instead of putting their twin-cam 750 on to the market straight away, they waited and developed their bike into a 1000cc monster which would not only be bigger and faster than the opposition but also lay the ghost of the frighteningly rapid H1 500 which took the world by storm in 1968. The prototype 1000s which were sent for evaluation to America returned with the summing up which nobody at Kawasaki expected: they were too quick. So, the final design for the export market was based around a mere 903cc unit. After emission controls took their toll of performance, the full 1015cc unit was put on the market several years after the 'King's' introduction. The 750 version was marketed in Japan, however, where larger machines were prohibited.

A yet later version of the 1000 is the Z1R which has a revised engine, different body panels and a neat fairing. This bike is intended as a stop gap until Kawasaki's six-cylinder range is ready.

The famous Z1000 engine is a four-cylinder four-stroke twin-overhead-camshaft unit which uses four carburettors and roller bearings for the big ends. All in all, the unit is remarkably smooth and produces its power in a turbine-like manner. The Z1R has 7bhp more than the standard Z1000, which puts the figure at an amazing 90bhp produced at 8000rpm. The bike's top speed is 131mph, while it will rocket through the quarter mile in just 12.1secs from a standing start. When all the performance is used, fuel consumption is very high and the rider, if he has time, can watch the fuel gauge, which sits next to a matching ammeter, go down.

At high speed, the little fairing comes into its own and does divert the wind away from the face and body, even though it does look no more than a cosmetic item.

The brakes on the Z1R are three cross-drilled discs which are meant not only to save weight but also get rid of water in the wet, thus making them more efficient. In reality, however, they work no better than the usual stainless-steel discs and that is not a compliment. The bike, at 542lb, is quite heavy and the brakes need to be gripped strongly in the dry, too. Even though the Z1R is one of the fastest bikes available, the American market has a quicker version which utilises a turbocharger. Not surprisingly, with around 25% more power, the Turbo Z1R is not so much a quick bike but more a road-going drag racer.

34 KAWASAKI Z650

The middleweight Z650 Kawasaki looks a lot like its larger stablemate, the Z1000, but they are quite different and just share the same appearance and basic specification.

The heart of the bike is a four-stroke twin-overhead-camshaft four-cylinder engine which, with four carburettors, produces 64bhp at 8500rpm and 42lb ft of torque at 7000rpm. With the bike weighing 465lb, this gives a top speed of 121mph and enables it to cover a quarter mile from a standing start in 13.3secs. Unlike the bigger bike's power unit, the Z650 uses plain main bearings but they detract nothing from the smoothness of the unit which is one of the quietest around. However, when accelerating hard, the normal purr is turned into a roar at the end of the four-into-two exhaust system. As the engine is so efficient, fuel consumption can be very good at lower speeds, with 45mpg on the lowest grade of fuel being possible. A 3.7 gallon fuel tank should ensure that the rider does not have to stop too often on a long journey.

The bike's handling although not as vicious as the early 900s can be worrying if the rider corners near the limit of the tyres, for the bike will tend to wallow when power is applied. That is only when the bike is travelling at speeds which would be foolhardy most of the time on public roads, however. Braking is by a single disc at the front, while a drum unit is utilised for the rear, but they are not up to stopping the bike repeatedly from high speed as they tend to fade quickly.

Like Yamaha who build a 650cc twin, Kawasaki resurrected that particular engine size and gave it, in their case, an advanced multi-cylinder engine which, in outright performance, is inferior to the Z1000 but nevertheless in a smaller bike makes for an adequate road burner. To quell thoughts that the bike's main failing was dated looks, Kawasaki introduced two other versions, one, the SR, for America only, had high-rise handlebars and a dual-height seat, along with minor engine modifications, while the other is the Custom with alloy wheels, three disc brakes and minor styling changes: in all, a good-looking and very fast middleweight machine.

35   KAWASAKI Z750

Fitting neatly in between the Z650 and Z1000 four-cylinder bikes in the Kawasaki range is the Z750 which is a parallel twin with a touring rather than sporting image.

What Kawasaki have done is take the much-loved formula of

vertical-twin and added to it the technology of a modern age, complete with twin camshafts, balance shafts, anti-pollution devices and all.

The four-stroke Z750 has an engine of square dimensions of 78mm which gives a total capacity of 745cc and, breathing through two Mikuni carburettors and on an 8.5:1 compression ratio, the power output peaks at 55bhp at 7000rpm. Outright power at the top end of the rev scale does not make full use of the bike, however, as it pulls strongly from low revs thus putting an accent on to fast touring rather than sprinting. Unlike the other big twins on motor cycling history, the Z750 does not vibrate a great deal, this being achieved with contra-rotating swing weights which oppose the primary forces. Another point which demonstrates the technology put into the bike is the fact that it has crankcase ventilation which recycles gases back through the carburettors, thus reducing hydrocarbon emissions. Of course, the twin overhead camshafts are also part of the specification usually set aside for sports multi-cylinder machines.

Power is fed through a gear primary drive to a five-speed gearbox which, in turn, drives a conventional chain to the disc braked back wheel; there is a single disc at the front, also.

Early Kawasakis were not renowned for their handling qualities, but the 481lb Z750 with its sturdy duplex frame copes remarkably well, even though it is not in the 'road-scratching' class; the high touring bars are no help when the rider tries hard, either.

Unlike Yamaha and Suzuki who were the first to develop self-cancelling indicators, Kawasaki on the Z750 use the ordinary audible system which bleeps in time with the flash of the warning light. What Kawasaki did introduce, however, is a neat safety device which cuts off the starter circuit when the clutch is engaged. This means the lever has to be pulled in before the engine can be fired.

36 LAVERDA 175

Zündapp of Munich produce a range of small two-stroke machines themselves, while for some time they have also marketed their engine/transmissions separately for other manufacturers to use. When Laverda decided to market some small two-stroke bikes themselves they decided that it would be easier to buy the proprietary German units rather than spend a great deal of money developing their own. When the 125 and 175 Laverdas were announced, they were seen as typical of the company's products, whether caravans, farm equipment or bikes: expensive but brilliantly engineered and immaculately finished with a modern style unique to them.

The Zündapp engine is a 163cc single which features water cooling for better efficiency and quieter running but, unlike larger machines which require water pumps, this unit relies on the thermosyphon system whereby hot water from the jacketing rises into the radiator while the cooled liquid there follows that elementary law of physics and goes down to the engine again: simple but effective. Because the engine is small and doesn't produce that much heat, a fan is not needed, either.

The oversquare engine (62×54mm) produces 17bhp at 7000rpm which gives the bike a top speed of 75mph, while fuel consumption is around 70mpg. The performance is not spectacular for a 175 and many 125s are not far off that in top speed, but the extra capacity does make things a little easier and less fussy, while the engine's smooth and quiet operation means that the Laverda can be cruised at high speed without the tiresome nature of a smaller air-cooled unit. A five-speed gearbox is fitted on the bike.

The rest of the machine reads like a who's who of expensive and high-class parts manufacturers. The electrical system is Bosch, suspension by Marzzochi, brakes by Brembo (disc at the front and rod-operated drum at the rear), tyres by Dunlop, while the wheels are alloy units from Campagnolo, some of the most expensive made.

The frame, of course, is Laverda's own and is simple yet sturdy which makes handling virtually viceless.

As can be imagined, the 175 Laverda is an expensive bike, and costs more than most 400s and almost as much as some 500s, but Laverda compete with other bikes on paper and specification rather than on price, and they have never found that a problem.

37   LAVERDA 2TR

Laverda of Breganze, a small town in the shadow of the Dolomites in northern Italy, is famous for its large roadster bikes, but over the past few years it has produced several off-road machines, from competition 125 and 250cc motocros and enduros, to the all-purpose 250cc 2TR, a bike which is basically for trail riding but which can also be used for small trial or enduro events. Laverda have collaborated with the Swedish Husqvarna concern on many matters and use their engines on competition machines. The 2TR, however, has a Laverda power unit which was designed by the Husqvarna team, being a simple piston-ported two-stroke single.

With square 68×68mm dimensions and a 10:1 compression ratio, the 247cc motor produces 30bhp at 7000rpm, a figure which is better than most road-going twins. Due to its off-road gearing, the Laverda has a lower top speed than a roadster style machine, but at 75mph it should be enough for a machine using knobbly tyres. Acceleration away from rest is very rapid and it is quite easy getting the front wheel airborne. Fuel consumption depends a great deal on conditions and terrain, but 40mpg is quite possible if mostly ridden on tarmac.

The 2TR is the most adaptable off-roader made and this is due to its easily adjustable steering geometry. The forks are pivotted at the top and there is a bolt which secures the unit in one of three positions. Basically, they are with the fork near vertical for trials riding; in the intermediate position for general off-road work or enduro; or angled forwards for easier road riding.

Another important feature which should ensure minimal maintenance is the enclosed rear chain which keeps it out of the harmful way of dirt and stones.

The Laverda is more rugged in appearance than many trail machines, and it has none of the appendages that might get in the way and hinder performance, the one exception being a neat little carrier mounted on top of the tank which has a window for a map: very useful if proper trail riding is undertaken.

A version of the bike better equipped for road use with twin instruments and chrome mudguards is manufactured and des-ignated the 2T.

38 LAVERDA JOTA

Jota is the name of a Spanish dance which is in triple time, and is also the name of the 1000cc three-cylinder sports bike in the Laverda company's range. The bike was developed using factory endurance racer parts and was finished off at the British importers with more efficient exhausts than standard, but which were also very noisy and illegal in most European countries.

The bike's engine is an air-cooled four-stroke three-cylinder unit of 980cc which with a 10:1 compression ratio produces 90bhp at 7250rpm. Breathing of the engine is by three carburettors and twin overhead camshafts, while drive is through a five-speed gearbox (with right-foot change). Top speed of the bike is just on 140mph, while it will accelerate to a quarter mile from a standing start in a little over 12secs; fuel consumption will average out at around 40mpg. The performance of the bike is quite different from other large bikes and is not at all turbine smooth or silky. It is, in fact, rather brutal and, like the rest of the bike, not the sort of thing for the faint hearted.

The gearbox casing is massive and more what one would expect to see on combine harvesters made by the same company, and the gearchange is hard and imprecise at low speeds with neutral just about impossible to select at rest. The bike's frame is a large duplex unit which gives the 475lb bike sure-footed handling, while cast-iron Brembo discs on the cast-alloy wheels make the braking just about as good as is possible.

The Jota is a very large bike and quite a handful for riders under 5ft 10in, and the absence of a side stand does not bolster the confidence of the smaller person. However, that apart, the Laverda should suit everyone for the riding position is completely adjustable. The clutch and brake lever can be adjusted for reach, the bars themselves can be adjusted for height (either almost flat, or the more popular racing position) and the gear pedal can be re-positioned on its splines to suit.

One aspect where the Jota's performance is not up to the rest of the bike is in the electrics. The starter motor does not always have the power to turn the engine over, especially after a run with the headlight on, for the alternator just doesn't produce enough. Bump starting is difficult, too, with such a high compression engine.

In all, the Jota is a powerful bike, but it does need a powerful rider who can overcome the heavy clutch, gearbox and heavy low-speed handling.

39   LAVERDA 500

The Laverda 500S Alpino is an updated version of the older plain 500 which at one time had the name Alpina, although this is also the name of a company marketing performance parts for BMW cars and so could have been confusing. The main difference between the two bikes is in the engine, where the later version has a balance weight geared from the end of the crankshaft.

The engine of the 500 is a 180° twin of air-cooled four-stroke design and features four valves per cylinder operated by twin overhead camshafts, driven from the centre of the crankshaft. In an attempt to minimise vibrations, the S model has a bob weight gear driven from the left hand side of the crankshaft and turning in an opposite direction to the crank itself. In reality, it makes the new bike a little smoother than the old one but it is not that noticeable. The S also has a higher compression ratio which gives it a little more horsepower and torque, but since the new bike Laverda have stopped quoting power figures. The older 500 had 44bhp at 10,300rpm and approximately 33lb ft of torque, which is excellent for a half-litre machine, and the revised version has around 4bhp more with roughly the same torque output.

Top speed of the S is 111mph, while it takes exactly 14secs to cover a quarter mile from a standing start. Fuel consumption is approximately 42mpg. The Laverda is fitted with a six-speed gearbox, the ratios of which are very close together, but it would probably get by just as well with a five-gear unit. Unlike the larger bikes from the factory, the 500 has the gear pedal on the more conventional left side.

The bike has a single down-tube frame which is siamesed at the bottom of the crankcase to cradle the engine, and is of sturdy design to make the handling of the 375lb bike predictable and fuss free; Pirelli tyres help roadholding, too.

Laverda use cast alloy wheels made in their own foundry for the 500 and the larger bikes in the range, and in this case are fitted with twin discs at the front and a single at the rear, all of cast iron and manufactured by Brembo. They are a lot easier to handle in wet weather than stainless steel items, and they give the bike excellent stopping power. Prototype 500s were fitted with a one-piece tail/rear mudguard the same colour as the tank and front mudguard, but the 500S has separate chrome units, all of a high standard and not the shoddy and easily rusting items at one time associated with bikes of the Italian industry.

A 350 version of the 500 is available for the Italian home market where it is in a cheaper tax bracket.

40 LAVERDA MIRAGE

Laverda with their Jota had at one time the fastest motor cycle in production but with the arrival of the 1000 Suzuki, 1100 Yamaha and CBX Honda, this was put in some doubt. To combat this, the Italian company produced the Mirage, an uprated version of their 1200 which itself was an update of the Jota but intended for touring rather than high-speed 'scratching'. The Jota-style 1200 is quite similar to all the other machines in the upper end of the Laverda range, thus sharing the unusual three-cylinder engine.

The Mirage is a four-stroke triple with its pistons mounted on a 180° crankshaft with the outer two at top dead centre while the centre one is at bottom dead centre. The more usual arrangement is the 120° layout à la Triumph Trident. In effect, the Mirage has a four-cylinder engine with one cylinder lopped off so that it misses one beat every three firings. Laverda claim that this arrangement breaks up the rhythms which cause high frequency vibration, but instead it makes the big bike sound and feel quite unlike any other.

The Mirage uses the same 8:1 compression of the 1200, the modifications being Jota type high-rise and larger overlap camshafts and more efficient but noisier silencers. Laverda do not quote figures for the bike, but it should have approximately 90bhp and an abundant supply of torque, enough to give a top speed approaching 140mph and plenty of acceleration. Again like all the other triples, the Mirage features an oil-cooler to help keep the engine temperature down.

Where the Mirage does differ from its stablemates is in the suspension, although the same robust double loop frame is still used. The bigger bike no longer has the forward rake forks which made the Jota rather heavy to handle at lower speeds and this has further been helped by the adoption of the flatter bars from the 500. The rear dampers are inclined more on the larger model, too, and they give more wheel travel for the same amount of deflection than the more upright 1000 models.

Other differences of the larger bike are a more shapely saddle for increased pillion comfort, a grab rail for said passenger, different fuel tank and the inclusion of a side stand, as standard.

41   MORINI 500

Morini were intending their 3½ to be a full 500 before it was announced but then decided it would be a little less risky and made it a 350 so that it would be more popular because of its lower tax rating. It was not until mid 1978 that a production version of the half litre machine was ready. Like the 3½, the 500 is a vee-twin of 72° configuration and is exactly twice the capacity of the 250 at 478.6cc. Also as with the other Morinis, the 500 uses a Heron-type head: instead of having a combustion chamber in the cylinder head, it is situated in the piston and so the head can be flat and cheaper to produce. Valves in the 500 are at 90° to the piston and drop down into recesses in them. Drive to the valves is from a single centrally mounted camshaft which itself is driven from the crankshaft by a toothed rubber belt. This has the advantage of not needing lubrication and having a much smoother and quieter operation. A compression ratio of 11.2:1 is used which would normally mean harder starting than the already difficult 3½, but the larger bike does have an electric starter, mounted unusually lengthways on the side, so that bevel gearing is needed to transmit its power through 90°.

Primary drive is by helical gear to the multi-plate clutch which is unusual in that it is dry and not, as is often the case, running in an oil bath; a five-speed gearbox is employed. The 500 does not have much more power than the $3\frac{1}{2}$, peaking in fact at 43bhp at 7500 (a DIN figure), but more important is the torque which is just under 32lb ft at its maximum, which is usefully down the rev range at 5100rpm. Maximum speed of the bike, at the red-line of 8200rpm in fifth, is 110mph, while fuel consumption is approximately 52mpg.

Like all Morinis, the 500 is blessed with excellent handling and this is helped by an adjustable steering damper. The bike is perhaps overbraked with the twin discs at the front and single disc rear easily stopping the 367lb bike, and great care has to be taken to stop premature locking. A major disadvantage for a rider used to Japanese bikes is the right-foot gearchange which is not the smoothest available and somewhat awkward in operation.

The 500 comes with cast alloy wheels as standard and a solenoid operated fuel tap which opens when the ignition is switched on.

42   MOTO MERIDEN CO-UNO 125

On the fuel tank of the Co-Uno 125 is the name Moto Guzzi with underneath, the word Meriden, so that it can be read as either the name of the bike's manufacturer or the name of the company that assembles it.

The workers co-operative at Meriden in the West Midlands of England, manufacture Triumph Tigers and Bonnevilles, the famous 750cc twins that have long been the backbone of one of Britain's most famous makes. The Meriden factory is large and could not run by making expensive and high-powered bikes alone, so with not nearly enough capital to build their own lightweight, they got together with automotive magnate of the Italian industry the Argentinian Alejandro de Tomaso to arrange to assemble Moto Guzzi 125s in England (de Tomaso owns the sports car company bearing his name, Maserati, Innocenti, Benelli and Moto Guzzi). This was agreed and production started.

The engine of the Co-Uno 125 is a further complication of matters being built at the Benelli factory on the Adriatic coast of Italy for the sister company of Moto Guzzi at Mandello del Lario in the lake district.

The unit is a simple piston-ported two-stroke which displaces

120.6cc and produces a healthy 15.4bhp at 7800rpm. Fuel, which is mixed in the bike's tank is put into the engine by a 22mm Dell'Orto carburettor.

Maximum speed of the bike is just on 70mph, while fuel consumption is excellent with a figure of 90mpg easily possible.

The engine is mounted in a proper cradle frame which is surprisingly stiff, making the light bike (212lb) a very taut machine indeed. The small Grimeca front disc and drum at the rear are not quite in keeping with that sporting image, however, and are a little suspect under heavy application.

Where the Anglo/Italian bike does take a distinct second place over Japanese rivals is in the electrics, for there is no battery to boost the system which is annoying on a proper motor cycle rather than acceptable for a moped. Although its overall looks are sporty and the bike is well able to stay with the opposition in performance and handling, the finish of the Co-Uno is more akin to a cheap economy model with a tiny speedometer as opposed to the more accepted norm of large twin instruments; no mirror is fitted as standard either.

That detracts, perhaps, from a nimble and sound motor cycle underneath.

43   MORINI 3½

The Morini 3½, so named because it has 'three-and-a-half-hundred' cubic centimetres in its engine, comes in two forms, a touring version called the Strada and the appropriately named Sport.

Both have a 72° vee-twin engine mounted longitudinally in the frame like Ducati, the other famous motor cycle manufacturer in Bologna. The engine is an interesting design for both con-rods work on the one crank throw which means that the offset of the two cylinders is very small and thus makes an inherently narrow engine design even narrower. Plumbing of intake and exhaust on such an engine design presents problems and indeed on the 3½ there is great difficulty when cold starting. The engine has two separate Dell'Orto carburettors and both have choke levers mounted on them which are very difficult to get to. As the engine is very sensitive when cold, the choke is quite critical and it does mean either waiting till the engine is hot before moving off or fiddling under the tank to get the right mixture until normal operating temperature is reached. That aside when the engine is running hot it is a very smooth sweet sounding motor indeed.

Both bikes are of 344cc, while the Strada has a 10:1 compression ratio to the Sport's 11:1. Power outputs are 39 and 42bhp, respectively, although these are SAE figures and not the more popular and accurate DIN ratings. In both forms, the engine is red-lined at 9200rpm and so with 14.4mph per 1000rpm in the highest of the six gears, the 3½s are obviously a little overgeared. However, a tall ratio in top helps the fuel consumption which is around 65mpg, excellent for machines in the sporting 350 class. Top speed is around 100mph for both bikes.

Unlike the 250, the 3½ has 12 volt electrics but does have one rather unique feature. A red warning light is mounted on the control panel which glows all the time the ignition is switched on, while a neutral indicator light would be a much better idea, especially as neutral is especially difficult to find with the bike at rest.

The most obvious differences between the two 350 Morinis is the styling, for the Strada is a two seater with straight handlebars, while the Sport features a neat racing-style saddle and clip-on type units. Both have a single disc brake at the front and attractive alloy wheels.

44 MOTO GUZZI LE MANS

The 850 Le Mans is the sportiest bike produced by Moto Guzzi from their factory by the shores of Lake Lecco in Italy, and has a low and lean look which reminds you of something straight off a race track. However, although the Le Mans is indeed a very quick bike, it is smooth and deep-throated and not like a screaming racer at all.

The bikes power unit is an 844cc 90° vee-twin which runs on a high 10.2:1 compression ratio. It produces 81bhp at 7300rpm and will rev to 8000rpm without harm, but also has an abundant supply of torque over a wide rev range, so it will pull strongly from low speeds even in high gears. Power is transmitted via a car-type single-dry-plate clutch to a five-speed gearbox and thence to a shaft drive. This makes gearchanging rather ponderous and the gears cannot be rushed at all. Top speed of the bike is 135mph, while it will accelerate over a quarter mile from a standing start in 13.5secs. Fuel consumption is an excellent 48mpg.

The 850 Le Mans sports Moto Guzzi's patented integral braking system which is both ingenious and simple. The right-side foot pedal goes to a master cylinder and, through simple valves, distributes 75% of the force to the left-side front disc and 25% to the disc at the back, so giving ideally balanced braking so that one wheel doesn't lock up prematurely. This saves the rider having to work out the required amount of co-ordination himself and is useful on wet roads and in emergencies. A normal brake lever on the handlebar operates the other cross-drilled cast-iron disc at the front and gives a little more retardation. The company says that it is for emergencies or sports riding, but it is more likely to give confidence to the uninitiated rider, for it would be far simpler to have all the brakes worked by the one pedal.

The Le Mans is styled in the manner of café racers with low bars and rear-set pedals. Early bikes had a single seat to give extra rear support for the rider but later models adopted a pillion cushion. However, the passenger will feel rather vulnerable on it as the rider will still be in the same crouched position.

A lot of criticism at one time was levelled at the tiny little nose fairing of the bike, but at high speeds it does indeed deflect the air far enough around the rider to make things more comfortable. Moto Guzzi, it should be remembered, have a massive wind tunnel in which they developed their famous dustbin-fairing-equipped racers so are unlikely to add a 'cosmetic' screen. Early models came with a wide dayglo orange band on the fairing, but this was dropped on later bikes.

45   MOTO GUZZI V50

The 500cc class V50 Moto Guzzi looks like a scaled-down version of the larger roadsters from the same Mandello del Lario company, but apart from all being 90° shaft-drive vee-twins, they are somewhat different. The V50 is a very oversquare unit with dimensions of 74 × 57mm bore and stroke which, with a compression ratio of 10.8:1 make it a high-revving two-valve twin indeed. Unlike the 850 and 1000s, the valves of the pushrod V50 are parallel working in conjunction with semi Heron-head combustion chambers set into the pistons. The 490cc unit produces 45bhp at 7500rpm, although the unit is red-lined at 9000rpm, and has a wide power band which makes for good acceleration, especially with the whole bike having a dry weight of a miniscule 334lb. Top speed is 105mph, while a 14.2secs time is possible for a standing start quarter mile.

The engine drives via a car-type clutch to a five-speed gearbox and then to the shaft driven wheel. The shaft does make gearchanging a little slower and more sensitive to engine revolutions, although this disadvantage is balanced out by not having to bother with chain adjustment and replacement. Braking is by Moto Guzzi's patented integral system where by using the foot pedal 75% of braking is given to the front wheel, while the rear gets the remaining 25%. The difference between the V50 and the larger Guzzis is that it has a very close fitting cover over the rear unit which is to keep it drier in the rain. If this does work and does not hinder the brake from dissipating heat, they could well be used on the front twin units as well.

The V50 is quite a low machine and has a very sturdy frame, with box-section alloy swinging arm at the rear. In true Italian tradition, handling is excellent (helped no doubt by the light weight), while Michelin tyres make roadholding superb, too.

Not like typical Italian machines of yore is the switching and instrumentation which is of high quality, although a combination of red, green, blue and yellow warning lights and switches may seem confusing at first. There is a lockable cover over the fuel filler cap (which gives access to the 3.6gals tank) and, nicely out of harm's and the element's way, the brake fluid reservoir.

A V35 350cc version of the bike is also available and is essentially the same as its larger stablemate, but more suited to Italy's tax laws.

The V1000 Convert Moto Guzzi is probably the ultimate touring machine, for not only is it built in the upright riding position style of the famous Electra Glide Harley-Davidson, but it also has the luxury of a semi-automatic gearbox.

The Convert uses a 949cc version of the famous vee-twin four-stroke engine which was designed for a small car to be used by NATO forces and which then found its way into military bikes and then to the famous V7 Guzzis.

In Convert form, it produces 71bhp at 6500rpm which gives the bike a top speed of 112mph and enables it to accelerate over a quarter mile from standing start in just over 14secs; excellent figures for such a machine. Fuel consumption is good, too, averaging at 43mpg.

Power is transmitted by helical-gear primary drive to a torque converter which has a stall gearing of approximately 3:1 and which locks when 1:1 is reached, so giving variable ratios in between. The Fichtel & Sachs converter then drives two gears which give ratios for either town work (low) or high speed (high), although the combination can be used if full acceleration is needed. A shaft final drive is used, too, like all large Guzzis.

The system differs from that of the Honda in that the Guzzi has no neutral as such, and a normal clutch lever is used for starting. The starting procedure is as follows: switch on, swing up side stand, which acts as a parking brake lever as well as an ignition cut-out, then pull in clutch lever and fire engine. The clutch lever can then be released and just a touch of transmission 'creep' will be experienced. From then on, the bike will drive like a pure automatic. One disadvantage of such a transmission is that there is little or no engine braking effect and, just like cars, the Guzzi's brakes have to be used more than normally. However, the bike has the famous integral Moto Guzzi system, so it is easier and far more efficient than would normally be the case.

Apart from neat tab spoilers on the crash bars ahead of the engine, the Convert shares the same styling as that of the 850 T-3 Californian with a large tinted, adjustable-for-height screen, running boards, 5.3gal tank and pannier cases.

The Moto Guzzi V1000 Convert is slower, thirstier and heavier than a bike with normal transmission, but for the serious tourer it offers many advantages which take the strain out of riding vast distances.

47   MV AGUSTA 350 SPORT

Like most bikes in the range of MV Agusta, the 350S is the most expensive machine of its capacity available, but also like its stablemates, it is fast, stylish and every inch a thoroughbred.

It may come as a surprise but the 350S does not have the multiplicity of cams, valves and gears that MV are renowned for with their racers, but instead is based around an ordinary air-cooled four-stroke twin-cylinder engine which features overhead valves actuated by pushrods and rockers. The unit is of 349cc actual capacity and breathes through two Dell'Orto carburettors, with the mixture being compressed at a ratio of 9.5:1 in the cylinders; power output is 34bhp at 8500rpm, while the engine feels unburstable right up to the 10,000rpm redline. However, the engine vibrates and clatters a great deal, so restricting revs to the level at which maximum power is produced should give a smoother ride and increase the life of the engine. Due to the high compression of the motor, kick-starting can be difficult, and the engine can hold an average side rider at the top of the kicking stroke quite easily. A right-foot operated gear pedal, in the old tradition of British and Italian bikes, is used with an unusual one-up-four-down change pattern; again, this is reminiscent of vintage bikes.

Although the bike does shake and vibrate, it does have a good performance with a top speed of 104mph and the ability to cover a standing start quarter mile in 15.3secs. Fuel consumption is good, too, if a restrained throttle hand is used, and can average out at over 60mpg. With a massive 4.2gal fuel tank, a touring range of over 250 miles can be achieved, which is a lot better than many pukka touring bikes, and nobody can ever mistake the middleweight MV as a tourer.

With an excellent racer-like chassis, the 350 is endowed with remarkable handling and roadholding qualities, and has earned praise as one of the best bikes in this respect in the world.

MV commissioned famed Ital Design car stylist Giorgetto Giugario to design the bodywork of the 350 and, like the Italjet's designer Tartarini's work with Ducati, the result is simple but very attractive with a one-piece tank/seat/tail fairing unit. Although it is just possible to squeeze a pillion aboard, there are no rear pegs so it will be uncomfortable for everyone concerned. To further complement looks, a full dolphin racing-style fairing is available, while on the other hand a touring version with the same mechanical specification can be purchased in Italy. The difference is that the 350GT has flatter bars, a proper dual seat and blue-and-gold paintwork to replace the famous fire-engine red of the 350S.

48 MV AGUSTA 125

Like all machines in the Meccanica Verghera range, the 125 Sport is very expensive for its size, and a quick appraisal of its specification and performance would reveal that on this bike there is not a great deal of sophisticated engineering or luxury extras to warrant its high price tag. If MVs were marketed under another name, they would probably lose a lot of prospective owners, for the name is automatically linked with the famous fire-engine-red racers which have won no less than 37 World Championship road racing titles. On all bikes leaving the factory, there is a sticker on with 37 stars to indicate this.

The little 125 shares a lot of its technology with the bigger 350 in that it has a pushrod engine, in this case a single-cylinder unit of 123.5cc. The motor is light alloy with a cast iron barrel and on a 9.5:1 compression ratio produces 14bhp at 8500rpm. Maximum torque is just over 7.5lb ft at 7000rpm which is not a great deal. Performance, therefore, depends a great deal on the weight of the rider, but the MV should reach a top speed of just over 70mph. Fuel consumption is as one would expect from a small four-stroke, and the 125 can return an overall figure of 84mpg.

A wet-multi-plate clutch is used and a five-speed gearbox is fitted which has the foot pedal situated on the traditionally Italian right-hand side. Braking is by a disc at the front and drum at the rear.

The frame is similar to that of the 350 with a pair of strong tubes running straight from the headstock to the tail of the bike, with a single downtube which bolts to the engine and triangular centre section meeting the rear of the engine by the pivot for the swinging arm. The whole unit is extremely rigid and probably able to handle many times the power of the 125. As it is, it copes easily with the bike's 228lb weight, and handles as well as any machine currently in production.

Other features on the bike are both good and bad for, while, for example, the 125 has electronic ignition, the brake light works only on the rear unit, which is a little out of keeping of what is expected of a modern bike. One neat touch is the seat which, like the 750 series, is suede covered. When the rider wishes to carry a pillion, the tail section can be slid back on those frame tubes to reveal more of the cushion. In standard position, it is a rear rest so that the rider can make full use of the clip-on-style bars and racer-like handling. To complete the image, a full dolphin fairing can be ordered.

49   MV AGUSTA MONZA

MV Agusta have never seriously produced motor cycles at all, in the context that Count Agusta made a living from manufacturing Bell helicopters under licence. It was his hobby to make motor cycles and the fact that his 'fire engine red' machines have won 37 World Championships, far more than anyone else, is just coincidental.

The company has also produced a range of touring and sporting roadsters, the most famous of which have had engines very similar to the four-cylinder four-stroke twin-cam units fitted to the famous racers.

The MV Monza is developed from the double identity (touring/sports) America 750S, and differs in that it is an out and out road-going racer.

The distinguishing aspect of the big MV is the engine which is an awesome sand-cast alloy unit, indeed from the same moulds of the track bikes. The unit differs in that it has only two valves per cylinder, instead of four, but it has the same twin overhead camshafts driven from the centre of the crankshaft by gears, an expensive but very accurate means. Breathing through four 27mm Dell'Orto carburettors and with a compression ratio of 9.5:1, it can be imagined that the 837.7cc engine is in a high state of tune. Indeed it is for it produces 95bhp at 9500rpm, and is safe right up to 10,000rpm. Ignition is, interestingly, by a car-type distributor. Top speed of the bike is in the region of 140mph, although it is geared for something approaching 160mph. Primary drive is by gear and goes to a wet-multi-plate clutch and thence to a five-speed gearbox and shaft drive. The change is light and positive and suffers none of the slowness associated with many drive shaft layouts.

The power unit sits in a sturdy but low frame which keeps the centre of gravity down and so enhances the excellent handling and roadholding characteristics.

An extravagant and unnecessary part of exclusive Italian bikes is the black suede seat which although gripy and soft stays soggy for days after a shower of rain. Like the smaller 125, the rear fairing can be slid back to accommodate a pillion.

Wire wheels and twin front discs and drum rear are standard, but triple discs and alloy wheels are optional, as is a full fairing. Although it helps high-speed riding, the engine tends to overheat in traffic with the close-fitting body. If the performance of the bike is not up to requirements, a tuned version called the Arturo Magni Special, with special engine preparation on an 861cc unit by the company's famed developer, is available.

After that, a special 116bhp 1100cc version, the Grand Prix, with chain drive for lightness, is offered in Germany.

50   MZ 250 SUPA 5

The 250 Supa 5 is the top of the East German Motorradwerk Zschopau's range and like most machines from iron curtain countries is a practical rather than super sporty and good-looking machine. However, the MZ is a good performer and its appearance is very deceptive.

The bike is based on a large-looking (due to the amount of cooling fins) two-stroke single-cylinder engine which uses ordinary piston porting. The 243cc motor using mix of 50:1, produces 21bhp at

5350rpm and an impressive 19lb ft of torque at 4850rpm. Performance is to the order of an 80mph top speed, while acceleration from a start over a quarter mile takes 17.9secs. The little bike is surprisingly frugal and superior to most of its competitors, in that it can cover up to 80mpg.

Interestingly, the clutch is mounted on the engine side of the primary drive chain and this is felt when the bike is accelerated, for it holds its speed for a little longer, something that is rather disconcerting at first, even though it presents no problems.

Although performance is quite good, the brakes are not up to it at all, and the small drum at the front needs a very firm grip before it stops the bike in anger. However, with an enormously long (11in) rear brake lever acting on the same size brake at the rear there is the reverse problem. The rider can get so much leverage on it that it is extremely easy to lock the wheel altogether which gets rid of most of the retardation found. Liberal use of rubber mountings give the Supa a pleasant ride and negate the effects of single-cylinder vibrations while the seat, although not over padded, is nevertheless comfortable. The fuel tank looks odd in front of the seat, as it is much taller and not tailored in at all, but it does hold a generous 3.8gals which gives a range of an incredible 300 miles. The finish and looks of the MZ are strictly utilitarian, but the amount of standard equipment offered is, again, quite the reverse. There is a 12-piece tool kit along with a puncture outfit, chain link and hand-pump; a tachometer and rear-view mirror are also included in the price.

What does not look too attractive but is otherwise extremely worthwhile is the casing which covers the whole of the driving chain, so keeping dirt and grit off and extending the maintenance intervals and the life expectancy of the chain itself.

51 NORTON COMMANDO

The Norton Commando, before production ceased in the middle of 1977, was steeped in British tradition, being well made, fast, economical and almost racer-like in the handling stakes. However, time had caught up with the beast that had given the famous Norton four-stroke pushrod twin a new lease of life in 1967, just prior to the new tide of multi-cylinder 'superbikes' which effectively killed it off. The big Norton started off in 750cc guise, but was soon upped to 850 form in a bid to keep its performance competitive with the growing competition. In fact, the Commando had to adapt quite a lot just to stay alive, with the gearchange pedal placed on the left, opposite to the traditional right-hand side, to suit the Americans, along with the adoption of electric start, which later models proudly advertised on their side panels. Disc brakes, too, were part of the bike's specification even if older Nortons had managed well enough with drum units.

The Commando last appeared in Mark 3 guise and then was a well loved and excellent bike. With 58bhp and plenty of torque available from its 828ccs, it could reach 112mph and accelerate strongly from almost any speed in any of its four gears. There was an added bonus, too, and that was that the fuel consumption would be upwards of 40mpg, with almost 60mpg possible if the bike wasn't pushed too hard. Firing a Commando into life is not as easy as the side panel might suggest for, although able to restart the big twin with ease when hot, a cold start usually presents more problems. The technique needed is to have everything switched on and then to use the kickstarter while at the same time pressing the starter button. That way the starter motor helps take the strain out of kicking and so easing the low-compression motor over to fire. On its own, the starter will not guarantee a start and is a good way of getting the battery flat. However, a Norton owner will usually be quite happy to except things that way.

Once on the road, the bike will be transformed, for its frame is one based on the famous featherbed Norton which set new trends in handling in its day, and since the technology of the cycle hasn't progressed as much as that of the motor, the Norton is still streets ahead of most of the opposition.

With Norton-Villiers-Triumph (NVT) concentrating on Easy Rider mopeds and the Commando out of production, it was thought that big Nortons were a thing of the past. However, NVT had its mind, and money, on other sights: a monocoque-framed Wankel rotary of the equivalent of 1200cc. It was due for production in early 1979 with performance predicted that would not need improving to stay with the opposition.

52 QUASAR

The Quasar looks more like an eccentric styling exercise than a production motor cycle, but late 1977 did indeed see the unusual car-like two wheeler get into production from the company based near Bristol in the west of England. Everything about the Quasar is different from the normal concept of a bike and even the frame would seem more suited to a car.

Made from Reynolds 531 tubing, the frame features two overhead bars which support the Quasar's roof and also protect the rider in the event of the machine overturning. The engine of the bike is mounted under the steering head and is in fact the alloy straight-four water-cooled four-stroke as used in the small Reliant cars. Of pushrod-valve design, the 848cc engine produces 40bhp at 5500rpm and 46lb ft of torque at 3500rpm.

The Quasar uses the clutch and gearbox of the Reliant too, and a great deal of difficulty was encountered when trying to adapt the synchromesh unit to work in a bike manner. The finished machine has in fact two gear pedals, one above the other, and the upper is pressed to change up while the lower is pressed to change down; nothing at all happens if both are pushed at once, so there is no chance of ruining the gearbox that way. Naturally, as can be expected, the actual changes are more time consuming and positive than on a conventional bike. A final drive featuring a shaft is used but is quite separate from the swinging arm.

A standard suspension layout is used at the rear, while the front uses a leading swing arm on a pivoted fork so that braking stresses do not affect suspension movement. In reality, the Quasar has to be steered rather than banked to turn, but once learnt the procedure is quite simple.

The most striking thing about the bike is that it has an all-enveloping body of sleek and sharp design. A gentle line from above the front wheel goes upwards over the riders head, past a luggage locker, where it ends abruptly to give a squared-off back. The rider sits inside in an upright position with both legs and arms forward, something like a sports car. This means that although quite comfortable most of the time, gravitational pull will more severely affect him under braking, where on a normal bike the body is

131

naturally balanced against it. A hammock is slung from the roof and so the riding position can be adjusted; in fact, a passenger can be carried at a pinch.

The obvious advantage of the Quasar is that it is well protected against the elements (there is even provision for a heater to blow warm air on the rider's hands), but what is not so apparently obvious is the machine's low centre of gravity and remarkable aerodynamics. Performance of the 650lb bike with standard engine is remarkable with a top speed of just on 100mph, and fuel consumption of around 70mpg. A turbocharged version has been in prototype form and it is hoped to put that into production.

The Quasar is a very well balanced machine and can corner at speeds that would make sceptics think again and wonder whether it is just an attention getter and more like the direction in which two-wheeled vehicles ought to be developed.

53   RICKMAN KAWASAKI

The Rickman brothers, Don and Derek, were at one time world class motocross riders on machines using their own frames and named Metisse, meaning mongrel bitch in Gallic. They set up their own factory in Hampshire, England, in 1962 and produced some excellent bikes for use both on the road and off. More recently, they have been busy manufacturing glassfibre bodies, top boxes and fairings which are marketed not only under various names of other outlets, but also under well known bike manufacturers' labels who hand out the work to Rickman Bros Ltd. As the accessory business built up, concentration of production was taken from the bike side, although the two brothers were too enthusiastic about their bikes to let the line stop completely.

They make chassis units for Honda and Kawasaki bikes, in both touring and café racer guise, with the most popular being the racer-like version with the 1000cc Kawasaki 'Z' engine.

The frame of the Rickman is fairly conventional in design and has no tricks, but is also very sturdy and well engineered. It is built of Reynolds 531 manganese molybdenum which when assembled is nickel plated. The finish is rather like chrome, except that it has a more golden tint to it. Lighter, stiffer and lower than the standard Kawasaki unit, the Rickman frame gives the bike more positive steering and far superior handling and, with famous Red Arrow Dunlop tyres, roadholding is excellent; braking is taken care of by three cast-iron discs mounted on attractive six-spoke alloy wheels.

The glassfibre bodywork of the bike can be purchased separately and fitted to a standard Japanese machine, and consists of a half-dolphin fairing, side panels, front mudguard, tank cover which fits over an alloy tank of 3.5gals capacity, and a tail/seat unit which can be either of single or double design. Handlebars are of clip-on type which with the rear set pedals and seat fitted well back give the rider a purely racing crouch riding position. Instruments are some of the few items apart from the engine that are taken from the standard Kawasaki bike. The others are the side and centre stands. Unfortunately, as the bike is a lot lower than standard, the centre stand is impossible to operate without help.

The Rickman has slightly lower gearing than standard, but this and a 40lb weight saving are all that affect straight-line performance. Top speed is roughly 130mph, while it will accelerate over a quarter mile from start in 12.1secs.

54 ENFIELD INDIA 350

The Enfield India 350 is a bike straight from the past which is still available today. For, back in the 1950s, Royal Enfield sold manufacturing rights of two of their bikes (a 175cc two-stroke and a 350cc four-stroke) to the Indian government who wanted a bike to mobilise their forces. The bikes were built in Madras and, in still almost the same form as then, they are built today.

Although somewhat crude to manufacturers and riders both east and west of its home country, the machine is popular enough for the Indian bike-riding populous, the Government and a small but thriving export market. In all, 11,000 or so Enfields are built each year. The bike uses a simple overhead-valve pushrod, single-cylinder, four-stroke engine of 346cc which produces a maximum of 18bhp at 5600rpm with its lowly 6.5:1 compression ratio. Powerful it may not be (although a top speed of just over 70mph should not be frowned upon), but frugal it is. Well over 70mpg should be possible in most conditions with the bike, while a figure nearer 90 will be achieved by those who use fuel sparingly. Acceleration, naturally, is leisurely but more than adequate to keep up with traffic in town; a four-speed gearbox is utilised.

Handling of the machine is surprisingly good, but there is one criticism and that is that the braking, like everything else, is as per 1950s British middleweight, and that compared with today's standards is not good. 6.5in drums front and rear cope with stopping the 350lb bike, but only just. Everything else is old, solid, reliable and sturdy, if not immaculately, finished. As a no-nonsense form of transport with character and a 'good old days charm', the Enfield 350 works well.

55   SEELEY HONDA

The Seeley company is a lot like Rickman, and Colin Seeley, like the Rickman brothers, has a great competition career behind him. The difference is that Colin was a side-car racer and at one time even looked after the production racing car side of the famous Brabham racing car company. However, during his time dabbling with three wheels and four, he made a succession of solo racers which were renowned for their excellent handling.

A lot of the thinking that went into those racers found its way into the Seeley Honda, the road bike he manufactures which is fitted with the four-cylinder CB750 engine.

Like the Rickman, the Seeley uses Reynolds 531 tubing for its construction but in this case is usually finished in attractive gloss white rather than nickel. The front of the frame does indeed resemble the Rickman in that it has a wide duplex cradle and bracing just above the exhausts. Standard Honda forks are used, however, which is probably the one weak point in the chassis set-up. Although a standard K series, or F1 or F2 engine is fitted as standard, an overbored 1000cc Seeley is also available, and the frame will easily stand up to the extra power. Full specification includes a four-into-two Jardine exhaust system, Lockheed brakes, S & W multi-rate dampers at the rear and the very expensive Lester alloy wheels, which are usually fitted with Dunlop Red Arrow covers.

A small nose fairing is fitted while the bars are flat rather than outright racer clip-on style. The most eye-catching feature of the bike is the fuel tank which holds a massive 5.5gals, enough to give the Seeley a touring range of well over 250 miles. Because of the large tank, no compromise has been made with the seating which is purely for the rider alone and has a large tail piece/fairing for support.

Naturally, the bike does not have to be clothed in such expensive trimmings, and many other items can be fitted to the base Seeley frame, which gives the rider all the advantages of a smooth and powerful Japanese engine with the manners of an excellent British chassis.

56 SUZUKI TS185

The Suzuki TS series is the company's range of two-stroke trail bikes which come in 100, 125, 250 and 185cc sizes. The 185 is typical of the range, being more an occasional trail bike than a serious full-time off-road conveyance.

The single-cylinder engine features an interesting induction system as used by Suzuki on their motocross world championship winning RM bikes, called the 'Power Reed'. Instead of being either piston ported or reed valve, the TS uses a combination of the two with the inlet tract split. One path goes straight to the cylinder, while the other goes via a reed valve to the crankcase. Timing of the piston port is mild to give the unit good torque characteristics at low engine speeds, while the reed-valve controlled crankcase port helps the engine breath more efficiently at higher speeds, so the bike should have good acceleration over the whole rev range. In practice, the 183cc power unit produces 17bhp at 6500rpm and 14lb ft of torque at 6000rpm, so the torque curve peaks quite near the maximum power figure. The torque does stay flat at lower speeds, however, and the bike's low speed acceleration is quite good. The top speed of the bike is a shade under 70mph, while it should return around 60mpg.

The suspension system of the TS185 is not as sophisticated as Yamaha's, but nevertheless works quite well, as it indeed should, again being based on the RM design. The rear set-up is the company's 'Tru-Trac' system with the coil spring damper units angled more horizontally than road units.

A lot of the bike's off-road performance is dictated by the tyres which have to cope with all weather performance on tarmac as well as trail blazing on the dirt, so they are something of a compromise and do not offer a great deal of grip in slippery conditions.

Also of compromise are the trimmings which would easily get broken or knocked off were the bike put down. However, that detracts from the TS185's sound design with its ample 9.1in ground clearance and long-travel suspension. While not as quick or as strong as many trail bikes offered, the 185 has its advantages with not too much power to get the rider into difficulty and not much weight (216lb) for him to pick up, and, for a novice rider, those points can be really important.

57 SILK 700S

Through no lack of talent and fertile minds, the British motor cycle industry was floundering by the late 1970s and, although designers could come up with plans for bikes that would have few peers from any country, a lack of money prevented them reaching fruition.

That is not the case with the Derbyshire-based Silk company, however, and they approach the 1980s with full order books and full design schedules. The machine produced is of 656cc two-stroke design and from the outside it looks like a latter-day Scott. One could be forgiven for that mistake for indeed the firm started off with a bike powered by an engine of that manufacture. Although it was not a great success on the race tracks, Silk thought that it would make an ideal roadster, but plans fell through with the owner of production rights to the Scott engine. The next best thing was for George Silk to build his own engine, which was to be of essentially the same design.

The power unit of the 700S is a two-stroke twin which is canted over forwards and which is liquid cooled. The large radiator is mounted forward of the engine and cooling is by the thermosyphon method which saves using a pump. Two-strokes are by nature very thirsty and dirty engines, but this has been cured to a large extent by the company's resurrection of Dr Schnuerle's loop scavenge system developed into a 'velocity contoured charge/scavenge' lay-out. It is essentially a complexly designed piston and port system which gets mixture into the combustion chamber more efficiently and gets it out again with the same vigour. It makes the bike cleaner and gives it an increase in low-to-mid-engine-speed torque as well as cures it of seemingly quenchless thirst. Maximum power of the single carburettor unit is 48bhp at 6000rpm, while maximum torque peaks well down at 3000rpm. The company do not quote specific torque figures, but the output is high for the maximum bhp figure corresponds to 42lb ft, which is remarkable. Being a two-stroke, the engine is quite light (a shade over 65lb) and this helps the bike's overall weight which is a miniscule 310lb. This along with a Spondon frame almost identical to that of their races, means that handling and roadholding of the Silk are of the highest order, while a disc at the front and drum at the rear stop the bike easily. Twin discs at the front or conical brakes of Campagnolo manufacture are also available, the latter built into Campagnolo alloy wheels. Other options available include panniers, top box and carriers, while Silk also have the patent on an ingenious centrally heated fairing.

If more performance is needed, a production racer is available, while the company is also developing a three-cylinder supercharged version of 1000cc.

58   SUZUKI X7

250cc motor cycles are popular largely because they are the biggest bikes available to learner riders and therefore it may seem to be a poor policy of Suzuki in advertising their 250cc X7 as a true 100mph machine, a point which will no doubt attract many novices to it. However, the X7 is a very good bike, and more than a match for bikes of almost twice its size.

The heart of the machine is a two-stroke air-cooled twin like its GT250 predecessors, the difference being that the X7 had adopted the 'Power-Reed' induction of the TS trail-bike series, which boosts torque at low to medium engine speeds. Maximum power is 29bhp at 8000rpm which does indeed give the 278lb bike a top speed of just on the magic 'ton', while acceleration over a quarter mile from standing start is just outside of the 'fourteens', standing at 15secs dead. As can be expected, the price one pays for performance from such a small engine is fuel consumption and the X7 will return just 36mpg.

A six-speed gearbox is used which makes sure that the engine can be kept spinning high up the range for maximum acceleration, although the torque of the bike is so good that the front wheel can be lifted with apparent ease without resorting to slipping the clutch.

The X7 is not intended as simply a drag-strip type roadster, however, for a lot of thought has gone into the bike's chassis, so that cornering too is sporting. The company advertises that the machine has a banking angle of 45° on the left and 46° on the right, although this will vary greatly on riders' weights; they assume the roads are dry, too, for such cornering.

Although many smaller four-strokes have the luxury of electric starting, the Suzuki just has a kick lever, but with a compression of 6.7:1 on a two-stroke that should be no hindrance at all.

Styling is very modern with carefully colour-keyed paintwork with shiny and matt-black contrasting well with the basic scheme and alloy wheels.

If the morals behind this '100mph learner' are debatable, Suzuki on the other hand should be praised for their cunning in just having 'X7' on the bike's side panels, so giving it a certain mystique and also saving the rider from letting on that his 'ton up' bike is a mere 250.

59   SUZUKI GS400

Suzuki have steadily developed their GS400 since it was introduced in early 1977, and it has become a very sophisticated and well-engineered middleweight machine.

The GS400 uses an air-cooled four-stroke engine which has twin overhead camshafts, like the larger multis in the range, and which is of 180° configuration. Drive for the camshafts is from between the cylinders on the crankshaft and the cam chain has the Suzuki Positensioner which, as its name implies, automatically keeps it at the right tension all the time. The engine produces maximum power at its redline of 9000rpm, a figure of 36.5bhp, while maximum torque of 23.9lb ft is produced at 7500rpm. The torque curve is quite interesting, for it more strongly resembles a horizontal straight line from around 3500rpm, with the figure just over 20lb ft all the way along. On the road, this makes the Suzuki a smooth and very responsive performer which is helped by the almost-universal-for-Japanese-four-stroke-twins balance system.

The bike has a six-speed gearbox which has a very slick and positive change and a virtually perfect set of ratios, although as the bike can easily reach maximum revs in top gear, a longer ratio would help cruising and ultimately fuel consumption. However, the efficient little engine makes the bike quite frugal anyway and it can quite easily cover over 60 miles on one gallon. Top speed of the GS is just over 100mph, while acceleration over a quarter mile from a standing start takes just under 16secs.

The flat bars on the bike make the riding position a little crouched and so uncomfortable around town, but they have the advantage of making it easier to exploit the machine's taut handling and good roadholding. Braking is by a single disc at the front (which is thinner than that of earlier models) and a drum at the rear which make light work of stopping the 380lb machine.

Styling of the GS400 is quite attractive with a neat seat/tail section under which is a small oddments tray and compartment in the rear. Instruments have the Suzuki orange glow at nighttime and there is the digital gear-position indicator which helps forgetful riders.

Not content with having the opposition produce similar bikes, in late 1978, Suzuki brought out a version with electronic ignition, alloy wheels and an overbored 425cc engine. The GS425 was, with its unique size, to run alongside the GS400 until 1979 when it would replace it.

60   SUZUKI GS550

Like Honda's bike which was uprated from 500cc, the Suzuki GS550 has a rather unusual engine size which the manufacturers hope will distinguish their multi-cylinder wares from the recent crop of half-litre twin-cylinder bikes which have appeared on the market. Of course, the extra capacity also gives a bonus of more performance and the GS550 has a very good turn of speed indeed. Like the larger 750 and 1000 Suzukis, the 550 has a four-cylinder air-cooled twin-overhead-camshaft power unit lying across the frame breathing through four carburettors. In this guise, the almost square engine (56 × 55.8mm bore and stroke) produces 51bhp at 9000rpm and 30lb ft of torque at 7500rpm. The power is transmitted through a six-speed gearbox (making the bike the largest capacity machine with as many ratios in production) and gives it a top speed of just over 110mph, while a standing start quarter mile can be covered in 13.7secs. Fuel consumption will work out at 45mpg. Although not as powerful as the larger multis in the Suzuki range, the bike has about 45lb less weight to carry so is more manageable in traffic and allows the rider to use the performance more.

With a smaller chassis, the GS550 is easier to handle on corners than its stablemates, although its ultimate roadholding will be roughly the same. However, the new generation Suzukis are among the best behaved bikes available and a long way from the machines that gave the Japanese industry the reputation for building sloppy and even dangerous bikes.

Braking is taken care of by two stainless steel discs at the front and a drum at the rear, which should make wet weather braking less nerve wracking. The instruments on the GS550 are excellent and radiate a warm orange glow at night time which is more pleasing to the eye than the usual green, while there is a neat digital gear-position indicator which glows red and which is certainly a help, as the smooth unfussed nature of the bike's engine makes it hard telling which of the many gears is selected.

The finish of the middleweight Suzuki is excellent and it comes with twin mirrors, pinstripe paintwork and an attractive four-into-two exhaust system.

61 SUZUKI GT750

The Suzuki GT750 was the only large two-stroke machine built with an accent on touring in the 1970s, even though a passing glance at its engine would have reminded you of something in a road-racing bike.

The heart of the big Suzuki is a three-cylinder triple which utilises liquid cooling and, from the outside, looks a lot like Suzuki's racer of the same capacity as used by Barry Sheene and team-mates in Superbike racing a couple of years ago which indeed did use the base 750GT motor. However, the GT's triple produces a 'mild' 70bhp at 6500rpm which is not enough for racing, but ample to push the surprisingly heavy (520lb) machine at quite high speed; a top of 122mph, in fact. In spite of the bulk, the GT's acceleration is brisk, too, and can reach 80mph from a standing start in just under 10secs.

One instinctively thinks of a two-stroke bike as being untractable by nature, but in the Suzuki's case nothing could be further from the truth, for the engine produces an enormous 61.5lb ft of torque at 5500rpm, which is a lot more than most other three-quarter litre bikes. This, along with the smoothness of a two-stroke and the quietness of a liquid-cooled engine, makes for an ideal tourer.

With the water jacketing, radiator and tall bars, the Suzuki looks cumbersome and ungainly and, compared with later models from the same company, the GT feels and handles that way, too. One benefit from its soft suspension, is the ride which is more comfortable than most on irregular surfaces, although the benefits of that disappear at the next corner where the bike wallows a little.

Braking is good with twin discs at the front and drum at the rear, although the discs do suffer in wet conditions, like most stainless steel units. Fuel consumption on a large 'stroker' would again be assumed as poor compared to a four-stroke, but in reality it averages out at a respectable 36mpg which is a lot better than two-stroke machines half its size manage at times.

The main failing with a two-stroke bike is that it is dirty and, even though it does not use a great deal of oil, the GT750 throws out a lot of smoke from its four tail pipes. That fact alone was enough to convince the manufacturers that the more complicated four-stroke was the best answer and so the four-cylinder air-cooled GS750 which ran alongside the GT for a while took over as the 750 of the late 1970s and early '80s.

62/63   SUZUKI RE5

Suzuki took on a big chance when they invested a vast amount of money on Felix Wankel's rotary engine, for they tooled up for a large production run and had to pay NSU a lot of money for the licence to build the unit. In the end, it was decided too late that the time was not right for the bike so everything was shelved in late 1977, just four years after the RE5 was launched.

Depending on your school of thought, the Wankel can be one of three capacities, but generally speaking the 497cc RE5 is equivalent to a 1000, being of single-rotor, three-chamber design. The motor sits in the frame with the eccentric shaft around which the engine rotates mounted crossways. Cooling and lubrication present problems and the bike has a wet slump which puts oil into the centre of the motor while there is a separate tank for the two-stroke oil for combustion. The lubricating oil passes through its own radiator, while due to the configuration, another radiator is needed for the liquid cooling. To add to that, there is a separate lubrication system for the gearbox. All in all, it adds a lot of weight to the bike and in some way detracts from one of the Wankel's advantages: simple layout and low weight. Also, in the RE5, smoothness and quietness of operation are not up to that achieved in NSU's Ro80 car, for example, and nowhere near as good as many four-stroke multis. However, the bike does have a fair amount of power with 62bhp at 6500rpm and, more importantly, 54.9lb ft of torque produced at a lowly 3500rpm and it does not drop off by a large amount until the engine is revving very near to its limit. In practice, such a wide power band means a more relaxed performance with less need for lots of gear changes. The RE5 has a top speed of 109mph, accelerates from a standing start over a quarter mile in 13.5secs but has a very poor fuel consumption.

Averaging out at just over 30mpg, the figure can drop to a little over 20mpg which is impractical even with a fuel tank which holds almost four gallons.

Along with the modern engine, the RE5 had space-age looks with, as its main attention grabber, matching instrument binnacle and rear light cluster, both being tubular in design. The instruments had a tinted perspex cover which, when the ignition key was inserted would slide back to reveal a speedometer, tachometer, water-temperature gauge and a multiplicity of warning lights. When the RE5 gave way to the updated RE5A, units similar to those on the GT750 took their place.

However, by the time the A version had appeared, the company from Hamamatsu had learnt its lesson and had shelved their rotary plans indefinitely, or until such times as the car manufacturers had pioneered their way with a second generation of Wankels and convinced the public that they are a viable proposition.

64 SUZUKI GS1000

The GS1000EC Suzuki looks a great deal like the smaller GS750 bike in the range, but underneath they are quite different machines indeed. Like its smaller stablemate, the 1000 uses an air-cooled four-cylinder four-stroke unit with twin overhead camshafts. However, as well as increasing the capacity of the engine to just over 997cc, they also took 10lb of weight from it by way of removal of the kickstarter, lighter crankshaft and different engine casting webs. In the rest of the bike, a further 25lb was added which is not a lot at all. So, the GS1000 has all the advantages of 1-litre power with none of the disadvantages of weight that is the bane of the other Japanese bikes in its class.

The engine produces 87bhp at 8000rpm and 61.3lb ft of torque at 6500rpm which gives the Suzuki a top speed of 136mph and enables it to accelerate over a quarter mile from standing start in 11.9secs. Fuel consumption is 44mpg. Where the bike has a significant advantage over the opposition is in handling, for the GS1000 has none of the frame flex that was so common with earlier bikes and its suspension is as advanced as any that is available, even on production Italian machines.

At the front, Suzuki use their race-proved air forks which are adjustable. A bicycle hand-pump is all that is needed to alter the

143

pressure between 11 and 17psi to give either ideal travel for a solo rider on bumpy roads or high-speed cornering with two up and plenty of luggage: two extremes, but anywhere in between can be used. Advanced air/oil dampers are used at the rear which again are completely adjustable. Braking is by three 11in discs while standard cross-spoked-style Suzuki alloy wheels are used.

A five-speed gearbox, like that of the 750, is fitted but the larger bike does not have the luxury of that digital gear indicator. Another luxury that is missing is shaft drive, but the company were planning to bring out a machine of basically the same design with that form of final drive fitted.

Styling of the bike is middle-of-the-road and may even be considered quite ordinary with no gimmicks or any obvious aesthetic embellishments, but the bike is efficient and does everything as well as, if not better than, its competitors.

65 TRIUMPH TRIDENT

The Triumph Trident first appeared in 1968 and was the first of the modern day superbikes with more than two cylinders. Soon after, the BSA Rocket-3 was launched, being essentially similar to its one-time rival except that its engine was canted forward by 15°, while that of the Triumph was vertical. After the BSA company went under, Triumph decided that they would use the BSA-style engine in their Trident which, apart from putting more weight on the front wheel to improve handling, would also enable them to fit an electric starter: one point that stopped the British bike from having the all-round appeal of its Japanese competition.

The late Tridents were sophisticated models indeed and it was unfortunate that the British industry could not persevere with its development.

The T160 Trident has a 120° four-stroke three-cylinder engine which produces 58bhp at 7250rpm and more importantly an abundance of torque, so that it will pull strongly from low speeds in each of its five gears; another improvement over the earlier models which only had four ratios.

Even though the engine is rather dated in that it utilises pushrod and rocker valve actuation, the tuned exhaust note gives it 'a distinct charm, and also that famous British reputation of being unburstable. With the ability to sustain revving at engine speeds over 9000rpm without damage, it is easy to see where the reputation came from.

With a top speed of over 115mph, the Trident is only a little away from its rivals, while the acceleration is not quite in the four-cylinder Japanese class, and only just quicker than the twin-cylinder models of the same company. Fuel consumption, too, is not a strong point and in normal riding over 35mpg is difficult to achieve. Oil consumption on the other hand is better than one would expect of a British bike and, while it is in the engine, is cooled by a radiator mounted above the unit just under the steering head. Although quite heavy for a triple at 503lb, the Trident is amazingly agile and few manufacturers can boast of a frame that is equal to that of the Triumph in rigidity. The bike's singular discs at either end are also effective in both wet and dry and make light work of stopping from high speed repeatedly.

The large Triumph is a good looking machine with its siamesed exhaust running from the centre cylinder and then splitting to by-pass the single down tube of the frame on either side, and it is a great pity that NVT or the Meriden Co-Operative had no room for it in their schedules. Although in latter years its performance was eclipsed by foreign opposition, it perhaps sums up the British industry when it was said that Triumph could not afford to develop their overbored prototype 850cc Trident.

66/67   TRIUMPH BONNEVILLE

The Triumph Bonneville, like the Norton Commando, has been part of British biking for many years, but it still appeals to riders who are not impressed with multi-cylindered sophisticated machinery and would rather settle for a well-bred 'iron' which can trace its parentage back many generations, something Japanese bikes can't do just yet.

The specification sheet of the latest Bonneville from the workers' co-operative at Meriden looks a little better compared to its foreign opposition, but is still rather dated.

The heart of the 'Bonny' is a parallel-twin engine of 744cc. Valve actuation is by pushrods and rockers and is fed by two Amal concentric carburettors which have built-in starting jets, and which conform to American regulations. Previously, to start the bike, a float chamber tickler had to be pressed until the unit flooded and only then could a hefty swing on the kickstarter fire the 7.9:1 compression ratioed engine to life. That is a thing of the past now, and only the big kick is needed.

The main modification over the older Bonnevilles is the adoption of electronic ignition which makes the bike faster, cleaner and more frugal; an uprated alternator, with more power at low engine speeds and a change from positive to negative earth. Power from the engine is unchanged and it produces 50bhp at 6200rpm and a useful amount of torque. The bike's top speed is 112mph, while fuel consumption is a little low for a British twin at 45mpg. The design of the Triumph engine may be a bit dated, but the gearbox is as smooth and light to use as any other bike; five ratios are used.

The chassis of the Triumph is excellent and with Dunlop tyres, Lockheed brakes (single disc at either end) and low 395lb weight, it is at home on the twistiest of roads.

The latest bikes have revised instrumentation and, although not nearly in the same class as the excellent Japanese units, are a great improvement over pre-1979 Triumphs. The finish of the machines is excellent and the pin-striping of the tank is all done by hand and far superior to any masked paintwork or transfers. The Bonneville comes in two versions: standard with flat bars and four gallon tank or 'US spec' with high rise bars and a smaller but more shapely three gallon tank. The 1979 models have reverted to chrome mudguards, too.

68   YAMAHA RD250

Although the Aermacchi-Harley-Davidsons and Kawasakis have recently been reaping the rewards on the race tracks in the 250cc class, Yamaha has produced many World Championship winning bikes and still produces machines for no less than 90% of the riders.

Their road-going two-stroke RD250 bears a strong resemblance to its brother racers, even though it is air rather than liquid cooled. The 54 × 54mm bore and stroke twin-cylinder engine produces 32bhp at 8000rpm with its lowly 5.8:1 compression and pushes the bike to a top speed of 92mph. Like the racers, the RD uses reed-valve induction which is claimed helps fuel consumption, and it returns 44mpg, although this is increased drastically if the engine is kept revving at a high rate.

The late model RD250s have six-speed gearboxes which is an improvement over the older versions' five. Interestingly, the earlier bikes had six gears in the housing but the highest one was blanked off, although it could be put into use after a strip down.

The handling of the RD again is akin to their racers and it is quite happy being thrown into bends at high speeds, something which is helped by its 340lb weight. Stopping, too, is easy with a disc brake at either end. Unlike Yamaha's four-stroke 250, the XS, the two-stroke model has no electric starter, but the low-compression engine is easy enough to crank over by hand, and is quite fuss free and willing to tick over without fouling its plugs, something that was definitely not the case with many 'strokers' of the 1960s.

The other large two-stroke roadster built by Yamaha is the RD400 which is basically the same except for the engine capacity and, with around 8bhp more and just 11lb extra weight, is a real flier and even more like the track bikes which share the same colour schemes.

69   YAMAHA DT250 ENDURO

The Enduro/Trail bike is a phenomenon of the 1970s, with the machine built purely for fun and the fact that it can be used as an everyday commuter an added bonus.

The Yamaha DT250 is typical of the breed and, although it has all the equipment necessary to make it road legal, it uses sensible fittings to ensure that it doesn't get damaged in tumbles on the rough.

The power unit for the DT250 is a single-cylinder, two-stroke which uses a reed valve for induction. This is a device with two stainless steel plates which are mounted in such a way that the engine with its 'suction' on the downward stroke will take in the right amount of mixture then, on the upward stroke, the pressure from compression and the natural springiness of the valves will shut so that mixture will not get in, thus avoiding the waste of usual piston-port two-stroke units. Yamaha have had great success in both motocross and road racing with their reed-valve engines.

The DT250 is not in a high state of tune like the competition bikes, however, and produces just 23bhp at 6000rpm, with the optimum torque produced at 500rpm less. This means that full use has to be made of the five-speed gearbox to keep the bike in its narrow power band. The engine is mounted in a high narrow frame which gives ten inches of ground clearance and, even if you have to make full use of it, there is a metal guard to protect the sump; helping in this respect too is the exhaust system which runs up and over the engine to exit level with the top of the rear wheel.

The frame itself is based on another famous Yamaha trademark, the cantilever monoshock unit where, instead of having two spring/damper units on either side running from the hub to the top of the frame, the DT has a whole subframe, which pivots where a trailing arm would be, to work a single large damper which rests in the top tube of the frame. The whole unit allows greater wheel travel for given suspension movement. It makes little or no difference on the road, but the benefits are felt if the bike is treated to its full potential on the rough.

The practical off-road capability is accentuated by the rubber-covered instruments, the indicators which are on rubber stalks and the plastic mud guards which don't shatter when the bike is dropped as often happens with fun riding on the trails.

70/71   YAMAHA SR500

Off-road bikes are usually of single-cylinder design and in Motocross Grands Prix, the norm is two-strokes of 400–440cc and four-strokes of around the half-litre mark. In recent years, the Japanese manufacturers have built similar trail bikes and, just like their competition counterparts, have too grown steadily in size. Yamaha produced the biggest of the lot with their XT500 four-stroke 'thumper' and suddenly everyone saw a lot more than an off-road bike. They remembered with fondness bikes like the BSA Gold Star and soon magazines expressed interest in project road bikes built around the Yamaha engine/transmission. Yamaha themselves took the hint and produced the SR500 saying that this was an obvious way to go as there was no new ground to break with turbine-like multis. Whatever the reason, the wheel had turned full circle and a new generation could savour the delights (and curses) of 'the big single'.

The SR500, in true Japanese fashion, is a well engineered bike and in most places the toil of owning such a machine has been developed out: like leaks, dubious electrics and general lack of reliability. The machine is powered by an oversquare engine of 499cc with valve actuation by a single overhead camshaft. Essentially the same alloy unit as the XT off roader, the SR differs in valves size and port shape so is a little more potent. A maximum power figure of 33bhp at 6500rpm is not a lot for a 500, but peak torque is just over 28lb ft at 5500rpm, and indeed the torque curve is remarkably flat from 2000rpm to that figure. A five-speed gearbox is used and the bike will reach a top speed of just on 100mph in the highest of them. Fuel consumption is a bonus feature of such a bike and the SR500 should have no difficulty in producing an overall figure of well over 50mpg.

Rather than try to get a starter to turn over a 500cc cylinder with a 9:1 compression ratio, Yamaha decided to leave firing to a hefty rider, although they do make it as easy as possible. A compression release lever is fitted and the engine is turned carefully so that the piston is at the top of its stroke. A little window on the camshaft cover indicates when this point has been reached. The bike should then fire at the first kick. A vacuum automatic advance and retard system (like that of the XS1100) also helps. Also dispensing with an electric starter helps save weight as again a plus point of a single is that it is quite light. Dry weight of the machine is 348lb so a single disc brake at the front and drum rear ably stop it. Handling is good, too, and the narrow bike instils a lot of confidence in the rider to make full use of it.

The SR500 Yamaha may not suit everyone, but it does take the tears out of 'vintage biking'.

72   YAMAHA XS400

Like Kawasaki, Yamaha have been trying to cater for all tastes and marketing machines with similar capacity in both two-stroke and four-stroke guises. The XS400 is the company's four-stroke machine in the popular 400 class and is completely different from the RD400 two-stroke which has a much sportier image, even if in reality both bikes are just about equal in performance.

The XS400's nearest relation is the similar-looking 250, and both have parallel air-cooled twin-cylinder engines driving through six-speed gearboxes. The single-overhead-camshaft unit is very oversquare with dimensions of 69mm bore by 52mm stroke, and it can rev to 9000rpm, which is quite high for a twin. Unlike the other 400 twins in the same class, the XS does not have counter balance shafts, which means the motor does vibrate more than the opposition, but this is not noticeable above 4500rpm. More important than the bike's 38bhp is the torque produced which peaks at 22lb ft at 7500rpm, but stays within 5lb ft of that figure right down to 4000. On the road, this means that the Yamaha will pull strongly and evenly over a large speed band. A top speed of 101mph can be achieved while acceleration over a standing start quarter mile takes a very creditable 14.9secs. There are single disc brakes at either end to stop the bike which are mounted on attractive alloy wheels which, in turn, help take away some of the bulkiness of the bike's looks. Yamaha have also devised neat paintwork on the tank and side panels which helps break up the lines, again to make the bike appear smaller than its 362lb would otherwise suggest.

The standard of equipment on the middleweight Yamaha is equal to that of many Japanese machines, and betters them with an ingenious indicator system which is worked by a linkage to the speedometer. This means that the winkers stay on for a certain distance which has no bearing on time but just distance travelled.

The indicator switch can be simply pressed inwards to override the unit.

73 YAMAHA XS500

Although looking like the smaller XS400 and XS250 bikes, the XS500 has a different twin-cylinder engine which features twin-overhead camshafts and four-valves per cylinder.

Although such an engine would be ideally suited to a sports motor cycle, Yamaha instead have used it in a state of tune for a bike they classify as a tourer with enough engine power to enable it to keep up with larger capacity machines.

The oversquare power unit displaces 498cc and with a compression ratio of 9.6:1 produces 49bhp at 8500rpm, just one brake horsepower down on the company's 650cc twin. A four-valve-per-cylinder engine is used because four small valves use space more efficiently than two larger valves, so that, in fact, more head area can be utilised which in turn makes the engine more efficient. Also the lower reciprocating mass of small valves means higher engine speed before 'bounce' is induced, and better ignition is helped by the sparking plug being central in the head, its most efficient position. The problem with the layout is that to get the valves in an efficient semi-hemispherical head, twin overhead camshafts have to be employed or a complicated system of pushrods and rockers which would negate the effect of the extra engine speed gained from the layout. The XS uses direct-operating overhead cams which make servicing more complicated and time consuming.

The Yamaha has pistons set at 180° unlike many four-strokes with their 360° layout with the inherent vibration difficulties. However, Yamaha had the problem of the crankshaft rocking with the alternate reciprocation, so to encounter this they use their patented 'omniphase' balance shaft.

The top speed of this 425lb bike is 105mph, while it will accelerate over a quarter mile from standing start in 14.3secs; fuel consumption is 46mpg. In all, the XS500 is deceptive for it is more advanced than it looks and 'four-stroke twin' specification suggest. However, although the engine is efficient and powerful, the extra complication of the valve gear means more complicated and expensive maintenance.

74 YAMAHA XS1100

When Yamaha announced their XS750 three-cylinder four-stroke, it was acclaimed as an excellent tourer with the best shaft drive of any machine available. If one thing was lacking it was outright performance for, although quick, it could not match the top-of-the-range models of the other Japanese manufacturers. The obvious idea would have been to graft an extra cylinder on the 750 to make it a 1000, but Mitsui Machinery decided to go one better and so the XS1100 was born.

The engine of the bike is an air-cooled unit of just a shade under 1102cc and, with its valves actuated by twin overhead camshafts, produces 95bhp at 8000rpm and 66.5lb ft of torque at 6500rpm. The whole unit is canted forward a few degrees and an oil cooler just under the steering head helps keep the motor running cool. Chain and gear primary drive goes to a wet-multi-plate gearbox and thence to a five-speed gearbox and the shaft drive which runs along the left side of the bike. The gear lever pedal is pivotted at the front so that it looks back-to-front but it does work in the normal one-down-four-up sequence.

Top speed of the big Yamaha is 138mph, while it will accelerate to a quarter mile from a standing start in just under 12secs; fuel consumption is 41mpg. The most awe-inspiring thing about the XS1100 is its size and mass, for it dwarfs just about everything apart from Harley-Davidsons. Once travelling at a few mph and the weight is forgotten, but it does affect the high-speed handling of the bike and the braking. Even though the Yamaha uses three 11.23in diameter discs, they are not up to stopping the 564lb bike repeatedly from high speed, although the 3.5in front and 4.5in wide rear tyres keep their grip.

Although the Yamaha has a sprint-like turn of speed, it is primarily intended for touring as its high bars and 5.28gal fuel tank prove. Not having to adjust the chain every 150 miles or so is a boon for long-distance travel, too.

The styling of the XS11ᴜ
instruments, indicators and refleᴄ
shape.

Standard equipment on the bike includes fuel gauge, a ᴜᴛ,
switch for the ignition should the bike fall over, self-cancelling
indicators and sockets for intercom, fog lamps or other accessories
that might be fitted.